SAN CARLOS BORROMEO.

Missions and Missionaries of California

New Series. Local History.

Mission San Carlos Borromeo

(Carmelo)

The
Father of the Missions

BY

FR. ZEPHYRIN ENGELHARDT, O. F. M.

*Author of "The Missions and Missionaries," "The Franciscans
in Arizona," "Mission Dolores," "Mission San Diego,"
"Mission Santa Barbara," "Mission San Gabriel,"
"Santa Inés and Purisima," "San Luis Obispo,"
etc., etc.*

Edited by *Fr. Felix Pudlowski, O. F. M.*

*"Colligite quae superaverunt fragmenta,
ne pereant," John, vi, 12.*

BALLENA PRESS

P. O. Box 711
Ramona, California 92065

1973

MISSION SANTA BARBARA
SANTA BARBARA, CALIF.
1934.

PREFACE

Numerous and competent critics, in this country and abroad, have acclaimed Father Zephyrin Engelhardt's historical works for their thoroughness, accuracy, and appeal. The books were regarded in another light by the venerable historian himself. He was wont to call them "His Children" —the cherished productions of his penetrating intellect and sympathetic heart.

Father Engelhardt worked painstakingly in libraries and archives, among dusty tomes and scarcely legible documents, to bring into being his monumental volumes on The Missions and Missionaries of California. He relinquished other enticing pursuits and devoted himself entirely to his historical labors to give them a superior character.

Old age with accompanying ailments, even serious illness, could not lessen this solicitude of the distinguished scholar of history. When it became apparent that his life's course was nearly run, his thoughts turned once more to the book on Mission San Carlos which he wanted so eagerly to finish and to give to the world in this sesquicentennial year of Father Serra's death. Before lapsing into a coma from which he never came forth, the dying historian softly queried: "How is the work getting on?"

The present volume is the answer to that final question of good Father Engelhardt, truth-loving historian of the Missions, loyal citizen of California and true son of Saint Francis.

The history of San Carlos is given, for the most part, as Father Engelhardt had prepared it. The narrative is exceptionally interesting. It treats of Father Serra's own Mission and Monterey, the civic capital and "puerto famoso;" of daring adventures upon uncharted seas, and pioneering expeditions into unknown lands.—But above all, the pages of this volume contain the story of Padre Junipero Serra, California's proudest boast!

In accordance with Father Engelhardt's constant practice in the past, grateful recognition is given herewith to those who have assisted in getting this work ready for publication. Special acknowledgement is made to Very Rev. Novatus Benzing, O. F. M., Provincial, who has been of exceptioanl assistance in the preparation of this volume; to Dr. Patrick Roddy, O. F. M., for much helpful advice and encouragement; to Very Rev. Gerald Gay and Rev. Silvano Baquedano of Monterey, for their assistance in obtaining valuable documentary material; to Frater Thaddeus, O. F. M., for his photographical work and to Brother Peter, O. F. M., for typing and proof-reading; to Mr. José Mojica for assistance in translating some of the documents; and to Mr. Edward Borein for the beautiful cover design.

In conclusion, as Father Engelhardt wished, may this volume be his tribute to Padre Junipero Serra in the sesquicentennial year of the latter's death. May it also be a lasting monument to good Father Engelhardt, who labored long and faithfully in collecting the beautiful fragments of California's Romantic Mission History, before they were lost forever.

THE EDITOR.

CONTENTS

CHAPTER IX.

CHAPTER X.

CHAPTER XI.

CHAPTER XII.

CHAPTER XIII.

CHAPTER XIV.

CHAPTER XV.

CHAPTER XVI.

CHAPTER XVII.

CHAPTER XVIII.

CHAPTER XIX.

CHAPTER XX.

CHAPTER XXI.

CHAPTER XXII.

APPENDIX

ILLUSTRATIONS

Page

THIRD MILITARY DISTRICT

V

SAN CARLOS MISSION

(1770-1845)

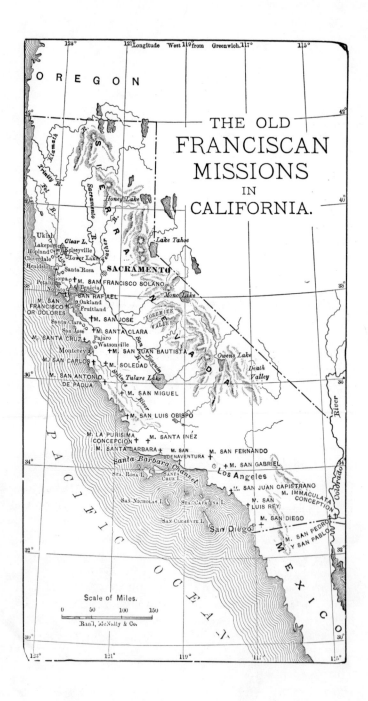

CHAPTER I.

Expedition of J. Rodríguez Cabrillo.—Expedition of Captain S. M. Rodríguez Cermeño.—Discovery of Old San Francisco Bay at Point Reyes.—Holy Mass First Celebrated.—Shipwreck.—Port Abandoned. —Monterey Bay Discovered.—Sebastian Vizcaíno.—First Holy Mass.—Discoveries.—Return to Mexico.

Mission San Carlos, together with the presidio or garrison, was first located on Monterey Bay. This had been discovered as far back as the year 1542, only fifty years after the discovery of America, by the Portuguese navigator, Captain Juan Rodríguez Cabrillo, then in the service of Spain. In two ships, the *San Salvador* and the *Victoria*, Cabrillo's expedition set out from the port of Navidad, twenty miles northwest of the harbor of Manzanillo, Mexico, on June 27th, 1542. "The vessels," says Professor George Davidson,[1] "were smaller than any of our coasting schooners. They were poorly built and very badly outfitted. Their anchors and their ironwork were carried by men from the Gulf of Mexico to the Pacific; they were manned by conscripts and natives; were badly provisioned, and the crews subject to that deadly scourge of the sea, scurvy."

Crossing the Gulf of California, the navigators reached Cape San Lucas on July 6th. They took in water and continued the voyage up the Pacific coast. On the eve of St. Michael's Day, September 28th, both vessels entered the port which for St. Michael they named San Miguel Bay. It is identical with San Diego Bay. Proceeding northward through the Channel, later called for Santa Barbara, on Thursday, November 16th, the *Relacion del Viage de Juan Rodríguez Cabrillo*, wonderfully in accord with the actual coastline, informs us, "the two ships found themselves at day break in a great bay, which came at a turn, and which appeared to have a port and river." They held on, beating about that day and

---

[1] See Bolton's *Spanish Exploration in the Southwest*, pp. 5-6.

night and on the following Friday, until they saw that there was neither river nor shelter.[2] In order to take possession they cast anchor in forty-five fathoms, but did not dare go ashore because of the high sea. "This bay is thirty-nine degrees, full,[3] and its entire shore is covered with pines clear to the sea." They named it Bahia de los Pinos, or Bay of Pines. That night they lay to until the following day.

The following day, Saturday, the ships ran along the coast, and at night found themselves off Cape San Martin.[4] "All the coast run this day is very bold. There are mountains which reach the sky. . .When sailing along near the land, it seems as if the mountains would fall upon the ship. They are covered with snow to the summit," and they named them the Sierra Nevadas. At the beginning of them a cape is formed which projects into the sea, and which they named Cape Nieve.[5]

It appears that Cabrillo, who was then very ill from a broken arm, dared not face the storms and the cold weather any longer, but a little north of Cape Nieve had his vessel move southward to winter at San Miguel Island or La Posesion, as he called it. There on January 3rd, 1543, the heroic commander passed away in consequence of a fall which he had suffered on said island and which broke his arm near the shoulder. After interring his body on the island, the crew named the island for him Juan Rodríguez Island. It is identical with Island San Miguel.

Cabrillo's voyage of exploration had no further consequences and was soon forgotten in the naval world. A brisk trade had, however, developed in the course of time between the Philippine Islands and Mexico. Merchant vessels with

---

[2] Both were there, but it needed going ashore to realize their existence.

[3] Rather thirty-six degrees and thirty-eight minutes. Owing to the defective instruments the calculations of the navigator were about two degrees too high.

[4] Perhaps some point north of San Simeon.

[5] Snow Cape, or perhaps Point Año Nuevo. Critics are all at sea on this and Cape San Martin.

their precious cargoes, would run up the coast of Japan, and thence, taking advantage of the ocean current, cross the Pacific Ocean in the latitude corresponding with Cape Mendocino. From there, about 200 leagues from the shore, seldom nearer, they would run southward to Mexico. The first of the Philippine ships, an exploring vessel, which ever landed on the coast was the *San Agustin* in charge of Captain Sebastian Meléndez Rodríguez Cermeño. Leaving the harbor of Manila on July 5th, 1595, and taking the usual course for the sake of avoiding contrary winds, the captain sighted the northwest shore on November 4th. Running thence southward till they reached the point of land since called Point Reyes, on November 6th, the captain had his ship round the point and was thus the first white man to face the little bay which there and then was named Puerto de San Francisco by the chaplain of the *San Agustin*, Fr. Francisco de la Concepcion, O. F. M. Here the ship lay at anchor for a whole month while the crew built a boat which was to be used for surveying the coast down to the Gulf of California.

Cermeño and his crew lodged in huts on the shore of the bay, where at least every Sunday Fr. Francisco celebrated holy Mass. During the week, however, it seems Fr. Francisco would offer the holy Sacrifice on board the ship for the benefit of the few men who guarded the vessel. Such doubtless was the arrangement then as it would be now. Hence the first holy Mass on the Northwest Coast of America was not celebrated by the Carmelites at San Diego or at Monterey Bay, but by the Franciscan, Fr. Francisco, on Old San Francisco Bay, since 1860 miscalled Drake's Bay, though that freebooter never came in sight of it. Thus the first Catholic worship was offered near the Golden Gate seven years before Vizcaíno and the Carmelites reached the shore of California.

Unfortunately, on November 30th, St. Andrew's Day, probably early in the morning before Fr. de la Concepcion had made preparations to go ashore to celebrate holy Mass for the crews on the shore, it being a Holyday of Obligation, the *San Agustin* was wrecked by a storm, and sank with all the men on board, Fr. Francisco included. Happily the survey boat *San Buenaventura* had just been completed. In it the survivors with Captain Cermeño on Friday, December 8th, set out to make the perilous voyage southward back to Mexico.

"On the following day, which was the 9th," he himself writes, "I coasted along the shore until sundown, when I anchored so as not to pass behind the point by night. Up to this point the coast runs northwest and southeast. I did not take the sun during the day because it did not appear. It was cloudy and there was much wind. During the day I traveled twenty-two leagues without discovering anything worthy of mention. Sailing close to the land, and at times within musket-shot of it, one could see plainly, and that it was bare, like rough broken country, although above on the mountains there were some pine and oak trees. The land seemed to be unpopulated, as no people were seen on it in the day time, and at night there was no smoke nor fire. Sunday morning (December 10th) I commenced to sail, and discovered a very large bay, which I named the Bay of San Pedro. It measures from point to point across the mouth a distance of fifteen leagues travel; and taking the sun in it I found that it was in latitude 37 degrees. Sailing seven or eight leagues toward the south, I anchored behind a point so as not to travel at night."

"This bay," (which Cermeño discovered and named San Pedro), writes Mr. Henry Wagner, "could be nothing else than Monterey Bay, and the distance he measured across it was probably measured from Point Año Nuevo to Point Cypress. The middle of the bay is in about 36 degrees 59 minutes. The point behind which Cermeño anchored may be Point Sur."[6]

Seven years later a Spanish fleet of three ships under General Sebastian Vizcaíno (Vizcayno) appeared at the bay

---

[6] *Voyage of Cermeño*, by Henry R. Wagner, page 15. The *San Buenaventura* eventually reached Acapulco on Wednesday, January, 31, 1596.

to which Cermeño had first given the name *San Pedro*. The three vessels had left the port of Acapulco, in the State of Guerrero, on May 5th, 1602. The ships named *San Diego*, *Santo Tomas*, and *Tres Reyes* respectively, had 200 persons on board. As their chaplains went along the three Carmelite Fathers, Fr. Andrés de Asumpcion, Fr. Antonio de la Ascension, and Fr. Tomas de Aquino. The object of the magnificent undertaking was the survey of the whole Northwest Coast. By the time the fleet reached what is now Monterey harbor, December 16th, at 7 P.M. several of the men had died from the scurvy, forty-five or more were ill from the same malady, and provisions were running low.

"Next morning, December 17th," the journal of Viscaíno relates, "the General ordered Ensign Juan de Alarcón to go ashore, and to build a hut in which holy Mass could be celebrated, and to see if there was any water, and what the country was like. He found that there was fresh water, and a great oak near the shore, where he erected the hut for saying holy Mass. The general, commissary (Fr. Andrés), admiral, captains, ensign, and the rest of the men landed at once[7] and Mass having been said, and the day having cleared, there having been much fog, we found ourselves to be in the best port that could be desired; for besides being sheltered from all winds[8] it has many pines for masts and yards, and live oaks and white oaks, and water in great quantity near the shore.

"In view of the fact that we had so many sick; that the pilot of the admiral's ship (*Santo Tomas*) and his assistant

---

[7] Scarcely possible. Alarcón could not have come back to the flagship until late in the afternoon, too late to celebrate holy Mass. The priests could not have been expected to wait so long, especially as it was Tuesday, not a Sunday. Therefore all waited till next day, Wednesday, December 18th. Then all landed and holy Mass was celebrated to the Holy Ghost for light to see what should be done, as Torquemada has it; but even he does not give the date, which is rather strange.

[8] An error, which in 1769 caused Portolá and his expedition to miss the bay. This port is protected against the storms from the southeast, but not from those that come from the northwest.

FIRST HOLY MASS AT MONTEREY, DECEMBER, 1602.

were very ill; that there was a shortage of sailors for going
forward (northward); and that the supplies were becoming
exhausted owing to the length of the time we spent in coming;
it seemed to the general impossible to complete the exploration at this time without a new supply of men and provisions.
He therefore at once (after the holy Mass as noted by Torquemada) called a council of the officers to consider what
should be done.

"It was decided that the admiral's ship (*Santo Tomas*)
should return as a messenger to the viceroy of New Spain
with a copy of the records of the discoveries as far as this
place, carry back those who were most ill, ask for further
supplies of men and provisions to complete the exploration of
the remainder of the coast; and that we, with the captain's
ship, (*San Diego*) and the frigate (*Tres Reyes*) should go on
to Cape Mendocino, and farther if the weather should permit
. . . . .The admiral's ship accordingly left on Sunday night
at 8 o'clock, and on the 29th of said month of December."

"We ourselves," the Diary of Vizcaíno continues, "remained, making preparations necessary for our voyage to
Cape Mendocino. The men worked under great difficulties
in taking on wood and water, because of the extreme cold.
This was so intense that on Wednesday when New Year's
Day, 1603, dawned, all the mountains were covered with
snow, and that the hole from which we were taking water was
frozen over more than a palm in thickness; and the bottles,
which had been left full over night, were all frozen so that
even when turned upside down not a drop ran out. So urgent
was our situation that necessity compelled us all to act with
energy, especially the general, who aided in carrying the
bottles and in the other tasks, with the support of Ensign
Alarcón and Captain Peguero, who, although ill, aided, while
the pilots spared no efforts to advance our preparation, so
that by Friday night, the 3rd of said month (January), we
were all ready."

"On this day (Friday 3rd)" the Diary continues, "the
general, with the commissary (Fr. Andrés) and ten arque-

busiers, went inland toward the southeast, because they had
heard of a copious stream which ran into the sea and of
another good headland, and in order the better to see the lay
of the land and its people and animals. They proceeded about
three leagues, when they discovered another good port into
which entered a copious river[9] descending from some high,
snow-covered mountains having large pines, white and black
poplars, and willows. It had an extensive river bottom, and
in it were many cattle as large as cows, although they apparently were harts. Yet their pelts were different; for their
wool dragged on the ground,[10] and each horn was more than
three yards long. An effort was made to kill some of them, but
they did not wait long enough. No people were found because
on account of the cold they were living in the interior. The
general sent Ensign Juan Francisco with four soldiers to a
rancheria to see what was there. He found it to be depopu-
lated, and therefore returned.''

Vizcaíno and his company boarded the *San Diego*, and
with the aid of a favorable wind moved out of the bay at
midnight, the same Friday. The ship reached the vicinity of
Port San Francisco, so named by Cermeño seven years previously, but did not enter, although it was recognized and
pointed out by Bolaños, who had been with Cermeño. On
January 12th the ship reached Cape Mendocino. By that
time almost the whole crew was incapacitated. A council
therefore decided to return to Mexico, which they did with
indescribable hardships and the loss of many of the officers
and men through death from scurvy. For details the reader
must be referred to our larger work.

---

[9] Rio Carmelo, so named in honor of the Patroness of the Carmelites,
Our Lady of Carmel. The bay or port was likewise named for the Patroness of the expedition Carmel Bay.

[10] Elks, doubtless.

CHAPTER II.

The waters of Monterey Bay were not again disturbed by
white navigators for more than a century and a half. The
Spanish Government then discovered that the Russians were
planning to establish themselves all along the north Pacific
Coast. In the beginning of 1768, therefore, Inspector General
Joseph de Galvez, who at that time endeavored to restore
order in Lower California, was directed to take the necessary
steps to secure the country discovered by Sebastian Vizcaíno
for the Spanish Crown.

Galvez, accordingly, made preparations to fit out two
expeditions, one by sea and the other by land. Each expedition was to consist of two divisions. For the voyage by sea
the packetboats *San Carlos* and *San Antonio* were chosen. The
former, in charge of Captain Vicente Vila, was ready and lay
at anchor in the Bay of La Paz at the beginning of the month
of January, 1769. At the request of Galvez, Fr. Junipero
Serra, the presidente or superior of the California Missions,
boarded the ship for the religious ceremonies. "On the sixth
of January of this year 1769," he writes in his *Diario*, "finding
myself in the port of La Paz with His Excellency, the Inspector, I blessed the packetboat named *San Carlos*, sang the
High Mass aboard, and blessed the flags. The Litany of Our
Lady and other devotions were sung. Finally His Excellency
made a fervent address which inflamed the hearts of those
who were to go in that ship to the ports of San Diego and
Monterey. He told them that theirs was a glorious task, inasmuch as they were going to plant the standard of the holy
Cross among the heathens. In the name of God, of the king
and of the viceroy he then charged them to respect the mis-

sionaries, and to maintain peace and harmony among themselves."

"On the morning of the 9th of January," Fr. Palou says, "all who were to sail made their confession, received holy Communion, and assisted at Holy Mass." Fr. Serra continues to say, "all embarked on the 9th at night, and on the 10th set sail. The commander determined upon for the expedition by sea was Don Vicente Vila, famed as a pilot on the seas of Europe. Don Miguel Costanzó went as engineer, and the chief of the troops of twenty-five Catalonian Volunteers was Lieutenant Pedro Fages. As chaplain for the expedition and missionary for one of the Missions I appointed Fr. Fernando Parrón, who had been my companion at Loreto since we arrived in California. All joyfully sailed away on the said 10th of January."

The other packetboat, *San Antonio* in charge of Captain Juan Perez, at Cape San Lucas received an overhauling similar to that of the *San Carlos*, and on February 15th was ready for the voyage. Fr. Presidente Serra had gone to join the land expedition, as will appear presently; but he had named Fathers Juan Vizcaíno and Francisco Gómez to accompany the navigators. On February 15th the Inspector General ordered all who were to embark on the *San Antonio* to prepare for their task by making their confessions and receiving holy Communion, which they did during the High Mass sung by one of the Fathers, not named, in honor of the patron of the expedition, the Patriarch St. Joseph, for the success of the undertaking. Thereupon Galvez exhorted the men and officers as he had done those of the *San Carlos*. All then embarked and sailed away for San Diego and Monterey.

In the meantime preparations had been made for the land expedition, which also consisted of two divisions. The first division composed of Captain Fernando Rivera in command of twenty-five leather-jacket soldiers, Fr. Juan Crespi, Don José Cañizares, three muleteers for the pack train, and forty-two Christian Indians for whatever work might arise in the way of opening roads and repairing bad passes. The whole company set out from the Mission San Fernando de Velicatá on March 24th, 1769, and reached the port of San Diego on May 14th, Pentecost Sunday.

The second division, under the military commander and governor of Lower California, Don Gaspár de Portolá, was composed of the commander, Fr. Presidente Junipero Serra, Sergeant José Francisco de Ortega, Leather-Jacket soldiers, muleteers, two serving boys, one for the commander and the other for the Fr. Presidente, and forty-four Christian Indians. This expedition set out from Mission San Fernando de Velicatá on the day after Pentecost Sunday, May 15th. They followed the road taken by Rivera, and arrived at the port of San Diego on July 1st. Next day, the feast of the Visitation of the Blessed Virgin, a High Mass was sung in thanksgiving in honor of St. Joseph, the patron of both divisions.

The packetboat *San Antonio*, which had sailed from Cape San Lucas on February 15th, with many sick aboard, dropped her anchor in the bay on April 14th. The *San Carlos*, which had left La Paz on January 10th, reached the bay and anchored on April 29th, with most of the crew ill from the scurvy. After the sick had been transferred to the camp on the shore near the mouth of the Rio San Diego, the *San Carlos* for lack of able-bodied men lay idle in the harbor for fifteen months before it could begin the return voyage to Mexico.

In the meantime Commander Gaspár de Portolá set out from the camp to lead his expedition northward in search of Monterey Bay. Accompanied by Fathers Juan Crespi and Francisco Gómez this land expedition set out from San Diego Harbor on Friday, July 14th, 1769, after a High Mass offered to Almighty God in honor of St. Joseph for the success of the undertaking. Two days later Sunday July 16th, bearing in mind the chief object of the missionaries in California, Fr. Serra, assisted by Fathers Juan Vizcaíno and Fernando Parrón, founded the first Mission in Alta California under the title of San Diego de Alcalá. For the details of the happy event the reader is referred to our *Mission San Diego*.

Returning to Portolá, we have to note that he was accompanied on this eventful march, besides the two Franciscans mentioned, by Captain Fernando Rivera with twenty-seven Leather-Jacket soldiers, Lieutenant Pedro Fages with seven Catalonian Volunteers, Sergeant José Francisco de Ortega, Engineer Miguel Costanzó, two neophyte servants of the two priests, two servants of Portolá and Rivera, seven muleteers, and fifteen Lower California Christian Indians, in all sixty-seven persons. By order of Fr. Presidente Serra, Fr. Crespi kept a Journal of the expedition. It covers one hundred and forty-four pages in Fr. Palou's *Noticias*. The military commander Portolá, Pedro Fages, Costanzó, and Sergeant Ortega each likewise kept his own record of the journey. Ortega generally preceded the main body in order to direct the clearing of the road and the locating of the camps.

As a rule, holy Mass was celebrated every Sunday and on the principal feastdays of the Spanish calendar. For further details on the march, the reader is referred to our second volume of the *Missions and Missionaries of California*. The road taken ran, so far as practicable, in sight of the ocean and then through the Sierra de Santa Lucía in the vicinity of the later Mission San Antonio, and finally to the Salinas River on September 27th. Proceeding down its course, the expedition Sunday, October 1st, camped within a league and a half of the river's mouth and of their own destination.

"Shortly afterwards," Fr. Crespi writes, "the commander, the engineer, and myself, accompanied by five soldiers, went to examine the beach. We ascended a little hill (doubtless Mulligan's Hill on the Moro Cojo Ranch) which is not very far from it, and from the summit beheld a grand enseñada or open bay, and we conjectured that it was the one which Cabrera Bueno places between Point Año Nuevo and Point Pinos de Monterey; for we saw the latter covered with tall pines, so that near it must be found the Port of Monterey." That is to say, as Bancroft aptly remarks "believing yet doubting they look out over the bay and harbor of Monterey, then pass on wondering where is Monterey."

"We saw not a single Indian around here," Fr. Crespi notes.

"We accordingly returned to camp, and the commander decided that the captain (Rivera) should on the following morning go forth to examine said point." Rivera with eight men on Monday morning marched southward along the shore of the bay. They crossed Point Pinos, and on the other side discovered "a small bight formed by the said point and another south of it, with an arroyo flowing down from the mountains, well wooded, and a slough into which the said stream discharges its waters." They had discovered Carmelo Bay and Carmelo River and Cypress Point. It is remarkable that on recrossing Point Pinos, and standing near the ravine at the foot of Presidio Hill, as they must have done, Rivera and his men failed to recognize the port. From that point of vision the bay is just what Cabrera Bueno described it—egg form.

The exploring party returned to the camp on Tuesday evening, and all declared that no port had been discovered. Portolá thereupon decided to call a council of his officers and the two friars. At his request on the following morning they celebrated holy Mass to the Holy Ghost for light in the matter. Next day, October 4th, Fr. Crespi gave vent to his feelings in these words: "This is a grand day for all the children of St. Francis, whose feast we his sons celebrate in this corner of the world, without any other church or choir than a wilderness, having constructed a brushwood shelter for the celebration of the holy Sacrifice of the Mass, which each of us offered up with as much devotion as possible, praying the Holy Ghost, through the intercession of our Seraphic Father, to enlighten the officers so that they might determine what is conducive to the greater honor and glory of our king."

"Holy Mass concluded," Fr. Crespi reports, "The commander called all the officers, and, when all had assembled in the Name of God, he laid before them the lack of provisions, the many sick we had (who were seventeen men, half crippled and in no condition for hardships), the distance already traveled, all that the men still able suffered from the excessive burden of guarding the stock at night, having to perform

sentinel duties, and continually making explorations and surveys. In view of what had been said, and that the Port of
Monterey had not been found in the latitude in which it was
supposed to be, he wished each one to give his opinion freely,
in order to determine what might be judged most expedient.
all the officers voted that the march should be continued as
the only expedient remaining, in the hope, with the favor of
God, of reaching the desired Port of Monterey, and of finding
in it the packetboat, *San José*, which would relieve them of
all necessities; and that, if God should permit that in search
of Monterey all should perish, we shall have complied with
our duty to God and to men. We two religious also attended
this council, and we voted the same way."

Before starting out to execute this resolution, Ortega with
his men moved out early on October 5th to explore the country
to the northward in the hope of reaching the other point of
the bay or roadstead, as it appeared to them, which it was
thought might be Point Año Nuevo. The explorers returned
on Friday evening, October 6th, and reported that no harbor
had been found.

The main hope of Portolá and his party now rested on the
supposition that they had not as yet arrived in the latitude
where Cabrera Bueno and Sebastian Vizcaíno located the
Port of Monterey, that is to say in thirty-seven degrees. Fr.
Crespi calculated that Camp Santa Delfina, where the expedition had been resting since October 1st, lay in thirty-six
degrees and fifty-three minutes; Costanzó observed thirty-six
degrees and forty-four minutes. The march was therefore
resumed on Saturday, October 7th. Instead of finding Monterey Bay, however, which lay before them unrecognized, after
undergoing indescribable hardships, the expedition on October
31st discovered and at once recognized San Francisco Bay
behind Point Reyes. "We have therefore left the Port of
Monterey behind," Fr. Crespi and the advance guard under
Sergeant Ortega exclaimed!

After they had surveyed the bay region sufficiently,
Portolá and his officers were now convinced that the expedi-

tion must go back to Point Pinos in order to find the Port of Monterey, and in it the *San José* with supplies waiting for them. The weary return march was begun on November 11th, and on Sunday 26th the explorers found themselves back at Camp Santa Delfina near the mouth of the Salinas River. Next morning they forded the stream above tidewater, passed by sand dunes, and halted for the night near a small lagoon in view of Point Pinos. On November 28th they crosssed the pine-covered hills and pitched their camp back of Carmelo Bay, probably on or near the spot where later on Mission San Carlos was established. Costanzó found the latitude the same as that of Cadiz, Spain: thirty-six degrees and six minutes.

Portolá now ordered a close survey of the coast. While Captain Rivera, some soldiers and six Lower California neophytes examined the surrounding country and shores, the men in camp suffered exceedingly for want of food; for neither game nor fish, not even clams could be obtained. Only the animals fared well, Fr. Crespi remarked, because there was plenty of grass. Hunger drove the men to kill sea gulls and pelicans. Finally a mule was slaughtered, but only the Catalonian volunteers and the Indian attendants would eat the flesh. Cold weather added to the general distress. Rivera on the night of December 4th returned and reported that he had failed to discover the Port of Monterey; and that the only certainty he had was that they were at the foot of the Sierra Santa Lucía, but that there was no way of passing it along the coast.

Portolá accordingly called a council for the 7th of December. On the 6th and on the 7th also the two Fathers celebrated holy Mass for the intention that the officers might reach the right decision. The majority decided that the return march should begin at once, since the supplies had dwindled to fourteen sacks of poor flour, snow was covering the hills and might render roads impassable, and the cold was already excessive. Next day, Friday, December 8th, the feast of the Immaculate Conception, "we two priests," Fr. Crespi writes, "celebrated this day the feast of our Most Beloved Superioress* by offering up the holy Sacrifice of the Mass at which all attended. The weather was rough and stormy, and did not permit us to leave the place. On Sunday, December 10th, we both celebrated holy Mass, and every one attended. Before we departed, a large cross, framed for that purpose, was raised (on a hillock near Carmelo Bay, which likewise had not been recognized). On the cross were carved the words—'Dig at the base and thou wilt find a writing.' The document, which related the arrival of the expedition, the failure to discover the Bay of Monterey, the discovery of San Francisco Bay, and the necessity of returning to escape starvation, was placed in a bottle and buried at the foot of the cross."

On December 11th, the disheartened explorers left the camp at Carmelo Bay, crossed the pine-covered peninsula, forded the Salinas, and for the night camped near the spot which they had occupied on September 30th. Here both Fathers on the 12th celebrated holy Mass in honor of the feast of the day, Our Lady of Guadalupe. The march was then continued and pretty much the same route traveled as in coming until they arrived at the camp of San Diego Bay and were welcomed on Wednesday, January 24th, 1770.

---

* "Fiesta de Nuestra Amantisima Prelada," as Fr. Crespi has it.

CHAPTER III.

Bancroft's Conclusions.—Explanation.—Second Land Expedition Successful.—The *San Antonio.*—Fr. Serra Founds Mission San Carlos.—
The Presidio.

"It is and must ever remain more or less inexplicable,"
Bancroft feels constrained to confess, "that the Spaniards
should have failed to identify Monterey Bay at this time. All
that was known of that port had resulted from Vizcaíno's
visit, and this knowledge was in the hands of the explorers
and in the works of Venégas and Cabrera Bueno. The description of the landmarks was tolerably clear, and in fact
these landmarks had been readily recognized by Portolá's
party at their first arrival on the bay shore. Moreover, the
advantages of the harbor had not been greatly exaggerated,
both Torquemada, as quoted by Venégas, and Cabrera Bueno
having called Monterey simply a *famoso puerto*, the former
stating that it was protected from all winds, and the latter,
from all except the northwest winds. Yet with the harbor
lying at their feet, and with several landmarks so clearly defined that Vila and Serra recognized them at once from the
reports at San Diego, and penetrated the truth of the matter
in spite of their companions' mystification, the Spanish officers
could find nothing resembling the object of their search, and
were even tempted to account for the port's disappearance
by the theory that since Vizcaíno's time it had perhaps been
'filled up with sand.' "[1]

Fr. Francisco Palou, on the other hand ventures an explanation, and Bancroft acknowledges that it would be difficult to prove the theory inaccurate. "When the venerable
Fr. Junipero Serra," writes Fr. Palou, "conferred with the
inspector-general (Galvez) about the first three missions
which Galvez had directed him to establish in the New (Alta)
California, seeing the names and patrons which had been

---

[1] History of California, vol. i, p. 152.

assigned, he said to him, 'and is there to be no mission for our Father San Francisco?' Don Joseph de Galvez replied, 'If San Francisco wants a mission, let him cause his port[2] to be discovered, and it shall be placed there.' The expedition went up; it reached the Port of Monterey; it halted and planted a cross there; yet not one of those who went there recognized it, although they made out all the marks in the history. They went up forty leagues farther; came to the Port of our Father, San Francisco,[3] and at once recognized it from the conformity with the description which they had brought along. In view of this, what else must we say than that our holy Father wanted a Mission at this port?"[4]

Fr. Palou's inference, that the eyes of the explorers must have been held so that they should not see,[5] is corroborated by the narrative of the puzzled Fr. Juan Crespi. "In view of what has been said of the Sierra Santa Lucía," he writes, "which this sierra back of our camp doubtless is, and that we do not find in this neighborhood the celebrated Port of Monterey, although the examination was made at their leisure by men of character, who are capable, intelligent, and versed in navigation, who came expressly to survey this coast by order of the king, we have to say that they did not find it after the closest investigation made at the cost of much labor and hardship. Possibly it may have to be said that it has been filled up and destroyed in the course of time; but, inasmuch as we see no reason for such a decision, I suspend my own judgement on this matter. What I can say with certainty is that efforts have been made on the part of the commander, the officers and the soldiers, yet no such port has been discovered, although God permitted that we should reach and recognize the Port of San Francisco."[6]

The situation at San Diego the reader will find fully de-

[2] Cermeño Bay, or Old San Francisco Bay.
[3] Cermeño Bay.
[4] Palou, *Vida*, cap. xviii.
[5] Allusion to Luke, xxiv, 16.
[6] Crespi, *Diario*, December 5th.

scribed in our *San Diego Mission*, along with the description
of the preparations made for a second attempt to reach Monterey Bay. Two expeditions, one by land the other by sea,
were ready about the middle of April, 1770. In the *San
Antonio*, commanded by Captain Juan Perez, Fr. Junipero
Serra, Miguel Costanzó, and Dr. Pedro Prat took passage,
when it sailed for its destination on April 16th. The second
land expedition in charge of Commander Portolá, accompanied
by Fr. Juan Crespi and Pedro Fages, set out next day, April
17th. On Ascension Day, May 24th, the land expedition
reached the bay on which they had camped in the previous
December. Lieutenant Fages, Fr. Crespi and a soldier who
had been present at the raising of the Cross, accompanied
Portolá to search for the *San Antonio*. When they approached
the sacred emblem of eternal salvation they observed with
amazement that it was surrounded by feather-topped arrows
and sticks driven into the ground. From one of the sticks a
yard from the Cross, dangled a string of sardines; and on the
other side to another stick was fastened a piece of meat. At
the foot of the Cross lay a heap of clams. Evidently the
savages had placed these things there as offerings, but the
motive for the action was not learned until some time later.

"As soon as the recently baptized Indians had begun to express themselves in Spanish, and the Lower California neophytes, who had come along understood the language of these
natives," Fr. Crespi relates, "they on various occasions explained that the first time they saw our men they noticed
that every one wore on his breast a small, glittering cross;
that when the Spaniards had gone away and left this large
cross on the shore, the Indians dreaded to approach the sacred
sign, because at night they would see it surrounded by brilliant rays which would even dispel the darkness; that the
cross appeared to grow larger so as to reach the skies; that in
the daytime, when it stood in its natural size without the
rays, they would approach it and offer meat, fishes and mus-
sels in order to enlist its favor, lest it harm them; and that,
when to their amazement, they saw that the cross did not

consume these things, they would offer their plumes and arrows in token of their desire to be at peace with the people who had planted it there." This explanation, Fr. Palóu remarks, different Indians at various periods and without the least variation repeated to Fr. Presidente Serra when he returned from Mexico in 1774.[7]

Portolá with Fr. Crespi, Pedro Fages and the one soldier now turned to the harbor to see whether the packetboat had appeared. As the day was very clear they observed that the bay was formed by Point Pinos and another point which runs out much farther into the sea, and which had always been judged to be Point Año Nuevo. They observed that the whole immense bay was as calm as though it were a grand lagoon, and that countless seals were swimming and barking therein. They also noticed two large cub whales very near the beach, not farther than five yards away, which was evident proof of sufficient depth.

While walking along the same beach a short distance they soon perceived that the bay was locked in by Point Año Nuevo and Point Pinos in such a way that the grand body of water resembled a round lake like an O. At sight of this all three with one voice exclaimed: "This is the Port of Monterey for which we are searching; for it is to the letter as Sebastian Vizcaíno and Cabrera Bueno describe it!" To make sure that they were not deceived, the commander resolved to await the arrival of the *San Antonio* on the other side of Point Pinos where they had camped on December 10th, 1769, at the Rio Carmelo, because the water on the north side proved brackish or insufficient for their needs.

Meanwhile the *San Antonio* had been battling with heavy storms which drove her as far south as degree thirty. She made her way back and continued as far north as the farallones, southwest of Point Reyes. From there she sailed along the coast southward until she reached Monterey Bay and cast her anchor in the evening of May 31st, just one week after the

---

[7] Palóu, *Vida*, chap. xxii; Noticias, tom. ii, chap. xxi.

Mision de Sta. Cruz

Mulligan Hill, whence the explorers viewed the bay

R. de San Antonio now Salinas River

MAP OF

MONTEREY BAY

ALEXANDRO MALASPINA

1791

N.

S.

Pta. de Pinos

Presidio de Monterey

Pta. de Cipreses

Mision de San Carlos

Ensenada de Carmelo

Rio del Carmelo

Pta. del Carmelo

1 2 3 4 5

Escala de 5 millas maritimas

arrival of the land expedition. Portolá now immediately ordered three fires lighted, the signal agreed upon to let them know that the land expedition had arrived. The *San Antonio* at once responded with the counter-signal, the firing of a cannon, as token that the watch-fires had been seen. Next day, June 1st, Portolá, Fages and Fr. Crespi crossed the peninsula of Point Pinos from Carmelo, and heartily welcomed Fr. Serra and the whole crew of the packetboat.

Orders were now given to remove the camp from the arroyo near the Rio Carmelo to the newly discovered harbor of Monterey. The shore was closely examined, and then very near the ravine the pools of water and the oak trees were seen, especially the large one whose branches bathed in the sea when the tide was in, where holy Mass was celebrated in the year 1602 when Sebastian Vizcaíno's expedition anchored there. The ceremony of taking formal possession was fixed for Pentecost Sunday, June 3rd. Fr. Crespi describes the memorable event as follows:

"On June 3rd, 1770, Pentecost Sunday, on the shore of the Port of Monterey, there being assembled Commander Don Gaspár de Portolá with his officers, subalterns, soldiers and the rest of the expedition, Don Juan Perez, captain of the packetboat *San Antonio* with his sub-captain, Don Miguel de Pino, the whole crew and the rest of the sea expedition, and the Rev. Fr. Lector and Presidente of all the Missions, Fr. Junipero Serra, with Fr. Juan Crespi, an arbor (enramada) having been erected on the very spot by the side of the little ravine, and near the live-oak where in the year 1602 the Rev. Carmelite Fathers, who had come with the expedition of Comandante Don Sebastian Vizcaíno, had celebrated the holy sacrifice of the Mass, an altar was arranged, the bells were suspended, and the celebration began with the loud ringing of the bells.

"The Fr. Presidente named, vested in alb and stole, all kneeling, implored the assistance of the Holy Ghost (whose coming upon the small assembly of the apostles and disciples of the Lord, the Universal Church celebrated that day) and intoned with all possible solemnity the hymn of the day, the *Veni Creator Spiritus*. Thereupon he blessed water and with it the great cross, which had been constructed, and which all helped to raise and place in position, and then venerated. He then sprinkled the whole surroundings and the shore with holy water in order to drive away all infernal enemies. Thereupon High Mass commenced at the altar upon which stood the lovely image of Our Lady, which, through Inspector-General Galvez, the Most Rev. Francisco de Lorenzana, then Archbishop of Mexico, but now Archbishop of Toledo and Primate of Spain, had donated for the expedition to Monterey. This first holy Mass was sung by the said Fr. Presidente, who also preached after the gospel, the lack of musical instruments being supplied by the repeated salutes from the cannon of the bark and the volleys from the muskets and other firearms. At the conclusion of the holy Mass the *Salve Regina* was sung before the lovely statue of Our Lady, and then the ceremony terminated with the *Te Deum Laudamus*.

"When this first function of the Church was concluded, the commander proceeded to take formal possession of the land in the name of our King, Don Carlos III (God protect him) by raising anew the royal standard, which had already been unfurled after the erection of the holy cross. To this were added the customary ceremonies of pulling up some grass, throwing stones and earth to the four winds, and drawing up a record of all that had taken place. From this day began the Divine Worship, and the famous Port of Monterey came under the dominion and government of our King. Thereupon all the gentlemen together with the Fathers dined on the shore of the port, as did all the men of the sea and land expeditions, repeated volleys of the cannon and muskets in the meantime accompanying the various functions of the celebration.

"On the same day, June 3rd, Pentecost Sunday, 1770, on which Governor and Commander Gaspár de Portolá took possession of the Port of Monterey in the name of the king, and began the presidio of San Carlos, the Rev. Fr. Presidente of all the Missions, Fr. Junipero Serra, in the name of the king, and in the name of the Rev. Guardian and of the Ven. Discretory of the Apostolic College of the Propagation of the Faith of San Fernando de Mexico, began the new Mission under the title of San Carlos, naming as chief patron of the new church the most holy Patriarch St. Joseph, as he had been directed by the illustrious Inspector-General that two patrons should be assigned, one for the Mission, who was San Carlos Borromeo, and the other for the church, who was the most holy Patriarch St. Joseph. As our ecclesiastical head, he (Fr. Serra) took possession of it in the name of the said College, appointing as his companion missionary Fr. Juan Crespi, his pupil in philosophy, which he had taught him in the royal monastery of our Seraphic Father San Francisco in the City of Palma in the holy Province of Majorca.

"The first religious function, then, performed at this new Mission was that which I described before. An arbor of boughs served as the first church, and in it a table for an altar on which they continued to celebrate holy Mass until an apartment was completed which served as a chapel.

"On the same day on which the Mission was founded and possession had been taken, as soon as the holy cross was erected, as I have already said, and before the singing of the Mass, ecclesiastical burial was given to the body of Alejo Viño, the calker of the packetboat, who had died aboard the ship on the day before, after receiving the sacraments of Penance and Extreme Unction. The remains were interred close to the holy cross.

"As soon as in the royal presidio the apartment was finished which was to serve for a temporary church, the holy ceremony of its benediction having preceded, in it the solemn function of the Corpus Christi celebration was observed on its proper day, which was June 14th with a High Mass. The Solemn Procession with the Blessed Sacrament was held in the square already marked out and begun for the royal presidio. The procession made its way around accompanied by the peals of bells and repeated salutes from the cannons on the packetboat and from the guns and muskets of the soldiers. This function was for all a source of great rejoicings and extraordinary delight, as every Roman Catholic Christian will understand."

On the following day, June 15th, a soldier and a sailor, who both had volunteered for the dangerous errand, set out on horseback with the messages from Portolá to the viceroy which announced the discovery of Monterey harbor and other details. Going overland to Lower California they reached Fr. Francisco Palóu, the Superior of the peninsular Missions, and Governor Ármona at Mission Todos Santos on August 2nd. On the following day Fr. Palóu sang a High Mass in thanksgiving, and then Armona had the messengers transferred by ship across the gulf, and they eventually reached the capital. The news created great rejoicings at the viceroy's court and at the college of San Fernando in which the whole population joined.

Portolá toward the close of the month, as ordered by Don José de Galvez, turned over the command to Lieutenant Pedro Fages, and in the *San Antonio* on July 9th sailed for Mexico.[8]

---

[8] Palou, *Noticias*, tom. ii, chap. xxv-xxvi.

CHAPTER IV.

Building activities, as already indicated, began soon after
the arrival of the packetboat. The first structures were of a
primitive nature. Poles driven side by side into the ground,
the interstices filled out with twigs and branches and perhaps
covered with mud, and a roof of similar construction, constituted the first buildings. Lieutenant Pedro Fages, who at
the end of the month of June relieved Portolá of his command
gives some details. Reporting to Viceroy De Croix under
date of July 1st, 1770, he says: "Since the arrival of the
packetboat two warehouses have been erected, one for the
presidio and one for the Mission. A little apart from these a
smaller structure was built for the safekeeping of the powder.
I am staying at the presidio with the surgeon, Don Pedro
Prat, twelve men of my company (Catalonian Volunteers),
seven ordinary (Leather-Jacket) soldiers, and five sailors whom
Captain Juan Perez left here on account of illness, four of
them suffering from the scurvy."

The other building or warehouse, which Fages does not
describe, contained a room for the goods brought along, the
apartments for the two Fathers, and the chapel. Such was
the situation at the beginning of July, 1770. It would be interesting to learn how the indefatigable Fr. Presidente conducted himself under those circumstances. For one thing we
know that he speedily came to the conclusion that the immediate neighborhood of the site chosen was most unsuitable
for a Mission among Indians. As it had to be self-supporting,
agriculture and the raising of livestock, cattle and sheep
especially, were essential features of the establishments to be
founded for the native converts. Now the vicinity of the
presidio lacked sufficient land as well as water to irrigate the
land. There was, too, the proximity of the soldiers, Leather-

Jacket soldiers at that, who were not volunteers like the Catalonian band of Fages, but jailbirds and convicts allowed their liberty on condition that they went to California. This class of mission protectors had proved pernicious to the Missions in Lower California. Hence it was that with the various reports which the *San Antonio* carried to Mexico went also a petition from Fr. Serra to the viceroy for permission to transfer the Mission to the Rio Carmelo across the peninsula of Point Pinos. He also asked for more missionaries. Both petitions were granted, as we shall see in the proper places.

Meanwhile the Fr. Presidente and Fr. Crespi made efforts to prepare the way for the conversion of the Indians; but as there was no one who knew their language the two apostles of Christ encountered insurmountable difficulties. Then it pleased God, Fr. Palóu relates, to open a way for them to the mind of the Indians. They had brought from Lower California an Indian boy, who by associating with the natives at length began to understand their language. When he had learned how to explain the intention of the missionaries; that they had come from far away to teach them the way to everlasting happiness in heaven, the natives showed willingness to listen, and thus the way was open to the hearts as well as the minds of the suspicious savages; and thus it came to pass, that Fr. Palóu could report with a glad heart as follows: "On December 26th of said year (1770) the first baptism[1] took place in that pagan nation. It was for the fervent and ardent heart of our venerable Father (Serra) an indescribable jubilee. In the course of time others were gained, and increased the number of Christians so that after three years, when I came up to that mission, there were already one hundred and sixty-five Christian Indians."[2]

[1] Eight months after the first Baptism of an Indian at Mission San Diego. See our *Mission San Diego*, page 126.

[2] In the same letter Fr. Serra informed Fr. Palóu: "That at San Diego they are already baptizing grown up people and they are also celebrating marriages. Here at San Carlos we, too, are approaching that point, for already the young people begin to express themselves in Castilian.

The missionaries received much support, or rather as Fr. Palóu writes in this connection, it was the principal basis for the important conquest, that God, our Lord, let the savages witness wonderful things and prodigies, so that they were filled with both fear and love for the Catholics: with fear, which restrained them, despite their great numbers, from treating the small number of Christians with insolence; with love of a kind, which made them listen with a sort of affection for the Evangelical Doctrine which had come to teach and move them to embrace the sweet yoke of our holy Law. In proof of this Fr. Palóu here quotes the incident with the shining Cross on the shore of Monterey Bay, which was reported by Fr. Crespi, and which we have already noted in the previous chapter.

A noteworthy event was the arrival on May 21st, 1771, of ten Franciscan Fathers from the missionary College of San Fernando in the City of Mexico. They had volunteered for the new Missions to be established in California. These new recruits were a source of great joy for the venerable Fr. Presidente, who had asked for more missionaries to spread the Gospel among the Indian tribes on the coast. An abundance of provisions had also been brought up in the packet *San Antonio*. Additional shelters of palisades had been erected where the ten friars could take up their abode until assigned to their posts.

As the feast of Corpus Christi that year fell on May 30th, the feast of the patron saint of their College, Fr. Serra resolved to utilize the opportunity of impressing the natives with the beauties of the Christian Religion by having a celebration with as much pomp as the circumstances permitted. At all events, twelve priests in their vestments following the Holy Eucharist borne by the Fr. Presidente proceeding under a baldaquin or canopy and guarded by the military in uniform, would be a sight never to be forgotten, and not likely to be repeated in a lifetime. So the celebration was held with all the solemnity possible. Solemn High Mass was offered up with deacon and subdeacon, the missionaries forming the choir, and the celebrant, doubtless Fr. Serra, preached the sermon. The great heart of Fr. Junipero, says, Fr. Palóu, seemed too small to contain the great joy which overflowed his soul on seeing such a magnificent worship rendered to God on the shore of Monterey Bay.

Thereupon the Fr. Presidente assigned the missionaries, only Fr. Juan Crespi and himself remaining at Monterey. Six of the friars sailed on the *San Antonio* for San Diego, whence they proceeded to reach their respective field of labor. Four others stayed awhile and eventually went to the Missions of San Antonio and San Luis Obispo.

The Fr. Presidente then started out to explore the valleys on the Carmel River whither Mission San Carlos was to be transplanted. He found a suitable locality, and ordered the felling of trees for constructing the habitations. For this purpose he left there three sailors, who had remained behind, and four Lower California neophytes. A guard of five men under a corporal directed the work and saw that the timber was prepared for the buildings of the Mission. In the meantime Fr. Serra journeyed twenty-five leagues southward to the Sierra de Santa Lucía, where on July 14th, 1771, he founded Mission San Antonio, and placed in charge the two Fathers Miguel Pieras and Buenaventura Sitjar.

Returning to Monterey about the end of July, Fr. Serra hastened arrangements for the Carmelo Mission, which he wanted to establish in person. At Monterey he left Fathers Joseph Cavaller and Domingo Juncosa, who were destined for San Luis Obispo Mission not as yet founded, to look after the spiritual welfare of the troops, and Fr. Crespi to take care of the convert Indians. He was to provide the converts with food, and to recite twice a day the Doctrina Cristiana. New applicants for the Mission family were ever kindly to be received but directed to the camp at Rio Carmelo.

When these preliminaries had been effected, the Fr. Presidente set out for the spot chosen at Carmelo, about a league from the presidio, and there to lead a sort of hermit's life in a little shack erected for him. He would act as overseer, and often as an ordinary laborer, until a dwelling had been constructed in which he could find shelter against the cold winds which are experienced in that canyon almost all the year round. The first work he ordered done was the framing of a large cross, which, having been blessed, with the help of the soldiers and servants was planted and stationed about the center of the plot intended for the quadrangle, which was between the shack that served for his habitation and another structure that served as a temporary church so that his company and all his delights were that sacred emblem. He would venerate it as soon as the morning dawned, and the troops would sing the *Alabado*. Before it, too, the servant of God would recite the Matins and the office of Prime, whereupon he would immediately celebrate the holy Sacrifice of the Mass, at which all the soldiers and laborers assisted. Thereupon all would commence their work, each one in his own line, the venerable Father acting as engineer and overseer of the operations. Many times during the day he would venerate the holy Cross, and before it recite the Divine Office (Breviary). "All this," Fr. Palóu relates, "I heard from the mouth of the corporal who served as sentinel on the place. In the same way he, (Fr. Serra) exercized himself at night after concluding the recitation of the Rosary. This example was followed by the soldiers and the Indians learned to do likewise.

"When the pagans visited the venerable Father," Fr. Palou continues, "and there was seldom a day on which they failed to do so, attracted by curiosity or by the little presents he gave them, the first thing he would do was to make the sign of the cross on them with his own hands, and then he had them venerate the holy cross. After the conclusion of these holy ceremonies he would regale them either with food of boiled wheat or corn he ordered for them, or with *atole*, mush made of those grains, or with beads and trinkets as much as he could, in this way learning from them the language.

"The Christians would also visit him. They would ask permission of Fr. Crespi at Monterey to go and see the Old Father, as they would say. With these he had his delight, showing them more affection as though they were his own children. He taught them to salute everybody with the pious words *Amar á Dios* (Love God). The custom spread in such a way that even the pagans would utter this salutation, not only to the Fathers but to every Spaniard. It extended over this whole vast region. It would touch the hardest heart to hear the pagans on meeting their companions, or Spaniards on the road saluting with the words *Amar á Dios*.

"As soon as the venerable Father had concluded building the chapel and necessary dwellings, which was at the end of the year 1771, he called from Monterey his companion, Fr. Crespi. The new Mission with all the Christian neophytes was moved to Carmelo, where both together began that spiritual conquest. This became his own peculiar Mission, where he continued till his death, when he was not bound to visit other Missions or make necessary journeys in virtue of his office of Presidente of the Missions."

Concerning the permanent buildings constructed under the eyes of Fr. Serra at Carmelo Fr. Palóu says, "they consisted of one room for a chapel. To this were added a dwelling of four rooms, and one larger room for a granary, besides a house for keeping the boys, and a kitchen. All these structures were of wood and had a flat roof, and all were surrounded by a stockade. At one corner of the stockade a house with a flat roof was built to serve as a room for the guards and within sight some corrals for the mules and cattle were erected."

The new Mission San Carlos was located in a delightful spot, upon a hill in sight of a broad plain through which runs the Rio Carmelo. In the vicinity of the Mission were several villages of pagan Indians, who soon began to frequent it and whose conversion Fr. Serra and Crespi ere long brought about.

Owing to the delay in the arrival of the supply ships and the increase of converts, a severe dearth of provisions was felt at the two Missions of San Diego and San Gabriel. Military commander Pedro Fages, now captain, hastened over 2000 lbs. of flour to San Diego. Fr. Presidente Serra had, on April 13th, 1772, Fr. Crespi go along to substitute for Fr.

MISSION SAN CARLOS. ETCHING BY HENRY CHAPMAN FORD.

Dumetz who was seeking aid in Lower California. On passing
Mission San Gabriel, Fr. Crespi wrote that he saw the missionaries there already "tightening their girdles." At San
Diego he learned that for a long time the two Fathers there
each had been subsisting on half a pint of corn, twenty ounces
of flour and a little milk each day.

Soon the lack of supplies was felt also at San Carlos and
San Antonio. Writing from San Carlos to Fr. Palóu in Lower
California on August 18th, 1772, Fr. Serra related: "The
principal supporters of our people are pagan Indians. Through
their sympathy we live as God wills, though the milk from the
cows and some vegetables from the garden have been the
chief subsistence, but both sources are becoming scarce. However, the long, vexatious delay of fourteen months is coming
to an end. News has arrived that the ships are bringing
abundant supplies."

Meanwhile, in order to procure some relief for Monterey
and the two Missions in the north, Captain Fages sent a hunting expedition to the Valley of the Bears, fifty leagues southward, where Mission San Luis Obispo was established in the
following September, 1772. The hunters were successful.
During their three months' raid they killed so many bears
that they could send back to Monterey twenty-five packmules laden with about 6000 lbs. of meat.

Writing to Viceroy De Croix under date of June 26th,
1772, Captain Fages reported the incident thus: "No ship
has arrived, wherefore we are at present very much in want
of provisions, for they will last scarcely two months. I have
ordered two parties to go hunting for bears, and they succeeded in killing thirty to help us to much food. Greens and milk
aid us much. For the presidio there were sown four fanegas
of wheat and two of barley." That means the soldiers went
to work to raise supplies for themselves and families. Would
that they had kept it up throughout the Mission Period and
not expected the neophyte Indians to support them. Later
we shall see to what straits the idleness of the soldiers reduced
the Missions.

Next day, June 27th, Fages wrote to De Croix that he had received the despatch announcing his promotion by the king to the grade of Captain of the Infantry.

Indeed as early as June 20, 1771, he reported to Viceroy De Croix under the heading: *Noticia* del Cultivo de Tierras, que hay existentes en este Reál Presidio de San Carlos de *Monterey* as follows: "There is a garden 130 varas long in which were sown and harvested different kinds of vegetables by means of irrigation. Its width is in parts 40 and 50 varas, and the narrowest portion is 25 varas wide. In this plot were sown in the prepared soil one fanega of wheat and another fanega of barley. In another cultivated plot about a quarter of a league to the east, half was sown with a fanega of wheat and the other half with a fanega of barley. To the north of the same garden, about a quarter of a league they have culti-vated a piece of land 77 varas wide and 150 varas long, where they planted two fanegas of beans. In the same garden they have planted two almudes of rice. (This is the first mention of rice). They have also made a canoe (flatboat?) seven varas long and five wide to carry salt from the saltpits (salinas), and poles for corrals." (This shows the soldiers were kept busy for their own and the presidio's good).

The *San Carlos* as well as the *San Antonio* with supplies for the missions and presidios arrived at San Diego during the month of August, 1772; but the captains notified Fr. Serra that owing to the contrary winds, the ships could not continue the voyage to Monterey, and that therefore the provisions in-tended for Missions San Antonio and San Carlos would be unloaded at San Diego, whence they could be brought up by packmules. As Captain Pedro Fages was about to go south anyhow, Fr. Serra accompanied him in order to persuade the captains of the packetboats to change their minds. On the way down he founded Mission San Luis Obispo on September 1, 1772. At San Diego he and Captain Fages showed Captain Perez of the *San Antonio* how impossible it would be for want of packmules and necessary guards to transport the goods and supplies to Monterey overland, one hundred and seventy leagues. They both therefore begged the captain to trust in God, and to brave the contrary winds in order to bring the sorely needed provisions to their destination. The worthy navigator agreed, set sail again on September 27th and safely reached Monterey harbor.

Fr. Serra now thought it time to proceed to the founding of Mission San Buenaventura for which the Inspector General himself had packed the church goods three years before. Captain Fages, who had already tried to interfere with the affairs of the Missions, declined to lend his assistance, and what was worse, he gave the Fr. Presidente to understand that this was a matter which pertained to him and not to the missionaries. This was an assumption and contrary to the explicit orders of the viceroy. Moreover, from a letter written by the new viceroy Antonio Bucareli it was clear that the missionaries had been misrepresented by Captain Fages. To avert all future disputes or interference, the missionaries, who could be assembled at San Diego, with the Fr. Presidente decided that one of their number should have to confer with the viceroy in person so as to obtain an authoritative decision regarding their rights towards the Indian converts. All moreover were of the conviction that no better representative could be found than the Fr. Presidente himself. On October 20, 1772, accordingly, Fr. Serra sailed for Mexico in the *San Carlos*, in the company of an Indian youth, one of the first baptized at Monterey, and reached the port of San Blas on November 4th. On February 6th, 1773, with his young companion he was welcomed at the College of San Fernando in the Capital. On August 4th, Juan Evangelista, the boy companion then fifteen years of age, was confirmed by Archbishop Peralta, as the first Upper California Indian favored in that manner.

The Fr. Presidente had several conferences with the viceroy, who entirely reversed his opinion of the California missionary, and eventually in writing granted nearly everything Fr. Serra desired. The main point, which had brought him to Mexico was the one which clearly stated that the missionaries of California stood in the same relations to the Indian converts as do fathers to their children, *in loco parentis*, as the term adopted read. This precluded all further usurpations on the part of the rulers in California regarding the Indian Missions. Notwithstanding his eagerness to sail for California, Fr. Serra was detained till the middle of September. It was during this period that he most probably sat for the picture painted of him, and which is reproduced in this volume. Accompanied by his young Indian and by Fr. Pablo Mugártegui, a new recruit for the Missions, Fr. Serra bid farewell to the community of San Fernando and then with the blessing of the Fr. Guardian, set out for San Blas overland. On January 24, 1774, they were at last enabled to board the *Santiago* for San Diego. From there he journeyed by land to visit the Missions along the *Camino Reál*, which as yet was scarcely more than a trail. He finally reached Monterey on May 11th, and was welcomed at his own Mission by Fr. Palóu, who had meanwhile come up from Lower California, after turning over the Missions there to the Dominican Fathers. The Fr. Presidente was received with every mark of affection and joy by the Indians and missionaries at finding their father back after an absence of nearly two years.

FATHER JUNIPERO SERRA, O. F. M.

CHAPTER V.

Before proceeding, and by way of explanation, we must
note here that, when Fr. Junipero Serra early in 1769 with
Commander Gaspár de Portolá left Lower California to found
the Missions in Upper California, he named Fr. Francisco
Palóu his successor for the Missions on the peninsula. While
Fr. Serra was on his way to Mexico, as stated in the preceding
chapter, the Missionary College of San Fernando ceded the
missionary field of Lower California with all its Missions to
the Dominicans. Most of the Franciscans returned to the
College. Fr. Palóu and some others, by permission of the
College, chose to join their brethren in Upper California, Fr.
Palóu retaining his office as acting superior during the absence
of Fr. Serra. Thus it was that Fr. Francisco Palóu and Fathers
Fermín Francisco de Lasuén, Gregorio Amúrrio, Juan
Prestamero, Vicente Fustér, and José Antonio Murguia on
March 13th, 1773, arrived at San Diego Bay; Fr. Palóu was recognized as the temporary Superior of the Upper California Missions. Stationing his companions at the various missions on
the road and on November 2nd welcomed at San Luis Obispo
by Captain Pedro Fages, the acting Presidente at last reached
his destination, Mission San Carlos.

"On the 13th of November, 1773," he himself relates, "at
nine in the morning, about one league before we reached the
presidio of Monterey, I saw Fr. Juan Crespi, who had come
out from Mission San Carlos to welcome us. Great was the
joy I had at meeting him, for since we were boys we had
grown up and studied together, almost from the first letters,
until we both finished theology. More than five years had
passed by since we had seen each other. After giving vent to
our old friendship, we continued on our way and at about ten
o'clock we arrived at the presidio. There we were welcomed

amid the *salvos* of the whole artillery and the ringing of bells."
On the following day Fr. Palóu sang High Mass and made an
appropriate address to the soldiers of the garrison.

In the afternoon Fr. Palóu, accompanied by Fathers Crespi,
Juncosa, and Captain Fages, escorted by twelve soldiers and
some of the Catalonian Volunteers, proceeded on his way
to Mission San Carlos, where Fr. Francisco Dumetz surrounded by the convert Indians received their new Superior with
rejoicings. "I did not conceal my satisfaction," Fr. Palóu
writes, "to see myself at Monterey, because I can with entire
truth declare that for years not only since the conversion of
the Indians was undertaken, but since the year 1750, when I
read Father Torquemada, the voyage of Sebastian Vizcaíno,
the conversion of the Indians of Monterey impressed me so
strongly that I would have with greater pleasure come to
these Missions than I felt when in the same year obedience
sent me to the Missions among the Páme Indians of the Sierra
Gorda. However, after so long a time it has pleased God that
I should obtain this special favor, which I recognize to be a
great one for me, and for which I owe Him many thanks and
render Him, although in a poor manner. I beseech His holy
love and grace to let me labor in this vineyard during the
days He deigns to grant me life. I offer them from now on
for His holy service and the welfare and the conversion
of these poor, dear souls redeemed with His Most Precious
Blood. Gladly I offer mine own, if it should be necessary, for
the conversion and subjection of even a single one, hoping in
His Most Holy Majesty that through His infinite mercy He
will save mine, and give it the reward in the eternal glory
through the intercession for me, unworthy sinner, of those
whom I may succeed in sending to heaven."

The delay of the supply ship again caused distress at San
Carlos and Monterey early in 1774. "The worst kind of a
famine that was ever endured in the regions about Monterey
visited us," writes Fr. Palóu. "For eight months milk was
the manna for all from the comandante and the Fathers
down to the least individual; and I shared it with the rest.

Thanks be to God! However, all are in good health. At this Mission of San Carlos for thirty-seven days we were without a tortilla or as much as a crumb of bread. The meals consisted of a gruel made of garvanzos or beans ground to flour with which milk was mixed. In the morning a little coffee* took the place of chocolate." This statement was corroborated by Captain Juan Bautista Anza, who at the end of April, 1774, on his way back from Monterey to Sonora met Fr. Serra on the road coming from the south, as related in the preceding chapter. Anza told the Fr. Presidente that provisions at San Carlos had become so scarce that there had not been left even a small cake of chocolate to offer him for breakfast; and that all the food remaining consisted of milk and herbs without bread or anything else. On this account the neophytes were permitted to rove around the country for seeds or on the beach digging for shelfish or by fishing. The arrival of the *Santiago* on May 9th and of the Fr. Presidente on the 11th, relieved the distress, whereupon the Indians rejoined their Mission.

On Saturday morning, May 23rd, just as High Mass was about to be celebrated aboard the *Santiago* in thanksgiving for her safe voyage, Captain Fernando Rivera y Moncado arrived at Monterey to relieve Don Pedro Fages as military commander of California. Captain Fages, after having arranged the prescribed inventories, then set out for San Diego overland, and on July 19th sailed away in the *Santiago* for San Blas.

Captain Juan B. Anza, in company of the Franciscan Fr. Juan Diaz of the missionary College of Santa Cruz, Querétaro, and escorted by six soldiers from Sonora and two California guards reached Monterey on April 21st, 1774. By order of the viceroy this little expedition had started out from the presidio of Tubac, Sonora, on January 8th, 1774, for the purpose of ascertaining the practicability of a road overland to Monterey, so that in the future the expensive voyage by sea

---

* "un poco de cafe," This is the first time in California history that coffee is mentioned as the part of a meal. (*Noticias*, iii, cap. xlii, 149).

might be avoided. Captain Anza a few days later began the return march and found himself with his companions back at Tubac on May 26, 1774, thus demonstrating that the overland road was feasible.

By order of Viceroy Bucareli, Captain Rivera headed an expedition of sixteen soldiers and a muleteer in charge of packmules bearing provisions for a journey of forty days. It was to survey the port of San Francisco for the purpose of discovering sites for a presidio and a Mission. By order of Fr. Serra, Fr. Palóu with a young Indian servant and an Indian altarboy joined the expedition on November 23, 1774. The whole party set out that afternoon. On the journey holy Mass was offered up on Sundays and holydays; but the Rosary was recited in common every evening. Having surveyed the country about the bay and the Golden Gate, the expedition returned to Monterey on December 13th. Fr. Palóu closed his diary of the expedition in the following words: "May it please God that in my days I may see them (six different sites found suitable) occupied by Missions, and all the Gentiles that inhabit the surrounding country collected in them; and that none of them die without holy Baptism so that with them the number of the children of God and His holy Church and of the subjects of our Catholic monarch may be increased. This I ask of His Divine Majesty at this Mission of Monterey on the 14th of December, 1774."

Even before the preceding expedition had been undertaken, Viceroy Bucareli, in keeping with the royal aims, had ordered a sea expedition to survey and occupy the northwest coast to the sixtieth degree. The viceroy also asked the Fr. Guardian of San Fernando to assign a chaplain for the voyage. This chaplain was charged with the duty of taking observations for determining the latitude, and of making the demarcation of the coast of the countries which should be visited. He had also to take note of the character of the pagans found and of other matters that would lead to a full knowledge of those unknown lands. Fr. Juan Crespi of San Carlos was eventually named to accompany the *Santiago*, which under Captain Juan

Perez was to navigate the unknown shores of the far north. Fr. Thomas de la Peña was also directed to accompany Fr. Crespi on the voyage.

"On Thursday, June 9th, 1774," Fr. Crespi wrote, "Captain Juan Perez requested that on the following day a holy Mass should be sung on the shore in honor of Our Lady for the success of the voyage. On Friday 10th, the altar was erected under a shelter of boughs, and on the very spot where the holy Mass was celebrated on December 17th (18th?), 1602, during the expedition of General Sebastian Vizcaíno and on June 3rd, 1770, when a settlement was established at this port, and the first High Mass was sung by the Rev. Fr. Presidente, he likewise sang the holy Mass today. Fathers José Murguia, Francisco Dumetz, and we two, who were going with the new expedition, formed the choir. We all dined together near the old oak which Sebastian Vizcaíno saw. After dinner we went aboard the ship. We found that the condition of the boatswain, who had taken sick a few days previously, was worse. He made his confession to my companion, and I administered Extreme Unction to him. Shortly before five o'clock he passed away. The captain sent the corpse to the presidio that it might be given ecclesiastical burial."

Details on the voyage will be found in our second volume of *The Missions and Missionaries*, chapter ix. Suffice it to state here that the *Santiago* sailed from the Port of Monterey on June 11th, reached the highest point north in fifty-five degrees, and returned to Monterey on Saturday, August 27, 1774. "Thanks be to God and to His Most pure Mother Mary," Fr. Crespi exclaimed, "who has permitted us to arrive safely at this port, though we suffered the disappointment of not having gained our chief end, which was to go as far as sixty degrees of latitude, there to go ashore and to raise the standard of the cross."

Viceroy Bucareli was not satisfied with the results of the *Santiago's* voyage, and therefore had the *Santiago* in command of Captain Bruno de Ezeta (Heceta) and the *Sonora* in charge of Juan Francisco de la Bodega y Cuadra, sail from San Blas on March 16, 1775, with orders to reach latitude sixty-five degrees if possible. With them went as chaplains the Franciscans Fr. Miguel de la Campa and Fr. Benito Sierra. Particulars on the expedition will be found in our volume ii, chapter x. The *Santiago* reached degree forty-nine and was then compelled to turn back, on account of the illness of nearly the whole crew. She entered Monterey harbor on August 29, 1775. The *Sonora* arrived at latitude fifty-eight degrees, and then found it impossible to continue on account of contrary winds and the sickness of all but six men. She also cast her anchor in Monterey Harbor on October 7th. Eight days later officers and crew went out to Mission San Carlos in accordance with a vow made to Our Lady of Belén, the image of which was highly venerated there. In thanksgiving for their deliverance from many dangers, they had a High Mass offered up, during which all received holy Communion.

On June 27, 1775, the *San Carlos*, in charge of Lieutenant Juan Bautista de Ayala, accompanied by the Franciscan Fr. Vicente de Santa Maria, dropped her anchor in Monterey harbor. Besides supplies for Monterey, the vessel brought a personal letter from Viceroy Bucareli for Fr. Presidente Serra. Therein the viceroy explained the object of the coming of the *San Carlos*. He wanted the country around the Bay of San Francisco examined with a view to placing there a presidio and a colony, and in the district two Indian Missions. In conjunction with the expedition by water, a land expedition was to go up to the same district. Whilst the *San Carlos* set out from Monterey on July 27th, the land expedition under Captain Ezeta of the *Santiago* started out by land with three sailors, a carpenter, nine soldiers and a mule bearing a small canoe. Fathers Palóu and Campa, by order of Fr. Serra, joined the expedition as chaplains and to select a suitable site for Mission San Francisco. Details of these expeditions will be found in our volume ii.

When from Captain Anza's report Viceroy Bucareli had become convinced that communication between Sonora and Monterey overland by way of the Colorado River was practic-

able, he resolved to send another expedition on a grand scale
for the purpose of establishing a presidio, a colony, and two
missions at the Port of San Francisco. He also requested Fr.
Serra to have two friars ready at Monterey when the expedition should arrive in order to found the two Missions contem-
plated. Anza was placed in command and in reward for previous meritorious services made Lieutenant-Colonel. The
whole body of marchers consisted of Colonel J. B. Anza, Pur-
veyor Mariano Vidal, Lt. José J. Moraga, Sergeant Juan
Pablo Grijalva, eight veteran soldiers, twenty recruits, the
wives and children of the sergeant and the twenty-eight soldiers, ten veterans who were to return with Anza, four families
of settlers, twenty muleteers, three cattle herders, four Indian
servants and three Indian interpreters, in all two hundred and
forty persons. The train was composed of five hundred and
thirty horses, about three hundred and fifty head of cattle,
and one hundred and sixty-five mules laden with provisions.

This brilliant expedition set out from San Miguel de Horcasitas, Sonora, after a High Mass for the success of the undertaking on September 29, 1775. The Franciscans who went
along were Fr. Pedro Font, Fr. Hermenigildo Garcés and Fr.
Tomás Eizarch. Only Fr. Font, however, was to remain with
the immigrants till Bay San Francisco should be reached, and
then to return with Anza. On the journey holy Mass was
celebrated every morning, and in addition on Sundays and
holydays a sermon was preached. Just as the march began in
the morning Fr. Font would intone the *Alabado* which was
taken up by all the people. All travelled by horseback. At
night the Rosary was recited by each family, whereupon the
evening devotions closed with the *Alabado* or the *Salve Regina*,
sung in common. Omitting details of the route, it will here
be sufficient to note that the expedition arrived at Monterey
in the afternoon of Sunday, March, 10th. Fr. Serra was at
once notified, and invited to assist at a High Mass of thanksgiving on the next day. Early in the morning, therefore, the
Fr. Presidente, Fathers Palóu, Murguia, Cambón, and Peña
hastened over to the presidio, joyfully embraced Fr. Font,

and cordially welcomed Col. Anza and his people. Fr. Font sang High Mass and preached a fervent sermon. In the afternoon the guests were received at Mission San Carlos amid the ringing of the bells and the singing of the *Te Deum Laudamus*. Here the colonel and his little party of officers and guards took up their quarters, while the main body remained at the presidio. "On St. Joseph's day," Fr. Font notes, "there was a solemn High Mass with deacon and subdeacon in honor of St. Joseph. The Fathers sang and I with my instrument (violin) accompanied. Fr. Serra preached the sermon. Col. Anza and all were present."

"When we arrived at the presidio" (on the afternoon of March 10) Fr. Pedro Font writes in his *Diario* of that date, "everybody was overjoyed. We were welcomed by three volleys of artillery, consisting of some small cannons and the firing of muskets by the soldiers."

Fr. Font was a close observer and never hesitated to express himself clearly on what he saw. Hence we can expect a true statement on the situation at Monterey. "The royal presidio of Monterey is situated in a plain formed by the Sierra de Pinos, which ends here. It is close to the sea and about a quarter of a league from the Port of Monterey. Its buildings form a square, on one side of which is the house of the commander and the storehouse in which the storekeeper lives. On the opposite side are a little chapel and the quarters or barracks of the soldiers, and on the other two sides there are some huts or small houses of the families and the people who live there. All are built of logs and mud with some adobe; and the square or plaza of the presidio, which is not large, is enclosed by a stockade or wall of logs. It is all a very small affair, and for lack of houses the people live in great discomfort. Nor is this for want of materials, for there is lime and timber to spare. The commander (Anza) indeed had to lodge in the storehouse, and I in a dirty little room full of lime, while the rest of the people accommodated themselves in the plaza with their tents as best they could. . . . . . . The patron of the presidio is San Carlos, and it is therefore called San Carlos de

Monterey. In this title participates also the nearby Mission, which for this reason is called San Carlos y San Joseph, the latter in honor of the most Illustrious Señor Don Joseph De Galvez (Inspector-General of Lower California who directed the occupation of Upper California in 1769), who gave the Mission a beautiful image of Señor San Joseph, as the principal patron whom he invoked for that whole establishment: and it is called Carmelo (San Carlos de Carmelo) because this is its original name, given at the time of the first discovery made by sea by General Don Sebastian Vizcaíno.

"In the morning (March 11) the Very Rev. Father Presidente of the Missions, Fr. Junipero Serra, came from the Mission of San Carlos de Carmelo with four other friars, those assigned to the two Missions which were to be founded on the Port of San Francisco, namely, Fr. Francisco Palóu, Fr. José Murgúia, Fr. Pedro Cambon and Fr. Tomás de la Peña. They came with the royal surgeon to welcome us, one of the two missionaries, Fr. Juan Crespi and the missionary of Mission San Antonio, Fr. Miguel Pieras, who was sick, remaining at the Mission, and Fr. Francisco Dumetz. Great and very special was the joy which we all felt on our arrival, and after we had saluted each other with many demonstrations of affection it was arranged to go and sing the Mass. . . I sang the Mass at the altar as an act of thanksgiving for our successful arrival, and the five Fathers assisted, singing very melodiously and with the greatest solemnity possible, the troops of the presidio and of the expedition assisting with repeated salvos and volleys of musketry.

"After the Gospel," Fr. Font writes that he preached a brief sermon on the purpose of their coming, incidents on the journey, etc. It covers seven pages, and must have lasted half an hour. Much too long for the occasion. All but the Fr. Presidente returned to Carmelo. "It was decided that we should (in the afternoon) go to the Mission to yield to the urgings of the Rev. Presidente, but principally because in the presidio there was no place for us to lodge. So in the afternoon, the lieutenant of the expedition remaining with the people we had brought, we set out from the presidio of Monterey, the commander (Anza) and I, with a few soldiers, the Rev. Presidente, the commissary, and the surgeon of the presidio. Starting at four o'clock, at five we arrived at the Mission of San Carlos de Carmelo. Here the Fathers, who were seven, welcomed us with singular joy and festive peals of the good bells there, especially a large one which they had brought by sea, to which the soldiers replied with volleys and a salvo, accompanying us to church, at whose door Fr. José Murguia was awaiting us, vested in cope. I sprinkled holy water on the commander (Anza) etc., we venerated the holy cross, and entering the church in procession, we intoned the *Te Deum* with much pleasure and with tears of joy for our arrival. Then, after having given thanks to God we went to the dwelling and hospice that had been prepared.

"The Mission of San Carlos de Carmelo is situated on a little elevation near the sea, and close to the Carmelo River, which empties into a little bay called by Vizcaíno the Puerto del Carmelo, which is formed here by Sierra de Santa Lucía, which ends here, and the Punta de Cipreses. It is an excellent site with very fertile lands. The temperature is cold in a desirable way and very healthful, although somewhat foggy, as is the case on the whole coast. The Mission has a rather spacious and well made church, although it is of palisades and tule for the most part, and it is somewhat adorned with paintings. Apart from it are three good-sized rooms of adobe for the dwellings of the Fathers. Separate from it are a kitchen, forge, and two or three other rooms. . . . .

"The Indians of this Mission, who already number four hundred Christians (hediondos) appeared to me to be rather tractable, not very ugly, nor so ill-smelling as those of San Diego. They devote themselves to fishing, for at this place many good fish are caught. Besides the sardines, which are plentiful, there are obtained also many good salmon which enter the river to spawn. . . Of this fish we ate almost every day while we were here. In short, although the rest of the Missions are very good, this one seemed to me the best of all."

THE FIRST BUILDINGS AND PATIO OF MISSION SAN CARLOS.

On account of the illness of Colonel Anza, the expedition tarried at Monterey and the Mission till March 22nd. In the afternoon Anza and Fr. Font said farewell to the Father Presidente and the other Fathers and went to the presidio, whence the expedition started out after holy Mass for the Port of San Francisco.

In his *Diario* on March 12th, Fr. Font has this delightful item: "I went to take a walk through the garden, which is a stone's throw from the Mission. It was a delight to see it so beautiful and full of vegetables, cared for by Father Palóu with such diligence that he spent all the day working in it and had it very well laid out. It is square and all around it has a border of azaleas already in flower, and the beds full of cauliflower, lettuce, and other vegetable and herbs. And the finest thing about that country is that without irrigation all such vegetables are raised, than which there are no better in Mexico. Indeed, one artichoke would ordinarily last from two to three days. . . . .They only water the plants by hand, throwing on each plant a gourdful of water after transplanting, and this suffices."

On March 22nd Colonel Anza, Fr. Font, Lt. Moraga, eight Sonora regulars, two presidio soldiers who made the journey with Fages before, servants and muleteers, in all twenty persons, started out from Mission San Carlos for the purpose of selecting a site for the presidio and another for the Mission of San Francisco as the viceroy had directed. Details will be read with interest in our *Mission of San Francisco*. The whole party again reached Monterey on Easter Monday, April 8th. Captain Rivera's erratic attitude assumed towards Col. Anza and Fr. Serra, not being a local matter will be best studied in the second volume of our General History. Leaving the colonists about Monterey, at the mercy of Rivera the Colonel and his escort accompanied by Fr. Font resumed their march for Sonora on April 14th, and arrived at San Miguel de Horcasitas, Sonora, on June 1, 1776.

Rivera followed Anza a few days later, and reached San Diego on May 7, 1776. From there he directed Lt. José J.

Moraga, still waiting at Monterey with the immigrants, to proceed to the Port of San Francisco with twenty soldiers and to erect the presidio on the spot chosen by Anza. Rivera might have issued such an order at Monterey; and he might have ordered work on the two Missions to begin at the same time. Instead, aware that Fr. Serra would keenly feel the slight, he instructed Moraga to postpone the founding of the Missions and so to inform the Fr. Presidente.

About this time, May 21st, the *San Antonio* arrived in the harbor, and brought along the Franciscan Fr. Benito Sierra. On June 3rd the *San Carlos* appeared having on board the Franciscans Fr. Vicente de Santa Maria and Fr. José Nocedal. Under orders from the viceroy this vessel took aboard all the property of the soldiers and colonists, the church goods, house furniture, and farm implements for the new presidio as well as for the proposed Mission of San Francisco. The expedition which moved out of Monterey on June 17, 1776, to establish the presidio at the Golden Gate, was led by Lt. J. J. Moraga, whose wife had remained in Sonora on account of illness. In addition there were five Indians in charge of the packmules and two hundred head of cattle. To be ready for any emergency, the Fr. Presidente directed that Fathers Palóu and Cambón, two Indian servants, two Indian neophytes from Lower California, and one neophyte from San Carlos go along to establish the mission. A number of packmules and eighty-six head of cattle for the proposed Mission were in charge of the Indians. Details belong to our *Mission San Francisco*. It so happened, however, that the Mission was established on June 29th, even before the presidio's foundations were laid, despite Rivera's prohibition, who was glad however that it had been done when he visited there later, as will be seen in the said narrative.

Rivera's change of mind, however, came too late to save his position. For his strange conduct, and his incurred excommunication at San Diego for the violation of the Spanish-ecclesiastical Law of Church-Asylum, had become known at the Capital of Mexico. In consequence Felipe de Neve was appointed first resident governor of Upper California, and Rivera was transferred to Lower California as lieutenant-governor of that territory.

CHAPTER VI.

San Carlos Mission.—Activities.—First Report of Fr. Palóu.—Missionaries and Indians.—Means Provided by Spanish Government.—Mission Routine.

We have now to turn back two years in order to learn details on the condition, activities and achievements at Mission San Carlos. Naturally, we may obtain the best information from Fathers Serra and Palóu themselves.

It will be remembered that while in Mexico Fr. Presidente Serra, at the request of the viceroy on March 13, 1773, drew up a report on all the Missions thus far established. It was the first report dealing with California. From personal knowledge Fr. Serra could describe the situation only to the end of the year 1772, when he left California. As regards his own Mission San Carlos, he tells the viceroy: "The first and most northern, and therefore the most remote from this capital, is Mission San Carlos de Monterey. It was founded on Pentecost Sunday June 3rd, 1770; but, as it stood for a year incorporated with the presidio, from where it was afterwards transplanted to the place it now occupies, it may be reputed as founded one year later. On the new site the first habitations were constructed as customary of poles, as was the case on the first site. In both instances it was more favored than the other Missions, because by nature the country abounded in timber of various kinds, all near by; and it is the portion where the soldiers applied themselves to work. God reward them. The inclosure or stockade of thick poles, close together and high, with ravelins at the corners, measures a little more than seventy varas in length and forty-three in width. At night the stockade is locked, but because for lack of nails they are not fastened together, it is easy to remove a pole from the entrance. The principal structure is seven varas wide and fifty varas long. This is divided into six apartments, each having its door and lock. The walls are of strong poles plastered inside and outside, and the principal apartments are whitewashed with lime. One of the rooms serves for the church. Adjoining the said house on the outside are the quarters or guardhouse for the soldiers; and adjoining this is the kitchen. Both are surrounded by a stockade. All these buildings have a flat roof covered with earth. Besides these structures, there have been erected out-kitchens and various little huts for the Indians. They have a thatched roof or of straw. A beginning was made for a little enclosed garden, but for want of a gardener it made little progress. I am informed that there have been planted three almudes (pecks) of wheat and some vegetables, which is all they could do. Having more means now in consequence of the new arrangements of Your Excellency, it is intended to increase as much as possible the planting and sowing, as we have from the beginning desired.

"With regard to the spiritual affairs of Mission San Carlos, I have to say that, when I left at the end of August (1772), they had already about thirty Christians, besides various little ones who have already gone to enjoy God. Most of these were baptized in our first year; for in the second year seeing ourselves unable to give them any food to keep them with us, we baptized but few, save in case of necessity. Some of these would give account of their days, even weeks; but when, after having been sought or not, they returned to the Mission, they would give as an excuse the need of searching for food, because it appeared to them that the milk from the cows with which we fed them was too scanty a meal. Although we saw that to such a report there was no reasonable reply we felt it very much, because they returned from among the pagans in such different condition that we scarcely recognized them. After my departure, the Fathers write to me, they had some more Baptisms, without saying how many, besides some marriages. They must have about forty adult Christians there now. I may add that they have almost the whole neighboring rancheria under instruction, who, impatient of delay, say that they want to be Christians even though they are given nothing to eat."

Fr. Francisco Palóu, Acting Presidente of the Missions in

Upper California, under date of December 10, 1773, signed an official report at San Carlos on the state of all the Missions, about a year later than Fr. Serra. It is the first report emanating from California and most complete. Regarding the Presidio and Mission San Carlos he makes the following statements:

Real Presidio de San Carlos de Monterey.

It is distant from Mission San Antonio twenty-five leagues —eighteen coming from San Antonio northward, and seven leagues northeastward to the presidio—because there is no direct road over the Sierra de Santa Lucía. It was founded on June 3, 1770. It faces the harbor of Monterey, and is distant from the beach about a gunshot. It is situated on the brow of the Punta de Pinos, on the side of an *estéro*. Its stockade is of timbers with ravelins on the four corners, in each of which there is a bronze cannon. Within the stockade is the adobe church with mud-covered roof. Adjoining it is a little room of the same nature for the missionary Father who comes (from San Carlos Mission) to celebrate holy Mass every Sunday and holyday of obligation. In the other wing, in front of the church, is the dwelling of the comandante also of adobe. It has also two other rooms, one for the kitchen and one for the wardrobe. There is another adobe structure which is used as a jail. Then there are two granaries built of palisades with an earthen roof which contain the provisions. In the two side wings are the quarters of the Catalonian Volunteer soldiers and the Leather-Jacket soldiers. There are also other rooms built of palisades and having earth-covered roofs. These contain the quarters of the muleteers and servants.

San Carlos Mission on the Rio Carmelo.

The Mission of San Carlos was founded on the same day with the presidio adjoining it, that is to say, on June 3, 1770. It remained in that place until the end of December, 1771, when by order of His Excellency, Marquis de Croix, it was moved to the banks of the Rio Carmelo, distant from the pre-

VIEW OF THE SECOND SITE OF MISSION SAN CARLOS.

sidio a short league, and from the beach about two gunshots. This site is indeed much more appropriate, and it has more facilities for a Mission than the port of Monterey. It has continued in this place. Here its little church is erected of pine boards and cypress wood with a flat roof covered with earth. The dwelling of the Fathers and their corresponding rooms are also built in the same manner, and surrounded by a stockade, as is also a building for the barracks of the soldiers. They are erecting another church more spacious. It measures forty varas in length, and nine varas in width, partly of adobe and partly of wood. The roof will be covered with tules, because it has been experienced that the flat roof of earth does not protect against the many rains until an intelligent master builder will appear to erect one as the climate demands.

"Since the founding there have been baptized, young and old, one hundred and seventy-five, of whom eleven have died. Thirty-two marriages have been blessed. Twenty-eight of these were pure Indian couples, recently baptized. Three Indian women were married to three Catalonian soldiers; and one Indian woman was married to a servant of the Mission. There are under instruction in the catechism others who do not live at the Mission because it has no means to feed them, not even enough for the Christian Indians. These find themselves compelled to go to the mountains in search of wild seeds or to the beach to fish. This necessity has arisen because the transport with supplies has not arrived, and because no corn could be harvested from seeds that had come too late for planting in the right time. At present they are sowing five fanegas of wheat which was all that had been harvested from the two pecks planted in the past year.

"The Mission has here much and good land, though not irrigable, because the river runs very low in the dry season. In the rainy season, indeed, the water is brought up easily through a ditch by its rapid current. However, according to experience we could obtain harvests from the many rains and from the humidity of the soil.

"The Mission also has its own good sites for all kinds of

cattle, as the pasturage is abundant and water also. There is much timber, such as pine, cypress, poplar, willow and red wood.

"The Mission now has forty-seven head of cattle, twenty-eight pigs, four breeding mares, one stallion, four tamed horses, two riding mules, and ten packmules with their harness, etc.

"There are implements for the field and carpentershop, but the mechanics and laborers as elsewhere are lacking. Church goods we also have sufficient."

Fr. Palóu's reference to agricultural implements, mechanical tools, and to livestock, indicates the nature of the work which the missionaries were expected to perform in addition to their spiritual activities, as well as the object of the establishments which they were to found among the natives of California. Not only were they to teach the truths of Religion and subjection to secular authorities; but they were to induce and guide the savages to learn how to live and how to support themselves in a rational manner. A stupendous task! Particularly in view of the brutish character and the filthy habits of the Indians, and the lack of means which should have been provided by the Spanish Government.

The missionaries were men of learning, indeed, priests versed in the sciences of philosophy and theology; but they were not farmers nor mechanics. They knew all about the duties of a messenger of Christ and how to impart the message of Christ, and were at all times ready to undergo any hardship to win the savages for Christ. This was all that might be expected of missionaries sent to rational peoples, who supported themselves but was not enough in California. The natives raised absolutely nothing to sustain life. What the earth produced of itself, or what moved or crawled over the ground satisfied them, cooked or uncooked. If they secured, or rather their women, enough of such food, they were perfectly happy. Idleness was their bliss. Exertion, mental or physical, they loathed. Their habitations were inexpressibly filthy; but they never thought of improvements. If their huts swarmed too much with vermin, the savages would simply set fire to them, and have the women erect another of brush wood or tules. To reason with such a people, as the first Apostles of the Gospel did, or worse, book in hand to read to them what was in the book for their instruction was useless. The California Indians knew and understood just one topic, and that was how to obtain food to fill their stomachs. Of abstract things or subjects which they could not see, or hear, or feel, they had not the faintest ideas nor words to express them.

Hence it was evident to the zealous Fr. Serra and his no less ardent companions that they must not directly address themselves to the dull understanding of the Indians, but indirectly through the stomach, so to speak, in order to impress them with the advantages and beauties of Christianity. They must supply food and clothing if they wanted the Indian to listen to their message, and more food if they desired him to stay with them, which was the only way to benefit him permanently and to render their efforts successful. No force could be applied. The Indian must be allowed to be free in his choice to join or not to join the Mission family. He was not permitted to enlist for life in the army of Christianity until he had learned what it involved; and he was not accepted, even if he volunteered, until he had given proof of his sincerity after a more or less long period of probation.

That brings us to the question of compensation for both the missionary and the convert Indian. Both were volunteers, but from altogether different motives. When the missionary aspired to the life of a messenger of Christ among Indians, he had to volunteer. It was regarded as an extra hazardous existence for both the body and the soul. No one was therefore coerced to subject himself to the dangers. He must have a motive stripped of all selfish considerations. He must have a pure desire to enlist out of sincere affection for his Divine Master. His interests must be the interests of Christ, who throughout his mortal life labored to save souls for heaven. The missionary may look for compensation, indeed, but it must be altogether celestial. Of such a calibre were the mis-

THE PIONEER TEACHER OF CALIFORNIA.

sionaries who followed Fr. Serra into California. Thus detached from any worldly compensation and from any selfish influence, these messengers of the Gospel, vowed to poverty, could make themselves all to all, in a word become like an Indian, so to speak, to win the natives for Christ.

The Indians, too, were volunteers for life in the shadow of the Cross, but in the beginning, at least, for the sake of receiving plenty to eat. Only by degrees it dawned upon them, while under instruction, that there was something else to be enjoyed and for which it was worth while to abandon their wild, aimless life. Then they became volunteers for this higher boon, the knowledge and conviction of being recognized children of God, who would reward them, as he rewarded the missionaries, with a joy not to be found on earth. Thus, by degrees they trusted and loved the missionaries who were moved by no other desire than to be united with their red children in the House of the Heavenly Father. The simpleminded Indians comprehended that much, and therefore yielded their liberty and themselves to the service of that Almighty God. Would that the missionary Fathers and their converts had been allowed to continue thus in happy union till death approached both! However, we must not anticipate.

We have now to consider what means the Spanish Government placed at the disposal of the missionaries in order to accomplish the Christianization and civilization of the California natives. When the viceroy of Mexico had ordered or approved the founding of a Mission under the patronage of some saint selected by him, two missionaries were appointed. Each of them was granted an allowance of $400 in goods, minus the freight charges overland and across the Gulf of California. These charges would reduce the amount granted from one-fourth to one-third. The corporals of the guard received exactly as much, and the ordinary soldiers received but fifteen dollars less. As to the governor, he was allowed $3,000 a year. What the missionaries were given could not be called a salary, as it was but a pittance; it was called *sinodo* or stipend. Yet the missionaries ranked with the governors in learning. The Fr. Presidente, on equality with the governor in his sphere, received no more than a corporal, $400 a year. When he was not in actual charge of a Mission, or one of the two missionaries, he had to get along without anything, as he was on a level with supernumeraries. The Spanish Government thus showed in a queer way that its chief aim was the spread of Religion, as it claimed, from the manner in which it rated the value of the missionaries. It is true, owing to their vow of poverty, they needed no more personally; but they were expected to attract savages who would do nothing without some sort of recognition. The more the Fathers could lavish on their wards, so much the more effective would be their words. As it was, the missionaries utilized their allowance, which was no salary, but regarded as an alms by themselves, for the purpose of gaining the good will of the Indians.

The next move on the part of a viceroy was to pay over to the *sindico* or representative of the missionary College the sum of $1,000 from the Pious Fund, that is to say from the income of the Pious Fund Estates which originally the Jesuits had established in Mexico with the donations of wealthy benefactors for the benefit of the California Missions. The allowance of the Fathers came from the same source, not from the royal treasury, which never contributed anything to the Missions in Upper California. With this grant of $1,000, which the viceroy in the name of the king of Spain allowed to be taken from the Pious Fund, the two missionaries were expected to establish, for instance, San Carlos Mission. When the College of San Fernando was first informed of the matter, the Fr. Guardian, Fr. Rafael Verger, who had himself labored among the Indians of Lower California, under date of August 3, 1771, wrote to Don Manuel Lanz de Casafonda in Spain: "To see clearly how ridiculous and how more like a Quijotean feat than something meant in earnest, is the founding of a Mission with only $1,000, we must bear in mind that Monterey is 780, according to some 800 leagues from this Capital, and that it is necessary to take along many things from this city; for instance, agricultural implements, ploughshares, pick-axes, hoes, and a complete carpenter's outfit, such as small and large saws, augurs, adzes, planes, chisels, compasses, hammers, etc.; all the tools of the masons; and cooking utensils, such as copper pots, kettles, plates, etc. A little dwelling, a small church, even though it be ever so poor, and a granary must be built. There must be cattle, not for one family, but for a whole settlement. Some yokes of oxen for cultivating the land. Horses, and mules, besides food supplies must also be provided. These things must be taken from Sonora, for the old Missions in Lower California are already exhausted and have need of what mules, horses and grain they possess. Even if no wages are paid, it is necessary to feed the men who do all the work. To think that especially the pagans, who do not as much as know how, will be willing to work, even after many years, is *solemn nonsense*. To this must be added the daily rations which, as the Inspector-General says, must be given the pagans who gather at the Missions for instructions. All this expense is to be covered with $1,000! I should like to see the remarkable genius stationed there who with it can accomplish what has been described."

Accordingly, agricultural, mechanical arts, and live stock raising for the support of the Mission family of necessity became the essential departments of Mission life around the Mission church. Not being able to pay for a superintendent, the missionary Fathers themselves superintended the work done in the various departments. They rolled up their sleeves, put on a rough apron, and led in the work to be accomplished, the four Lower California neophytes at San Carlos assisting and showing the natives how to follow the Fathers in their particular branch.

Lest confusion arise from different methods adopted by the Fathers originating from the various nations, the Mother College invented a way or system adapted to Indian manners and character. This was eventually prescribed in order to secure uniformity of action for all the Missions. It came to be known as the *Mission System*. The missionary by royal decrees was recognized in *loco parentis*, that is to say, as the father of the Indian family clothed with all the rights and duties of a father, and independent of the military and civil authority, except with regard to capital crimes, the Indian Mission became a family of which the missionary was the head.

The Mission Routine was likewise uniform at all the Missions, and dictated by the Mother College in Mexico. A missionary might be transferred from one Mission in the south hundreds of miles away, and would find the same order and routine to which he was accustomed.

The manner of enlisting the savages for Mission life was also the same.

The late Charles F. Lummis describes it as follows:

"Food with the savage was the first requisite. If he could be given the beans, meat, tortillas, hard tack of the soldiers and sailors, it would be like the sweetmeats of white children, for it was cleaner, tastier, than what he was accustomed to. It would be the one attraction, and he would in return do any kind of little tasks. If given as reward for anything done, he would find it much easier to fill his stomach than to go for it in search through the ravines and foothills, and quicker than to fish. Once the missionaries discovered as much, the first step in reaching the Indians was learnt. Give them eatables in reward and in pay and for every turn.

"Then the simplest kind of instruction as to babies and reward like babies to have them come often, and regularly, and lastly to stay for it at the mission church. No use to, with book in hand, tell them what the book says. The missionary was supposed to know all that they must learn, and it would have to come piecemeal. There were stated times, the simplest prayers, the one Christ Himself taught. Morning and evening, before and after meals, and at bedtime, in common, aloud, the oft-repeated words would at last stick. Then when the language had been acquired sufficiently those words of the prayers would be explained, and what was behind them all, just as babies are fed with them. Always some eatables in reward, or something that made a show especially with girls and women. That would delight and arouse the affections."

CHAPTER VII.

On February 5, 1775, by which date the Fathers had succeeded in bringing Mission San Carlos into accord with the regulations of both the College and the viceroy, Fr. Serra again reported to Viceroy Bucareli on the state of the Mission as follows: "Since the month of December, 1773, when I made my first and last report to Your Excellency on the state and progress of the five existing Missions, until the last day of December, 1774, this Mission of San Carlos exhibits the following additions:

Fabricas (Buildings): A building thirty yards long and seven yards wide. It is partly constructed of adobes and partly of palisades, and has a roof of straw. This serves for a granary. A structure of palisades, plastered, and with a roof of straw. It serves for a work-room. A building of same nature and size to harbor a married servant (Lower California neophyte).—Another somewhat larger, also of palisades, plastered, and roofed with straw, for another servant (Lower California Indian) married to an Indian woman recently baptized. —A structure of the same nature, but with a flat roof covered with earth.—It has two rooms, reception room and bedroom, for the doctor and his family.—Another dwelling of the same construction and size with two rooms for the blacksmith and his family.—A building of palisades and roofed with straw. This is occupied by the corporal of the guard and his family.— An oven of adobes for baking bread.—Some small furnaces of adobes used as kitchens by the Indians.

Church and Sacristy. Additions. A chasuble of black damask trimmed with silver tape and all its belongings.—A frontal and cope of the same material.—A new missal having the saints of our Order.—Crucifix of silver with its foot of the same metal more than a *tercio* in height, containing in its crystal reliquary an authenticated Relic of the True Cross.—

Two oil paintings a yard in height, both in frames, of San Carlos and San Buenaventura.—Another like them two yards high, in its moulding, of San Luis Obispo.—Two like those mentioned, large, both in frames, one representing heaven the other hell, well painted.—Another like them, half a yard high, represents St. Francis and St. Joseph in a frame. —A copper plate representing Our Lady of Sorrows, with frame, rays and sword of silver.—Another copper plate, half a yard high representing Calvary, con su mediacaña, y sus cortinitas de gaza.—A copper plate more than two yards high representing the Tree of the Seraphic Order.—A group picture of paper containing all the saints of our Order.—Another group picture showing all the Popes and Cardinals of the Order.—Another group picture showing all the Superior Generals of our Order.

A confessional of redwood with seat of the same material.— Two altar tables for two of the three altars.—Two wooden platforms for the said altars.—One baldaquin and chintz canopy more than two varas high.—Two stocks (pedestales) for the processional candlesticks (torches).—A niche more than two varas high with its cupola of redwood for the fine statue of St. Joseph.—Three chairs for the chancel with much raised work,—Three cushions and back rests of blue woolen cloth.—One brass Cross with the crucified figure.—Two sets of covers (sleeves for the Cross and candlesticks).—One holy water pot of tin-plated copper with a sprinkler of the same material.—Four cassocks of red cloth and the surplices for the servers.—One large bell and twenty-four stools.

Here may be added what Fr. Serra brought along from Lower California in 1769, and had sent up to San Carlos with the other goods.—One silver censer with boat and spoon, (from Mission San Ignacio).—One missal, secondhand, (from Mission Santa Gertrudis).—Some fine corporals.—(From Santa Gertrudis), and from Mission Santa Maria all the following: Oil stocks of silver; silver baptismal shell; one altar-bread iron; one silver chalice, paten and spoon; six purificators; some altar cloths; one set of glass cruets; two finger towels;

one tin altar-bread box; a frontal of silk stuff with large flowers.

Additions to Utensils of House and Field:

A large table of redwood.—Chair with back, both of redwood.—One dozen and half of cane-seat chairs.—Large clothes-press.—Three inkstands with their sand boxes of brass.—Brass shaving cup.—Bottle case with eighteen bottles for altar wine.—A forge and smith's complete outfit.—One frame saw,—one alembic of copper, tin plated,—one alarm clock,—two wash-rooms for the shepherds' use.—Six bridles and six pairs of spurs.—Two metal water jars.—Four locks and bolts, and another medium sized one.—Four small locks for chests,—one square,—one carpenter's plane,—two medium sized saws,—a rasp,—one plane and two plummets,—three thousand nails and tacks,—two axes for charcoal making,—three cowboy saddles,—two dozen sacking needles,—twelve pounds of twine,—twelve pounds of twisted twine, made of agave fibre,—twelve dozen ropes,—twenty mule loads of cowhide sacks,—a piece of coarse cloth for the sheepherders' use,—an olla of ordinary copper,—two gross of medals and two of small Crosses,—one gross of Rosaries.

Herds and Beasts.—Bovine herd, large and small......61
Hogs, Shoats and Pigs................42
Breeding Mares........................ 4
Colts................................... 3
Tamed Horses........................ 6
Riding and Pack Mules............14
An old Burro......................... 1

Grains, planted and harvested:

Wheat, planted......3 ½ fanegas   harvested......125 fanegas
Barley, planted......3   almudes harvested...... 20 fanegas
Corn, planted..........8   almudes harvested......150 fanegas
Beans, planted.......6   almudes about 5 fanegas, harvested
7 fanegas.   Total harvested............302 fanegas

Harvested in 1774: corn 540 fanegas; wheat 475 fanegas; beans 40 fanegas;—Total, 1055 fanegas.

Families and Persons in the Mission:

Baptized down to December 31, 1774—267; and under instruction—
100.

Died	" "	"	"	" — 23.
Marriages	" "	"	"	" — 36; including three soldiers with neophytes.

Individuals, Indians, at Mission   —244.

Families,   "   "   "   — 32; with 244 souls.

Apparently the prospects for both the spiritual and temporal progress were all that could be expected. The patriarchal family headed by the wise and gentle Fr. Presidente himself, aided by his faithful assistant, Fr. Juan Crespi, promised to be a model of peaceful Christian living.

The daily order uniformly observed at all the Missions was as follows: At sunrise the bell called to church all the adults, that is to say, all over nine years of age. Holy Mass was celebrated by one of the Fathers, whilst the other from the pulpit would lead in reciting the prayers and the *Doctrina* with the assembled Indians. At the conclusion of the holy Mass the *Alabado* was sung after a melody which was the same at all the Missions. The Fathers, Fr. Font humorously remarks, would sing along for the sake of conformity and encouragement even if they had no good voices. Before being dismissed, during certain seasons of the year only, an instruction in Spanish followed the celebration of the holy Mass. Thereupon all would take their places at the tables for breakfast, bless themselves and sing or recite *Grace* aloud together.

The breakfast consisted of *atole*, a kind of gruel made of corn or other grain which had been roasted before it was ground. It was prepared in large iron kettles at the *pozolera* or community kitchen. Every family sent for its share, which was ample, in earthen or bark vessels. The girls and single women and young or unmarried men took their meals in their respective apartments. After breakfast, which usually lasted about three-quarters of an hour, the men and larger boys went to the work assigned them in the fields, among the live stock, or in the various mechanical shops. The girls found congenial occupation under the care of a matron, in the early years usually the wife of the corporal. At noon the *Angelus Bell* announced the time for that short prayer and then all would reassemble at their respective places for dinner. This was served in the same manner as the breakfast, but consisted of *pozole*, a soup or broth to which were added according to the season, meat, beans, peas, lentils, garbanzos. Two hours were allowed for this meal and for rest. At two o'clock work was resumed, one of the missionaries, as in the morning, encouraging the neophytes in the field by his word and example.

At about five o'clock work would cease, and the whole Mission population then went to church for the recitation of the *Doctrina* or catechism and religious exercises, one of the Fathers leading as in the early morning. On these occasions the Father in his pulpit would add an instruction in Spanish or in Indian as might appear expedient for his polyglot audience. The *Alabado*, as usual, would conclude the exercises, whereupon or about six o'clock there would be supper. This was served as in the morning in the shape of *atole*, of which the Indians were very fond, and which was served without stint. The remainder of the evening was passed in participating in whatever amusements the neophyte enjoyed. Even the pastimes or games played in the pagan state were permitted so long as Christian modesty was not offended.

The children received special attention. "In the morning," say the regulations observed at all Missions, "as soon as the grown people shall have gone their way, and in the afternoon before sunset, the Fathers shall give instruction to the little boys and girls who are five years old and more, and they shall permit none to be absent." These children generally assembled in the *sala* or reception room, or in the outer corridor.

Furthermore the regulations direct: "The catechumens, those who are about to be married, and those who are preparing to comply with the precept of annual confession, shall likewise attend these exercises in the morning and in the evening, in order that they may be instructed before receiving said holy Sacraments. The same shall be observed with re-

Alabado.

gard to those who, despite the daily exercises, may have forgotten the *Doctrina.*"

"On Sundays and holydays the Fathers shall exercise great
vigilance lest any one neglect the principal Mass or the sermon
which must be preached during the holy Sacrifice. On such
occasions they shall explain the Gospel of the day, or the
mysteries of our holy Faith, and they shall endeavor to adapt
themselves to the dullness and the needs of the Indians. When
holy Mass is concluded, one of the missionaries shall call every
one by name from the Padron (list or record of the Indians by
families). The neophytes shall then approach one after another to kiss the priest's hand. Thus it will be seen when
anyone is missing. Those more capable and intelligent shall
be exhorted to frequent the holy Sacraments in addition to
complying with the precept of the Church, especially on great
feasts."

On Sundays and holydays of obligation no servile work
was performed. After the divine services in the forenoon and
after devotional exercises in the afternoon, the neophytes were
free to divert themselves to their hearts' content. There
would be all sorts of games, even those of savage origin, as
was said before, the only restriction being that there must be
nothing against Christian modesty.

The singing at the High Mass was, of course, Gregorian in
the language of the Catholic Church the world over. Instead
of organ accompaniment, instrumental music was employed,
every Mission having an orchestra according to means. Male
Indians composed the choir, and sang from square notes which
were written on parchment in different colors to indicate the
part which the respective singer had to follow. The afternoon
devotions consisted of the Rosary, the Litany of the Blessed
Virgin, and other short prayers in Spanish, hymns in the same
language alternating. All other devotional exercises, such as
the Way of the Cross, every Friday and more often in Lent,
the prayers and singing during processions, etc., were also in
Spanish. The girls would pass the evenings and other free
times singing the lovely hymns known all over California. In

truth, a more kindly, patriarchal life existed nowhere. It molested nobody, but brought happiness to the converts, who desired nothing more than that their temporal existence continue thus. It would have been remarkable if satan's envy had allowed it to go on. So we may be prepared to learn that afflictions of some kind or another came upon the happy Mission family through the malice, greed, ambition, and depravity of white men, who allowed themselves to be influenced by the envy and animosity of Christianity's arch-enemy more early than could be foreseen.

On June 17, 1778, the transport *Santiago* brought up from Mexico a most important letter from the College of San Fernando, notifying Fr. Serra that he had been empowered by the Holy See to confer the Sacrament of Confirmation, because it was not likely that any Bishop would ever appear in the country. The privilege had in fact been granted by Pope Clement XIV four years previously to any one Father of the College of San Fernando designated by the Franciscan Commissary-General. The latter, after the King of Spain had given his consent, and the viceroy had likewise added his approval, had on October 17, 1777, named Fr. Junipero Serra to exercise the authority in California. Thus by reason of all the formalities to be observed in keeping with the union of the Church and State under Spanish rule, four years had already been consumed of the ten for which the faculty was granted by the Pope. Only six years remained. Fr. Serra, therefore, resolved to make use of his powers without delay so as to bestow the benefit on all the neophytes and others in California. See for details our second volume of *Missions and Missionaries*.

The Fr. Presidente himself notes in his personal *Libro de las Confirmaciones*, in which he made all the entries himself for all the Missions, as follows: "On the day of the Apostles Saints Peter and Paul, June 29, 1778, the whole congregation having assembled for High Mass, which I sang solemnly, I, the undersigned, at the end of the doctrinal and panegyrical sermon on said holy Sacrament, having in the sermon impressed upon all that the ordinary minister of it is the Bishop only, and that they might not think it strange to see me administer it afterwards, I in a clear and intelligible voice, and in the language of the people (Spanish) read the Letters Patent, which, in order that they may be in evidence to any one who might read this book, are transcribed faithfully on the next folio."

Farther on in the beginning of the entries, Fr. Serra gives these particulars: "I, the undersigned, Fr. Junipero Serra, vested with the sacerdotal robes in which I finished singing the High Mass of this solemn day of Saints Peter and Paul, and assisted by Fathers Juan Crespi and Francisco Dumetz, missionaries apostolic of said College of San Fernando and fellow missionaries at this mission, with the holy chrism blessed by the illustrious Bishop of Guadalajara, the latest which is here or could be obtained, I confirmed according to the Roman Pontifical, and with the solemnity possible, the following persons." Here the Fr. Presidente entered in full the names of ninety-one small (Indian) children along with the names of the parents and the two sponsors of each child. At the end of the list Fr. Serra added this note: "After the antiphon, prayers and oration which the Roman Pontifical prescribes, I bestowed upon all the newly-confirmed, who in obedience to my previous charge had remained in said church, the holy blessing which the said Pontifical ordains. I also told and explained to the godfathers and godmothers the spiritual parentage and the obligations which they had contracted, and with this that first and solemn act concluded. In testimony whereof I sign together with the said assistant Fathers."

The zealous Fr. Presidente next prepared the grown people, both Indians and Spaniards, for the reception of the Sacrament. In this case special instructions had to precede. By August 23rd he had entered one hundred and fifty names, each one after the same minute form already noted. On the following day, August 24th, Fr. Serra embarked on the *Santiago* for San Diego where he disembarked on September 16th. At the Mission he confirmed after the same manner as at San Carlos. Then he visited each Mission on the way back overland for the purpose of bestowing the same Sacrament, and by the end of the year he was back at San Carlos. He had confirmed in all 1897 persons, nearly all Indian converts.

There were good reasons for the minuteness in recording every particular concerned with the exercise of his extraordinary powers, as we shall learn ere long.

CHAPTER VIII.

Felipe de Neve First Governor of California.—His Instructions.—Neve
Exceeds His Authority.—New Plans.—Disagreements.—Discour-
teous to Fr. Serra.—Alcaldes Introduced by Neve.—Failure and
Worse.—Forbids Fr. Serra to Confirm.

The territory of Upper California had heretofore been
ruled in the name of the King of Spain by a military commander. Gaspár de Portolá held the office temporarily for
less than a year. Captain Pedro Fages succeeded to the title
till May, 1774, when he was relieved by Captain Fernando
Rivera y Moncada. Rivera occupied the position till the
arrival from Lower California of Felipe de Neve, who landed
at Monterey on February 3, 1777. Neve came with the title
of Governor of California.

Viceroy Bucareli in a long letter dated Mexico, December
25, 1776, informed the Fr. Presidente of the change, and added
the momentous remark: *"Governor* Felipe de Neve is charged
to act in everything in accord with Your Reverence."[1] How
the new governor entirely disregarded this order of the viceroy,
and what sort of gentleman he was, the readers will have
occasion to judge for themselves from the facts related in the
following pages. Other acts, which more directly affect other
Missions, are not included in this narrative on Mission San
Carlos.

H. H. Bancroft, who, on general principles, shares the
animosity of the first governor for the missionaries and for
Fr. Serra in particular, while introducing Neve to Upper California, unwittingly gives his client away in these words: "It
was evident that Neve, *despite the viceregal injunctions,* was
already on bad terms with the (Dominican) Friars.[2] The new
governor soon manifested the same spirit in his new field of

---

[1] "El Gobernador Don Felipe Neve está encargado de que para todo
use de los acuerdos de Vuestra Reverentia." (See vol. ii, chap. xiii, *The
Missions*).

[2] *The North Mexican States and Texas,* vol. i, p. 741.

operation. "Neve every day had another notion," writes Fr. Palóu, "and broached new schemes for obstructing the progress of the missionary establishments which were then flourishing in temporal as well as in spiritual matters."[3]

One of the new governor's schemes for obstructing the advancement of the Missions was proposed by him early in 1779, only two years after his coming to California. Without consulting Fr. Serra as to its practicability or expediency, and in total disregard of the viceroy's injunction, Neve boldly demanded that the Indian neophytes at every Mission should from their own number elect an *alcalde* or magistrate and two *regidores* or councillors, for the purpose of accustoming the Indians to self-government. These new officials were to have a certain measure of control and to be exempt from corporal punishment. When it is remembered that at Mission San Carlos, for instance, the first adult Indian emerged from the savage state only seven years previously and that most of the others had escaped from filth and degradation at irregular intervals during the last five years, one feels amazed at the bare suggestion of such folly.

The project was entirely uncalled for. The neophytes felt perfectly happy in their new environments. Of self government, like children, they knew nothing and cared less. They found themselves treated kindly, wisely, and justly. Even the adults were just so many childish, unambitious, carefree, overgrown youths, perfectly satisfied to be governed by the solicitous missionaries. They were entirely incapable of being left to themselves and their dull wits for any position of responsibility. The project, if carried out, would therefore effect nothing good but cause grave disorders.

At any rate, Neve in this matter was exceeding his authority. The missionaries towards their Indian wards by royal orders stood *in loco parentis*, that is to say, the neophytes were by Spanish law regarded as minors and entrusted to the keeping of the missionaries, who, therefore, possessed all the rights and duties of parents concerning the convert Indians. It was

---

3 *The Missions and Missionaries*, vol. ii, chap. xviii.

their right and their duty to decide when these wards of theirs had reached such a state that they could be trusted to govern themselves and others. The governor had no jurisdiction over the Mission Indians save in case any individual among them had committed a capital crime against the laws of the territory or the Spanish law for short. Fr. Serra might have quoted the declaration of Viceroy Bucareli and his Council on this relationship between the missionaries and the neophytes; but Neve would haughtily interpret that regulation to suit himself, as he had done on the question of rations to the missionaries.[4] This he could do with impunity, because the direct jurisdiction over the seven northwestern States, including California, had been taken from the viceroy and vested in a personal friend of the governor, Don Teodoro de Croix, with the title of Comandante-General. Both were swayed by the same French philosophical ideas of their period. Fr. Serra might appeal to the viceroy; but it would take a year to obtain an answer. Meanwhile the hostile Neve might do as he pleased, confident that his action would be upheld by de Croix. Fr. Serra and the Fathers might refuse to serve under such unworthy arrangement, and demand their passports. Fr. Lasuén and Fr. Figuér at San Diego actually adopted this course when they heard of the foolish scheme of the malevolent governor. Their permit to retire could not be refused by Fr. Serra, because they both had served the regulation ten years, and were free to return to the College. Neve, however, would probably refuse the passport and the facilities for the journey to Mexico. He might, if all the Fathers took the same course, report the friars in revolt against the government, and de Croix would have sustained him. There was no telling what the haughty caballero might do. In this dilemma, to avoid any scandal, after he had spoken to the governor on the matter, Fr. Serra decided to advise the Fathers to reconsider their determination. In one of his longest letters, Fr. Serra wrote to Fr. Lasuén as follows under date of March 29, 1779:

---

[4] See our Volume on *Mission Dolores*, chap. viii; and vol. ii, chap. xvii, *The Missions*.

"I have pleaded for the rations and for the suspension of the (Indian) elections. Yesterday, Palm Sunday, which I celebrated at the presidio,[5] we exchanged but a few words before holy Mass, whereupon the governor said to me something so far from the truth that I changed my attitude and grew indignant. I told him that nobody had ever said such a thing to me, because nobody could have said it to me. He replied with a faint smile that he too was a logician, thus giving me to understand that what he said to me was inferred, though it was not true itself. To this I retorted that it was very bad logic, since not even by a long stretch of imagination did it allow such inference. With some irony he said that I should not be aggrieved because it would remain between us two. I told him that this was too much for my feelings, even though it remained with one only. Finally the dispute ceased. Such was my preparation for the holy Mass and on such a solemn day! I had great difficulty trying to compose myself before the altar. I celebrated holy Mass, and after a short talk on indifferent matters, I came here (San Carlos) to sing the Passion[6] with my companions as they had expected me to do.

"The dispute was about the (Indian) alcaldes. The rest of the day I was in distress unable to remove the impression, and I was making thousands of plans as to what was expedient to do. I set to work writing a letter to said Señor (Neve), and I

---

[5] Fr. Serra resided at San Carlos. He must have come to Monterey very early, and made the distance of about a league and one fourth afoot, as was his custom unless suffering from illness, when he would use a donkey. It was characteristic of Neve's manner to approach the priest just before holy Mass to embarrass Fr. Serra when he wanted to be recollected for the sacred functions. Besides he was still fasting. However, Neve towards the missionaries was ever brave and overbearing and lost no courtesies or considerations on them, as this instance proves. Hence we can explain his cowardice at Los Angeles when he was to lead soldiers against the Yumas.

[6] Probably as deacon. That was quite a feat for a man of sixty-six years and with his ailments. The ceremony at San Carlos would last about two hours.

intended to include the one from Your Reverence as well as the one from Fr. Juan Figuér, in which you ask me for permission to retire in case the elections were held, although I had already told the Señor in person along with many other things. In every clause which I wrote something inexpedient would appear; so I stopped and thought and thought again. After struggling with that wretched letter till about midnight, and attributing the failure to my internal agitation, I took a new sheet of paper and went to work writing a letter to Fr. Sanchez at San Gabriel, in order to see whether I should become myself again. This letter did not turn out to be a short one. I finished, closed, addressed, and put it in its place. Then I returned to the struggle, but with the same result; yet, when I reflected that the night had already far advanced, and that, unless I gave myself a little rest, though I did not feel drowsy, I should be unfit for anything the whole day, I resolved to put the letter off till morning. When I had entered the bedroom, and thought of lying down for the needed rest, I tried to raise my mind upwards, but found myself unable to do so. In desparation I exclaimed: '*What is it, Lord?*' It seemed to that my interior responded with perfect distinctness: '*Prudentes sicut serpentes, et simplices sicut columbae!*'[7] I sat up, and much relieved said, 'Yes, Lord! yes, Lord! so it shall be with Thy grace!' I then fell asleep, and at the accustomed hour rose to recite the Office. Soon after I sang the High Mass in thanksgiving for the birth of a daughter to the Prince de Asturias.

"Well, what I have thought out is that what the *caballero* (Neve) demands should be executed, but in such a way that it cannot cause the least commotion among the natives, nor in the government which Your Reverence has established. Let Francisco with the same baton[8] and coat, which he has, be the first alcalde. It is nothing more than a change in the name. Let the chief of one of the rancherias who comes from

---

[7] "Prudent as the serpents and simple as the doves." (Matt. x, 16).

[8] This Indian seems to have been the fiscal or police officer, who, as a mark of authority, wore a uniform and carried a baton.

fifteen to fifteen days[9] be the other *alcalde*. With regard to the *regidores*, who as such carry no staff, let the one be of the Mission and the other of any rancheria, whether he is chief or not, though it will be more expedient that he be a chief, and thus the things will remain without creating wonderment. For my sake and for your sakes I entreat Your Reverences in the name of God, without omitting a dot of the governor's instructions, make the arrangement in such a manner that the neophytes behold in the Fathers no less authority than they have observed before. I hope to God that thus the difficulties may not ensue which otherwise, it is almost certain, will result. We all have reason to lament; but speaking of these Missions it may be said: *"Miscebatur lamentatio matrum et ad coelum transibat oblatio parvulorum."*[10]

Alcaldes and regidores were accordingly instituted at all the Missions; but notwithstanding the precautions taken by advice of Fr. Serra, the consequences were even worse than had been feared. The moment the Indians chosen saw themselves clothed with a little authority, and exempt from the punishment to which all the other neophytes were subjected for misdeeds, they availed themselves of their privileges to gratify their inclinations without thinking of their responsibilities. Writing to Fr. Lasuén, less than five months after the innovation, Fr. Serra reported that "the Indian alcalde of San Luis Obispo utilized his office to work mischief. The alcaldes are much puffed up and regard themselves as lords. The alcalde of this Mission of San Carlos has not yet gone out of his cotton pants and his blanket, nevertheless he already complains (directly) to his Honor."[11] Neve had disregarded all the objections and warnings of the missionaries. He assured them that these alcaldes would keep order; that they

---

[9] Owing to scanty harvests at San Diego, many neophytes lived in their rancherias, but came to the Mission every fifteen days for Mass and Doctrina.

[10] "The lamentation of the mothers commingled and to Heaven ascended the offering of the little ones."—Fr. Serra to Fr. Lasuén, Monday in Holy Week, 1779.—See vol. ii, *The Missions*, chap. xx.

[11] See Appendix G, vol. ii, *The Missions*.

would make the rounds of the village at night; and that they would take the people to church so that the Fathers would have an easier life. Before a year had elapsed there was trouble at every Mission except San Antonio. Neve had eventually to acknowledge, to himself at least, that the Indians were incapable of holding a position of trust independently of the missionaries, or even of having an election without a guide.

At Mission San Carlos, Fr. Serra's own Mission, and in the very neighborhood of Neve's headquarters, the experiment proved especially disastrous. A certain Baltasar had been chosen alcalde. "No sooner had he realized his privileges, especially his exemption from chastisement," writes Fr. Serra to the governor on January 7, 1780, "than he did what he pleased. He seduced his own sister-in-law. He also beat with a stick a Lower California neophyte because the latter executed an order of the Fathers, as I reported to your Honor at the time. Besides the neglect of his duties, the whole population now sees that he is a runaway, lives in concubinage, sends messages to the people here, communicates personally with those who leave without permission, and exerts himself to increase his gang in the mountains by new desertions from the Missions." Fr. Serra in his long letter to the governor gives other instances from other Missions, and demonstrates clearly that the new plan can but end in universal disaster.

When Neve saw that his scheme, whatever the motive for introducing it resulted in nothing but disorders, and that the Fr. Presidente was forcing the responsibility on him, he deemed it prudent to keep silent. Neve evidently felt that he had over-reached himself and now that Fr. Serra held him responsible for the disorders caused by his unwarranted interference, he sought the assistance of Fr. Serra to undo the mischief. Had he proposed his plan in any courteous manner, listened to the experienced missionary, and left the execution of the plan to the missionaries, they would have proceeded in the way they were now adopting, i. e., keeping the elected subject to chastisement for misdemeanors as before. For details on the sub-

ject the readers are referred to vol. ii, chap. xx. With Fr.
Serra that was sufficient answer. He therefore wrote to Fr.
Lasuén: "With regard to the alcaldes, inasmuch as we are
permitted to govern in our own way, I do not perceive much
inconvenience. It may be that now we shall be permitted to
be at peace in this matter, for since the governor received the
dose he said nothing. Hence, according to the rule 'Qui tacet
consentire videtur, etc.,' I have written to San Luis Obispo
and to San Gabriel that they should give them (alcaldes)
what they deserve.

"I called the governor's attention to the manner of electing
alcaldes. He then said to Fr. Crespi: 'Your Reverences may
see to it that the Indians assemble and elect their alcaldes and
regidores like the Spaniards, and so they will be trained, etc.'
The first day of the new year came. One alcalde was wander-
ing a fugitive and is still roving about. The governor anxiously
waited for the election returns; but neither on that day nor
on the following feast day were there any elections. He could
wait no longer, but wrote to me that it was strange, etc. I replied that as I had not troubled myself about the matter, it
was enough for me to have said that they had to hold the
elections, and that they could hold them when they pleased.
He then wrote to me that with regard to the elections he had
always placed confidence not in them (Indians), but in our
prudence. He also employed flattering words and begged
that what could be done should be done, etc. The tenor of my
answer to him was that, if we were so good, and if we were
trusted with the elections of the alcaldes, as we had desired,
then he could also trust us to rear them, correct them, chastise,
etc. This was the letter to which he made no reply."

About this very period Neve seized the opportunity of
embarrassing the Fr. Presidente in another matter, whereby
he implied that the Fr. Presidente was subject to the governor
in purely spiritual affairs as well as in temporal things. In
consequence of the close union of the State and Church under
the Spanish dominion, which for the Church was really a sort
of slavery, the Pope could not exercise any authority in re-

ligious matters without the permit of the king. For instance, any address or document from the Pope to a Spanish Bishop had first to be submitted to the king for approval and signature. Thus the document which authorized the College of San Fernando, Mexico, to designate a member to exercise the power of administering the Sacrament of Confirmation, had to have the *Pasé* or Permit of the king. It then went to the viceroy for his permit or approval added to the original of the Pope. It then was turned over to the College, which retained the document and sent Fr. Serra a copy only with directions to exercise the powers granted. Fr. Serra never saw the document or Papal Bull.

When Neve heard that Fr. Serra was administering Confirmation, he demanded to know by what authority the Fr. Presidente administered the Sacrament of Confirmation. He wanted to see the Bull of the Pope to make sure it bore the signature of the king and of the Comandante-General. An insolent assumption! Fr. Serra was moreover warned that he should desist from confirming till the required document was presented. Thus it came to pass that Fr. Serra, to avoid any scandal or allow the Indians to believe that the governor had any authority over him in ecclesiastical matters, refrained from visiting the Missions for over a year, because he would create wonderment if he did not confirm also. On appeal, the College represented the case before the viceroy. Viceroy Mayorga notified Governor Neve that all formalities had been observed, and that the original document empowering Fr. Serra to confirm bore the *Pasé* of the King. Fr. Serra, therefore, was within his rights in exercising the power to administer the Sacrament of Confirmation for the period for which it was limited. Thus Neve had received the proper snub he deserved, but not a glimpse of the Pope's Bull. The discomfiture caused him much chagrin, which he nursed until the next occasion. For details on the subject, see vol. ii, *The Missions*, chap. xviii.

On August 17, 1779, King Carlos of Spain asked his subjects in America for contributions to pay the expenses of the

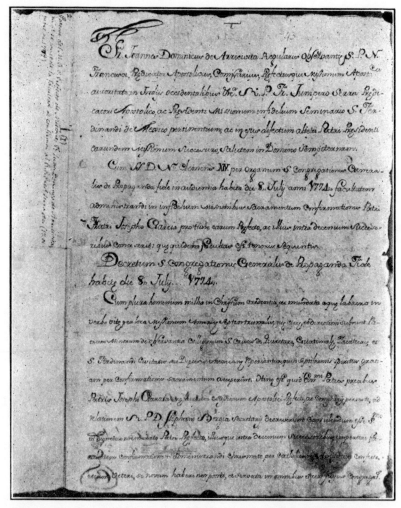

THE "PATENTE" NOTIFYING FR. SERRA OF HIS FACULTY TO ADMINISTER
THE SACRAMENT OF CONFIRMATION.

war with England. Mission San Carlos contributed $106. Its mayordomo, Ignacio, added $10 more for himself. See *The Missions*, vol. ii, chap. xxiii.

CHAPTER IX.

Returning to the internal affairs of Mission San Carlos, we find the Fr. Presidente writing to Fr. Lasuén at San Diego under date of April 22, 1779, among other things: "In the preceding year I had the consolation of seeing that all had complied with their Easter Duty when the last day of Easter time—Sunday Quasimodo—Sunday in Albis (White Sunday) arrived. This year, yesterday, the Third Day of Easter (Tuesday after Easter), with four days still to spare, only three are still missing." That was a fine record for the flock which included the guards. It is not certain, however, that the presidio people were included, though it seems so. It will be observed that, according to the Spanish custom, Easter Time for the fulfilling of the Easter Duty closed with the Sunday after Easter. In the United States the time extends to Trinity Sunday inclusive, the Sunday after Pentecost.

Now the Fr. Presidente, the man thoroughly at home in philosophy and theology, turns to something altogether outside of his sphere as a priest, but under the circumstances of more urgent importance—to cereals, vegetables and live stock. How he must have loathed it; yet for the sake of his beloved Indians he devoted himself to that department of Indian missionary existence as though he loved that too. Addressing Fr. Lasuén on September 28, 1779, Fr. Serra informs his equally learned colaborer in the California Missions as follows: "The barley harvest amounted to 420 fanégas and 3½ almudes, (700 bushels). Beans yielded nearly 100 fanégas (165 bushels). Wheat appears excellent and promises to yield 1000 fanégas (about 1660 bushels). Corn has just been shelled, and thus amounted to little more than fifty fanégas (about 85 bushels),

because horses, cattle, crows, and thieves left us only that
much, although God had provided abundantly."

It must be remembered that neither the missionaries nor
the converts knew much about farming. Then the implements
were of the most primitive kind. The plough, for instance,
was composed of two pieces of timber. One of these was formed of a crooked branch of such a shape that it constituted the
sole and the handle or stilt. A sharp piece of iron was fitted
to the point of the sole. The other was a beam of undressed
timber long enough to reach the yoke which was fastened with
thongs of rawhide to the horns of two oxen that drew the
plough. The beam was inserted into the upper part of the
main piece and connected with the sole by a small upright
piece of wood on which it could slide, and which was fixed by
two wedges. By withdrawing these wedges the beam was
elevated or lowered, and by this means the plough was regulated as to the depth of the furrow. The ploughman went on
one side holding the handle or stilt with his right hand and
managing the goad with the left. Only a rut could be made
and the soil could not be turned over deep; this necessitated
crossing and recrossing the field many times. A harrow was
unknown. Where wheat and barley were sown a bushy
branch was used to cover the seed. In places a log of wood
was drawn over the field. Corn was planted by hand in the
rut made by the plough, and the seed was covered with soil
by means of the foot.

In the same letter to Fr. Lasuén, Fr. Serra informs his
friend at San Diego, that, owing to his sore leg which had been
inflamed and pained him so, he had one day to omit celebrating
holy Mass. Next day he said holy Mass with much difficulty.
He passes the nights sleeping very little, although that is more
due to the head, (i. e., to Neve at the presidio) than to his leg.
For the solution of this puzzle about his leg, we must relate
that Fr. Serra coming from Spain in 1749, one night while
asleep scratched his leg so vigorously that on the following
morning the limb was found covered with blood and very badly swollen. For all that he kept walking till he reached the

PRIMITIVE PLOUGH AND MANNER OF PLOUGHING.

Capital, nor would he use any medical means to heal the wound. In consequence, periodically the sore gave him much pain and would at times make it impossible to celebrate holy Mass or to walk. On such occasions, to make a necessary journey he would have to mount a mule.

To spare his beloved Indians, Fr. Serra never exposed their shortcomings, though he explains fully enough other adverse circumstances. For instance, his letter to Fr. Lasuén of December 8, 1781, is replete with interesting items. "Already I shall believe that this year our plantings of corn, wheat, and garden seeds, etc., will be irrigated, and that the surplus water will run into the laguna near the granary so that it may never run dry, and that it may become a good warren for fish. Perhaps this may be realized in about eight days, and then with the help of God we shall proceed to work on the new church for which some stone has already been brought from the quarry. For the present year, however, we are most poor as regards wheat, because when the time had come for threshing, it was found that on account of the poor quality of the grain a sack of ears yielded less than two pecks. Of corn there was nothing nor likewise of barley. So wheat is the only grain secured. Holy Patience!

"As the exercise of the authority to confirm was lately restored, I went to use it at the Missions of San Antonio, San Francisco and Santa Clara. Since then I wore shoes because of an adventure which the mule provided while I was returning to this Mission of San Carlos; but I am told that all the ribs are still in their places. Today already the pain has moderated very much. Blessed be God for everything. The day on which the mule threw me was the same on which the first stone was laid for the temple of Santa Clara." The day for the corner-stone laying of Santa Clara church was November 19, 1781.

Two weeks later, December 2, 1781, Fr. Serra reported the number of male Indians, eighteen years and over, who resided at the various rancherias. We thus for the first time become acquainted with those Indian settlements. They were as follows:

Rancheria de San Carlos.......24
Rancheria de San Joseph.......14
Rancheria de Santa Teresa.....21
Rancheria de San Miguel.......17
Rancheria de San Francisco.. ..20

———

96

These Indians were all married, except five of whom three were widowers.

Furthermore Fr. Serra on the same date reported that at this Mission lives, as mayordomo, a Spaniard, Ignacio Vallejo by name. It was, as stated before, he who voluntarily offered his contribution of ten pesos as *donativo* to the war expense of King Carlos III.

At the end of 1782, or in the beginning of 1783, after having visited all the Missions in turn from San Diego northward, Governor Pedro Fages reported on the Missions as he had seen them. Regarding San Carlos he wrote: "Mission San Carlos de Monterey, distant twenty-six leagues from Mission San Antonio, is situated a short distance from the coast in a plain of the Rio Carmelo. It possesses much and good land, but as yet the arrangements for irrigating the lands from the Rio Carmelo are not complete. Nevertheless, good crops of all sorts of grain have been obtained. This is due partly to the fertility of the soil, and partly to the continual fogs. Its climate is disagreeably rough, and the locality of the Mission is always exposed to rough winds. It may be due to this reason and the presence of a lagoon of unwholesome water that the mortality of the Indians is so great.

"Placed in this sad predicament, and on account of their in-born laziness, and their lack of reasoning thus far manifested, the neophytes have contributed little to the advancement of their Mission. In addition, their constant stealing and killing horses and cattle have caused the backwardness of the Mission which it suffers. Nor have they ceased doing so notwithstanding the indefatigable zeal of their missionaries. Besides there are two languages spoken by the neophytes, one by the coast Indians and the other by the Sierra."

In 1787 Fages again reported and declared that "the natives (of California) are kept in order as neophytes only by the unremitting efforts of the friars, and they are as yet wholly unfit to become citizens."

Fr. Serra suffered a heavy blow when his former pupil in theology, and dearly beloved assistant at San Carlos, passed to his eternal reward at the Mission on January 1, 1782. Details will be found in the chapter on burials.

A heavier blow fell upon the Fr. Presidente in May, 1782, when the frigates *La Favorita* and *La Princesa* arrived at San Francisco. The mail was forwarded by courier to Fr. Serra. It brought a letter from the Fr. Guardian of San Fernando College. It contained unexpected news which not only crushed his hopes of starting new Missions, but threatened through Neve's machinations the destruction of those already founded. Neve had concocted a plan which reduced the missionary establishments to mere catechetical centers with but one missionary, who would have nothing more to do than to visit the Indians in their hovels, speak to those who would listen and then retire to his habitation. New Missions would not again be established as before. The plan had been tried at Yuma, on the Colorado and had resulted in the massacre of four Franciscans and all the soldiers together with Captain Fernando Rivera. This happened in July, 1781. Neve had not taken the lesson, but wanted the same system followed in California, and this had been the cause for the delay in the founding of the Santa Barbara Mission. There Neve had disappointed Fr. Serra, who had taken it as a matter of course that the Mission should be started along with the presidio.

The Fr. Guardian in a long letter explained the whole plot, and that de Croix and Neve had persuaded Viceroy Mayorga to supply no more means for new Missions. Fr. Guardian Francisco Pangua and his Councillors on the other hand insisted that the Missions must be established after the same system as the king had directed from the beginning or there would be no missionaries willing to expose themselves to such an aimless and fruitless life. Their unanswerable arguments and their fearless determination caused Viceroy Mayorga to report the matter to the king. His Majesty, Carlos III, as related by Fr. Palóu on August 16, 1786, decided: *"That the point in (Neve's) Reglamento which determined that the Missions should have but one missionary, is repealed, because it is unjust; nor is it the will of the king. It is the will of the king that we missionaries should be at the Missions in pairs."*

Hence, if the nine existing Missions continued and the subsequent twelve Missions likewise became such great schools for agriculture, horticulture, mechanical arts, and stockraising, and were not mere catechetical meeting places, it is due to the firm stand taken by the Franciscan College of San Fernando, Mexico.

Neve, the disturber of missionary peace and oppressor of the missionaries, had meanwhile been removed to take up the office of inspector-general in Mexico, and Pedro Fages in 1782 again became governor of California. He was happily in the agreeable position to let Fr. Serra know that Mission Santa Barbara could be established on the old lines. The news cheered the Fr. Presidente in his last days and his successor, Fr. Fermín de Lasuén, had thereafter much more pleasant times in governing the Missions of California.

California was now called upon to part forever with its heroic apostle. He had completed his last Confirmation tour by the end of 1783, and the term for which he had been empowered would expire on July 16, 1784. While he exercised his authority, the Fr. Presidente had visited every existing settlement of either Indian or white people. All had been afforded an opportunity to benefit by his presence and solicitude. By July 16th, Fr. Serra had confirmed as many as 5,307 persons mostly Indian neophytes.

The indefatigable Father now felt his end approaching. As was his custom he by letter communicated to the missionaries of all the Missions the news received by the recent vessels; but to those farthest south he bid farewell for eternity. Those nearest San Carlos he asked to send one of the two Fathers because he wished to confer with them. To Fr. Palóu at San Francisco, the now very ill Father wrote that he wished him to come to San Carlos by ship or by land. Fr. Palóu guessing the reason hastened to reach Monterey by land. Arriving at San Carlos on August 18th he found his old teacher in theology very feeble, although the Father was up and around. Nor would he cease going into the church for the customary Christian doctrine lessons and the prayers with the neophytes in the afternoon. With them he would also sing in conclusion the tender pious hymns composed by the venerable Fr. Antonio Margíl in honor of the Blessed Virgin. "On hearing Fr. Serra sing in his natural voice," Fr. Palóu writes, "I said to a soldier that the Fr. Presidente did not seem to be so very ill." The guard who was acquainted with Fr. Serra since the year 1769, replied: "Father, we must not be too confident; he is sick; but the saintly Father, when it comes to praying and singing is always well; now he is near the end."

"On the following day, the 19th of the month, he directed me to sing the High Mass in honor of the Most Holy Patriarch St. Joseph, as he was accustomed to do every month, and said to me that he felt very tired. I did so. Nevertheless, his Paternity did not fail to sing in choir with the neophytes, and to recite the seven Pater Nosters and other customary prayers. Neither did he in the afternoon fail to recite the prayers and to sing the verses of the Virgin. On the following day, which was Friday, as always he went the Stations of the Cross in the church with the whole congregation.

"Five days after my arrival at Monterey the packet-boat anchored in the bay. Very soon the royal surgeon came to the Mission to visit the Rev. Father. Finding him so fatigued from the trouble in his breast, the surgeon proposed cauterizing the chest in order to draw out the tumors which had accumulated in the breast. The Father replied that he might

apply as many of that sort of remedies as he pleased.* The
doctor did so, but with no more effect than to aggravate the
pains in the enfeebled body. Yet neither this powerful remedy,
nor the pains which he suffered brought out any demonstration of feeling, just as though he had no such pains,
always on his feet as though he were well. As the packet-boat
had brought some cloth, he began to cut it with his own hands
and to distribute the pieces to the neophytes so that they
might cover themselves.''

---

* This was remarkable, as he always declined to use any remedies for
his ills. Only a month before at Santa Clara he declined the offer of the
navy surgeon to treat the sore leg. "Let it go. We might lose all,"
he said.

CHAPTER X.

"On the 26th of August the Venerable Father arose more fatigued. He told me he had passed a bad night, and that he wanted to prepare himself for whatever God might dispose regarding him. He was that whole day in retirement without admitting anything distracting. At night he repeated with me his general confession with copious tears, and with a clear mind as though he were well. Having concluded, after a brief meditation he took a cup of soup and lay down to rest, without wanting any one to remain in his cell.

"At daybreak on the 27th of August I entered his room and found him with the breviary in his hand, as he was always accustomed to begin Matins before daybreak,[1] whereas when on the road he would begin them at daybreak. On inquiry how he had passed the night, he said to me that he had experienced nothing particular, but that, nevertheless, I should at holy Mass consecrate an additional host and to reserve it and then I should notify him. This I did, and on concluding holy Mass I returned to inform him. Then he told me that he desired to receive the Most Divine Sacrament as Viaticum, and that for this he would go to the church. When I told him that there was no need for going to the church; that his little cell would be adorned in the best way possible; and that his Divine Majesty would come to visit him there, he replied: ' *No*,' that he wanted to receive Him in the church, since as he could go there afoot, there was no reason that the Lord should come to him. I had to yield and to comply with his holy wishes. He then walked by himself to the church, which was more than 100 yards distant, accompanied by the comandante of the presidio, who had come for the function with a portion of the troops. The Indians of the village or Mission

---

[1] Hence by candle light.

accompanied the venerable sick Father to the church and manifested great affection and devotion.

"On arriving at the steps of the presbytery, the venerable Father knelt in front of a little table prepared for the ceremony. Re-vested I came out of the sacristy, and on reaching the altar, while preparing the incense to begin the sacred function,[2] the fervent servant of God with his natural voice, as sonorous as when he was well, intoned the *Tantum Ergo Sacramentum* whilst tears of emotion streamed from his eyes. I administered the Sacred Viaticum with all the ceremonies of the Ritual, and when the most holy function, which under such circumstances had never been witnessed, was concluded, the venerable Father remained in the same kneeling posture giving thanks to the Lord. When he had concluded them, he returned to his little cell accompanied by the whole assembly. Some would weep out of devotion and affection, others from pain and sorrow because they feared that they would be left without their beloved Father. He staid alone in his cell, lost in contemplation and seated in a chair by the table. Seeing him so recollected I allowed no one to enter to speak to him.

"I saw that the carpenter of the presidio went to enter the cell, but when I would not permit it, he told me that the Father had called him to make the coffin in which to bury him and he wanted to ask him how he desired it. This touched me deeply, but I gave him no permission to enter and speak to the Father. Instead, I ordered him to make it as he had made the one for Fr. Crespi. The venerable Father passed the whole day, seated in the chair, in absolute silence and profound recollection, without drinking anything else than a little soup during the whole day, and without lying down.

"In the night he felt more aggravated and asked me for the Holy Oils. He received this holy Sacrament seated on a low stool made of reeds. With us he said the Litany of All Saints and the Penitential Psalms. The whole night he passed without sleeping, during the greater portion of which he knelt leaning his breast against the boards of the bed. I told him

---

[2] For incensing the ciborium after opening the tabernacle.

to lie down a little, but he replied that in this posture he felt more relief. Other portions of the night he passed seated on the floor reclining on the shoulders of the neophytes who filled the little cell all through the night attracted by the great love which they had for him as the Father who had regenerated them in the Lord. When I saw him so much prostrated, and reclining in the arms of the Indians, I asked the surgeon what he thought of him? He replied, as the Father seemed very much oppressed: 'To me it appears that this blessed Father wants to die on the floor.'

"Soon after I went in and asked him if he wanted the Absolution and the application of the Plenary Indulgence. Replying in the affirmative, he disposed himself, knelt and received the General Absolution, and I applied to him the Plenary Indulgence of the Franciscan Order. With this he was very much consoled, and spent the whole night in the manner described. The day of the holy Doctor of the Church, St. Augustine, August 28th, dawned and the Father seemed alleviated, and without the suffocating sensation in his breast, although throughout the night he had not slept nor taken anything whatever. He passed the morning seated in his low reed chair leaning against the bed. This consisted of a few boards poorly planed and covered with a blanket, more to cover himself with than to soften the hardness for resting; nor was there a sheepskin as is the custom in the College. Even when travelling he observed the same custom. He would spread the blanket upon the ground, place a pillow at one end, and then stretch himself out on the blanket for the necessary rest. He always slept with a crucifix upon his breast which he held in his arms. The crucifix was about one foot long. This he carried along since the time when he lived in the novitiate of the College. He never left it behind, but carried it with him in all his journeys together with the blanket and pillow. In his Mission, and wherever he stopped for the night, as soon as he rose from the bed, he placed the crucifix upon the pillow. So also it was on this occasion when he did not want to lie down, neither during the whole night nor on the forenoon of the day when he had to surrender his soul to the Creator.

"About ten o'clock in the morning of the said day of St. Augustine, the officers of the frigate came out to see the Father. He received them standing with every mark of esteem, and ordered the bells to be rung. Then again seated on his stool he said: 'Gentlemen, I am thankful that you have been able to come to this distant port in order to place a little earth on my body.' When the gentlemen and all the rest of us heard this we were quite surprised, because we saw him sitting on his little reed chair, and yet we heard him speaking thus. They said to him: 'No, Father, we trust in God that you may yet recover and continue the work of conversion!' The Father, however, replied: 'Yes, Yes; please do me this charity and work of mercy of throwing a little earth over me and I shall be very thankful to you.' Then fixing his eyes on me (Fr. Palóu) he said: 'I wish you to bury me in the church next to Fr. Juan Crespi for the present, and when the stone church is built, you may place me where you will.'

"When the tears allowed me to answer him, I said to him: 'Fr. Presidente, if it pleases God to take you to Himself, it shall be done as Your Paternity desires. In this case I beg Your Paternity for the love and great affection which you always have had for me that when you reach the presence of the Most Holy Trinity, you adore It in my name, and that you do not forget me, nor forget to pray for all who dwell in these establishments, especially for those who are here present.' 'I promise,' he said, 'That if the Lord in His infinite mercy shall grant me this eternal happiness, which my faults do not merit, that I shall do so for all, and that the conversion of the great pagandom be accomplished which I leave still unconverted.'

"Not long thereafter he asked me to sprinkle the little room with holy water. I did so. On asking him whether he felt anything, he said: ' No,' but that I should do it so that he might experience nothing. Then he remained in profound silence. Suddenly, very much frightened, he said to me:

'Much fear has come over me. I am much afraid. Read for me the *Recommendation of the Souls*, and let it be in a loud voice, so that I can hear it.' I did so, assisted by all the gentlemen of the bark and also by his companion, Fr. Mathias Noriega, the surgeon, and many others of the bark and of the Mission. I read the Recommendation of the Soul for him to which the venerable dying man answered as though he were well, while seated in the little chair of reeds, arousing the emotions of us all. When I finished the prayer, he exclaimed full of joy: 'Thanks be to God! Thanks be to God! Fear has been entirely taken from me. Thanks be to God! Let us therefore go out.' We all went out to a little outer room with his Paternity, all astonished and thankful.

"He then sat down in the chair by the table, and taking up the Diurnal, (portion of the breviary containing the Little Hours) and prepared himself to pray. When he had finished the Office, I said to him that it was later than one o'clock in the afternoon, and asked whether he wished to take a cup of soup? When he said 'Yes,' he drank it, and after having given thanks, he said: 'Let us now go to rest.'[3]   He then walked to his little cell where stood his bed. Taking off his cloak only, he lay down on the boards covered with the blanket, the crucifix in his arms as said before, in order to rest. We all thought he was going to sleep, since in the whole preceeding night he had not slept at all. The officers went out to dine; but being somewhat solicitous, after a little while I returned to enter his cell. On approaching the bed to see if he slept, I found him just as we had left him a little while before, but he was already asleep in the Lord, without having given any demonstration or sign of agonies. His body remained without any more evidence of death than the absence of respiration; on the contrary it appeared to be sleeping. We all devoutly believed that he slept in the Lord a little before two o'clock in the afternoon of St. Augustine's Day in the year 1784, and that he went to receive in heaven the reward of his apostolic labors.

---

[3] They were his last words.

"He closed his laborious life when seventy years, nine months, and four days old. He lived in the world sixteen years, nine months, and twenty-one days. He lived as a Religious fifty-three years, eleven months, and three days. Of these he passed thirty-five years, four months and three days in the exercise of an apostolic missionary. As soon as I had made sure that we had been left orphans without the amiable company of our revered prelate, I directed the neophytes present to announce it by the bells. As soon as the double tolling spread the sad news the whole village flocked together bewailing the death of their beloved Father. All wished to see him in order to give vent to the sorrow, which oppressed their hearts, through the tears that filled their eyes. So great was the crowd of the Indians, soldiers, and sailors that it became necessary to close the door in order to put the body into the coffin. For the purpose of burying it nothing more was necessary than to remove the sandals, which the captain of the packet-boat and the chaplain, who were present, received as souvenirs. The body continued in the same shroud in which the venerable Father died, that is to say the habit, the cowl, and cord, without inner tunic, because the two which he used on the journeys he had ordered to be washed six days before his death together with a change of underwear, and these he would not use because he wanted to die only in the habit, cowl, and cord.

"As soon as the body had been placed in the coffin between six lighted candles, the door of the cell was opened. The sorrowing neophytes were already there with bouquets of flowers of various colors gathered from the fields to adorn the body of their deceased venerable Father. The body was left in the cell until the approach of night. There was a continual concourse of people. They would come in praying for him, and they would with their Rosaries and medals touch his venerable hands and the face, in a loud voice calling him *Padre Santo*, *Padre Bendito*, and using other epithets born of the love they had for him. They would also relate the heroic virtues which they had observed in his life.

"When night had come we carried the body in procession to the church, the neophytes of the Mission with the soldiers and sailors forming the line. After placing the coffin with the body upon a table amid the six lighted candles, the function was concluded with the Responsory (*Libera*) for the dead. They besought me to leave the church open in order to watch over him and to recite the Rosary for the soul of the deceased, changing about at stated hours, and thus passing the night in continual prayer. I yielded to this, but left two soldiers as guards who were to prevent any indescreet acts of piety or thefts, as all were eager to possess something which the deceased had used. The sailors and soldiers were especially anxious to secure something the deceased had used. Although I promised to grant their wish after the funeral this did not prevent them from cutting little pieces.from his habit, and also a portion of the hair of his crown, when they could do so unknown to the sentinel, if, indeed, he did not participate in this pious robbery. Such was their esteem for the venerable Father that they called such remnants by the name relics, despite my effort to correct them and to explain.

"The funeral took place on Sunday August 29th, the day after the Father's death. The naval officers, the chaplain and crew, except a few sailors who guarded the ship and fired a cannon every half hour, which was answered by a cannon of the presidio, the presidio officers and the garrison, participated with the neophytes in the solemnities, the officers bearing lighted candles." After chanting the Vigil, Fr. Palóu sang the High Mass of Requiem surrounded by five Franciscan Fathers who sang the *Libera me Domine*. At four o'clock in the afternoon the bells again called the people to the church for the last Rites. A procession headed by the cross-bearer and acolytes was formed, and the body was borne around the plaza, the bearers relieving one another, as all the officers of both the navy and of the garrison wished to enjoy the honor of having borne the deceased Father on their shoulders. Four stops were made, at each of which the *Responsorium* was sung. Returning to the church the coffin with the body was again

placed on the table in front of the sanctuary. *Lauds* were then sung, whereupon the burial took place on the Gospel-side in the presbytery amid the weeping of the unconsolable neophytes, whose dear Father had gone from them forever.

After the ceremonies the people, the marines and soldiers as well as the officers wanted some keepsake from their Father. Fr. Palóu gave a tunic to the commander of the packetboat with the request to cut it into pieces for those on board. The royal surgeon, Don Juan Garcia, received one of two handkerchiefs. A few days later he returned to the Mission, and thanked Fr. Palóu for the gift, and said: "With this little piece of cloth I expect to cure more people than with all my books and bottles. A sailor on board who suffered from a headache which gave him no rest, I gave medicine and tied up his head with the handkerchief. He fell asleep and next morning awoke cured entirely. I hope that piece of cloth will accomplish more than a whole drugstore."

Fr. Palóu relates other instances, but emphatically declares that he stated these cures not as miracles, since in his opinion these keepsakes had no miraculous virtue; but simply for the sake of showing what was the general opinion of the virtues of the Rev. Fr. Junipero, and the esteem with which his exemplary life was regarded, especially by those who had known him and associated with him.

For the seventh day Fr. Palóu planned the Commemoration for the deceased Fr. Presidente. The same officers of the navy and the crew and the troops from the presidio again participated. The solemn vigil was chanted by the same missionaries, and then Fr. Palóu sang the Requiem High Mass with the deacons who are not named. Father Antonio Paterna, who had been with Fr. Serra in the Sierra Gorda Missions, Mexico, and Father Buenaventura Sitjar conducted the singing of the choir Indians who had been instructed by the deceased himself. Then a great many scapulars made of the tunic given to the marines were blessed to serve as souvenirs. Finally Fr. Palóu gratified those who had as yet received nothing by distributing to them some medals which the deceased Father was in the habit of doing.

"We, however, who had been his subordinates, were left with the heavy grief and pain of having been deprived of our beloved Father, prudent Superior, wise and model teacher, who had kept all of us inferiors comforted. I dare say of him what Solomon said of that other wise man: His memory will not be blotted out because the works which he did while alive have been stamped upon the inhabitants of this new California, who in spite of the devouring elements of time, will perpetuate it to all generations."

At the time of his death, those who had been baptized (during the 14 years) numbered 5800.

Fr. Tomas de la Peña, who had served at Mission Santa Clara, but was then procurator in Mexico for the California Missions, under date of June 26, 1805, informed Fr. Baldomero Lopez, who had served at Santa Cruz Mission, that Fr. Serra had merited the esteem of the highest government officials; and that the College repeatedly had elected Fr. Serra Guardian, but that, owing to his absence at so great a distance, he could not be confirmed, which always necessitated the election of another Father to the office. (Santa Barbara Archives, No. 486).

CHAPTER XI.

After the funeral rites had been performed for the late Fr. Presidente Serra, Fr. Palóu returned to his own Mission, San Francisco, and remained there till the end of July, 1785. His last entry in the Baptismal Register was dated July 25, 1785. Thereupon he took up his residence at San Carlos, because on the death of Fr. Serra he had become temporary Presidente of the Missions.

Meanwhile, September, 1785, Fr. Fermin Francisco de Lasuén of Mission San Diego received a letter from Fr. Guardian Sancho of San Fernando College, Mexico, which notified him that he had been elected Presidente of the Missions, because Fr. Francisco Palóu was in possession of the permit to retire which Fr. Serra had asked for him. Moreover an order from the Most Rev. Commissary-General of the Indies had arrived at the College that Fr. Palóu should be recalled to the College as soon as possible. "For this reason, Your Reverence (Lasuén) will direct him to execute the command of the Most Reverend Commissary-General, and to use the permit which he has received from me."[1]

Fr. Palóu, while awaiting orders at San Carlos, very likely was made acquainted with this news in good time so that he probably returned to Mexico in the same ship which had brought up Lasuén's appointment.

From his *Noticias*[2] we learn that Fr. Palóu intended to

---

[1] See vol. ii, *The Missions*, chap. xxiv.—Fr. Sancho to Fr. Lasuén, Feb. 7, 1785.—*Santa Barbara Mission Archives.*

[2] Vol. ii, *The Missions*, chap. viii.

remain in California until his death. It is, therefore, surprising to read in Fr. Sancho's letter that Fr. Serra himself had procured for his friend the permit to retire to the Mother College. The disagreeable conditions, however, brought about by Governor Neve's meddling with Mission affairs had disheartened both Fathers. There was no telling what Neve, now Comandante-General over California, and residing in Mexico City, might attempt, if his subversive plans were not checked at the Capital of the nation. Neve, unknown to the two Fathers, died three months after Fr. Serra. Pedro Fages, however, had returned as Governor. He was trusted by neither Fr. Serra nor Fr. Palóu. At all events, at the viceroyal court Fr. Palóu could explain the needs and vicissitudes of the Indian Missions. He proved himself a match for all schemers, in and out of Mexico, against the Missions in California.[3]

There was another motive which justified Fr. Palóu's return. He had used his spare time to collect documents soon after his appointment to Lower California, and to compile a reliable narrative of all that had transpired in California from the date of the arrival of the Franciscans at Loreto, Lower California, and from 1769 to June 1783 in Upper California. It is not likely that he had received orders to employ his talents in that way for he had enough on his hands as missionary and occasional Superior of the Missions. At any rate, whether commanded or from love of the work, the result was his *Noticias de la California* in four volumes. It was most providential that Fr. Palóu provided posterity with this authentic document, and thus putting on record whatever concerned his brethren or their Indian charges. We can surmise what Bancroft and others would have made of that period had not Fr. Palóu's writings compelled them not to deviate from the truth more than they did. During his last years in California the former pupil and colaborer wrote the life of Fr. Serra under the title *"Relacion Historica de la Vida y Apostolicas Tareas del Venerabile Padre Junipero Serra."* "I have sometimes been tempted," Bancroft writes, "to entertain

---

[3] *Missions and Missionaries of Calif.* vol. ii, chap. xxiv.

a selfish regret that Palóu wrote, or that his writings were ever printed, yet all the same he must be regarded as the best original authority for the earliest period of mission history."[4] Good Father Palóu himself, in his short preface to the *Noticias*, clearly explains the object of his undertaking as follows: "This material, collected in the wake of the apostolical ministry, has no other purpose than to note down whatever has happened in this new vineyard of the Lord, and *with entire sincerity and truth* to set forth the events, and the deeds of the missionaries, just as they happened in both Lower and Upper California."

Bancroft's own historical works and the productions of many would-be historians could be regarded with more confidence if the authors had with *entire sincerity and truth* endeavored to set forth the deeds of the missionaries, and the events of their time, just as they happened, without craving to shine as literary lights.[5] Fr. Palóu had his facts shine, but himself he kept in the dark.

The manuscript of the *Noticias de la California* was transcribed and a copy went to Madrid, but it was not printed until 1857, when it was incorporated in the *Documentos para la Historia de Mexico*. Mr. John T. Doyle in 1874 published the work in four volumes at San Francisco. The only critical English edition was printed on the California University Press, Berkeley, and published by Professor Herbert E. Bolton in 1926. Instead of the usual introduction a sympathetic and judicious biographical sketch, covering sixty-seven pages, written by Dr. Bolton precedes Fr. Palóu's own brief foreword. This remarkable sketch describes the author of the *Noticias* from his earliest years down to the last days of his eventful life. After reading Dr. Bolton's appreciation, the thoughtful student will have come to the conclusion that Fr.

---

[4] Bancroft, *California*, vol. i, p. 420.

[5] Lovers of history have at last grown tired of literary vagaries. *The Fortnightly Review* (Arthur Preuss) accordingly declares (August, 1933, page 176): *"The first duty of a historian is not to be interesting, but to be truthful."*

Francisco Palóu was really one of the great men of both California who deserves some recognition as one of the ablest and noblest among the heralds of Christianity and civilization on this Western Coast.

With regard to his *Vida*, Fr. Palóu under date of August 16, 1786, wrote from Mexico to Fr. Lasuén: "In a short while you may read the Life of the Venerable Fr. Junipero Serra, principal founder. They are now examining it in order to give it to the press; for the expenses I have already some benefactors who without asking them have offered to bear the whole cost. If God grants me to see it, I shall forward for your Missions a number of copies. I believe that Your Reverence will be pleased with this news and all the other Fathers likewise; for in the *Narrative* is expressed what each of Your Reverences has done; and I believe it will circulate all over Europe (as the examiners tell me) because very much pleased that they will know more about the new conquests. . ."[6]

The death of Fr. Serra and Fr. Palóu's retirement were keenly felt by their fellow-missionaries, but the spiritual and temporal welfare of the Indians was not pursued less vigorously for that reason. At the close of the year, 1786, the Monterey district consisted of 626 adult Indian males, 667 adult females, 585 males under nine years and 436 female children under nine years, or in all, 2314 Indians. The military district of San Diego had 844 adult males, 741 adult females, 547 male children under nine years, 522 female children under nine years, or in all, 2654 Indians. Within the limits of the district of Santa Barbara there were 137 male adults, 94 female adults, 105 male children under nine, and 88 female children of the same age limit, or in all, 424. San Francisco contained within the limits of its district 243 male adults, 210 female adults, 355 males under nine years, 302 female children of the same years, or a total of 1110.

It is plain from the figures just cited that the missionaries were not slow to take advantage of the comparative peace which the Missions enjoyed during these few years, to make rapid strides towards the fulfillment of the object which had brought them to the shores of California. Two travelers with diametrically opposed views, visited San Carlos during this time and have left records of their impressions of the work of the missionaries at that place. Jean Francois Galoup de La Perouse reached Monterey in September, 1786. He and M. de Langle, in charge of one of the French frigates, received a royal welcome. They accepted the hospitality of the Fathers and were made acquainted with the Mission System. La Perouse, however, whilst forced to admit the admirable personal qualities of the missionaries and the incontrovertible evidence of advancement among the natives, was imbued with

---

[6] *Santa Barbara Archives*, no. 155.

that sort of philosophy which understands not the motives of the missionaries and hence could not correctly gauge the results.[7]

The two Spanish corvettes, the *Descubierta* or *Santa Justa*, under Captain Alexandro Malaspina, and the *Atrevida* or *Santa Rufina*, under Captain Joseph de Bustamente y Guerra were run into Monterey Bay, September 12, 1791, and remained twelve days. They also paid a visit to Mission San Carlos, but came away with impressions very much different from those that La Perouse saw fit to report about the place.[8] With Malaspina came the first genuine Yankee to the California coast in the person of John Ingraham, gunner on board the corvette *Atrevida*, unfortunately only to die here. See for details the Burial Register.

Captain George Vancouver, a British navigator, was another visitor to Mission San Carlos in the last decade of the eighteenth century. He left San Francisco Bay on November 25, 1792, and proceeded to Monterey where he stayed until January 14, 1793. He writes: "On Sunday the 2nd of December (1792), in consequence of a very polite invitation, I paid my respects to the Mission of San Carlos. This establishment is situated about a league to the south-eastward of the Presidio of Monterey. The road between them lies over some steep hills and hollow valleys, interspersed with many trees. Our reception at the Mission could not fail to convince us of the joy and satisfaction we communicated to the worthy and Rev. Fathers who in return made the most hospitable offers of every refreshment their homely abode afforded. On our arrival at the entrance of the Mission the bells were rung, and the Rev. Fermin de Lasuén, Father Presidente of the missionaries of the Order of San Francisco in New Albion, together with the Fathers of this Mission, came out to meet us, and to conduct us to the principal residence of the Father Presidente. This personage was about seventy-two years of age whose

---

[7] La Perouse, Tom. ii, chap. xi; also *The Missions and Missionaries*, vol. ii, appendix, i.

[8] *The Missions and Missionaries*, vol. ii, chap. ii, section 2.

manners, united to a most venerable and placid countenance, indicated that tranquillized state of mind that fitted him in an eminent degree for presiding over so benevolent an institution. The usual ceremonies of introduction being over, our time was pleasantly engaged in the society of the Fr. Presidente and his two companions, the priests regularly belonging to the Mission of San Carlos, who attended us over the premises. These seemed to differ but little from those at San Francisco or Santa Clara, excepting that the buildings were smaller, the plan, the architecture, and the materials exactly corresponding.

"In their granaries were deposited a pretty large quantity of the different kinds of grain before noticed at the other establishment, to which was added some barley, but the whole was of an inferior quality, and the return from the soil by no means equal to that produced at Santa Clara. Here also was a small garden on the same confined scale, and cultivated in the same manner as observed at the other stations. An Indian village is also in the neighborhood; it appeared to us but small, yet the number of its inhabitants under the immediate direction of this mission was said to amount to eight hundred, governed by the same charitable principles as those we had before visited. Notwithstanding these people are taught and employed from time to time in many of the occupations most useful to civil society, they had not made themselves more comfortable habitations than those of their forefathers; nor did they seem in any respect to have benefitted by the instructions they received. Some of them were employed at this time under the directions of the Fathers *in building a church* with stone and mortar. The former material appeared to be of a very friable nature, scarcely more hard than indurated clay; but I was told that upon its being exposed to the air, it soon becomes hardened, and is excellent stone for the purpose of building. It is of a light straw color, and presents a rich and elegant appearance in proportion to the labor that is bestowed upon it. The lime they use is made of seashells, principally from the era-shell, which is of large size and in great numbers on the shore; not having as yet found any calcareous earth that would answer this essential purpose.

"Their only method of reducing corn to flour is by two small stones placed in an inclined position on the ground; on the lower one the corn is laid and ground by rubbing the other stone nearly of the same surface over it. The flour produced by this rude and laborious process makes very white and well tasted though heavy bread; but this defect is said by the Spaniards to be greatly remedied when mixed with an equal proportion of flour properly ground."[9] Early in November, 1794, accompanied by the *Princess* and the *Chatham*, Vancouver with the *Discovery* entered the harbor of Monterey for the third and last time in order to prepare his charts and overhaul his three vessels. On December 2nd the little squadron sailed for England.[10]

Vancouver's statement that a new church was being constructed of stone at Mission San Carlos is corroborated by certain letters of Fr. Lasuén. In a letter of June 7, 1794, the Fr. Presidente informed Governor Arrillaga that he had placed the first stone of a new church at this place on July 7, 1793.[11] He wrote more at length to the governor on January 3, 1795: "Manuel Estévan Ruiz, a master-mason and stone-cutter, has agreed to teach his trades to the natives and to practice them therein, in consideration of 18 reales ($2.25) a day for a term of four years. He began to work at the royal Presidio on the 15th of June, 1791, and stayed until December 20, 1792, when Revilla Gigedo directed the mechanics to teach the Indians at the Mission. He came to San Carlos when there was no material at the Presidio." The arrival of

[9] M. de Langle, La Perouse's companion, had donated a handmill by means of which four women might produce the same amount of flour that without the machine required the toil of one hundred. Nevertheless, the women preferred their own method, and discarded the machine. (Vol. ii, p. 436).

[10] Vancouver, vol. iv, pp. 297; 310; Bancroft, vol. i, pp. 517-529; Greenhow, p. 232, etc.

[11] *Archb. Archives*, no. 63. Fr. Lasuén to Governor Arrillaga, June 7, 1794.

VIEW OF MISSION SAN CARLOS, SHOWING STONE CONSTRUCTION.

the master-mason apparently impelled Fr. Lasuén to begin
the construction of a more suitable house of worship; for he
continues in that letter: "Wherefore I laid the first stone of
the church on the 7th of July, 1793, and the work is quite half
finished." The mason's work was so satisfactory that the Fr.
Presidente gives vent to the hope that he might be allowed to
complete it. "But the term of the contract is not sufficient
either for this or for adequately instructing the apprentices
who have been placed with him." The missionary was careful
to state that the artisan not only did his work capably but
also was well behaved, for which reason the Father Presidente
begged that the contract be extended at least for a year or
a year and a half, at which time he thought that the church
would be completed and the Indians sufficiently instructed.[12]

The foregoing letter indicates that the missionaries lost
no opportunity of having the Indian neophytes instructed in
those manual arts which would be useful for them and for
which they showed aptitude. On the other hand the natives
cared nothing for book-learning, nor for anything which taxed
their mental faculties. It was a difficult task to impart even
the rudiments of Faith and morals. In view of this, some of
the more talented and industrious boys were taught to read
in order to render them capable of assisting at the altar and
in the choir; but to open regular schools before professional
teachers and the means to pay them could be procured was
out of the question. Nevertheless, when the official command
of King Carlos reached California commanding that, in all
towns of the governmental department, schools for the Spanish language should be established in order that the Indians
should learn to read and write it, and that they be forbidden
their native idiom, Fr. Lasuén sent a letter to all the missionaries telling them to execute this command to the best of their
abilities.[13] The white population of the Presidio stood in great
need of schooling likewise, though they were no more eager
than the Indians to acquire the rudiments of secular know-

---

[12] *Santa Barbara Arch.* Fr. Lasuén to Gov. Arrillaga, January 3, 1795.

[13] *Missions and Missionaries*, vol. ii, chap. v.

ledge. Governor Borica, however, determined to effect a re-
form in this respect in accordance with the royal orders.
Wherefore, in the Presidio of Monterey, José Rodriguez
taught the children in the carpenter-shop.[14]

Once, for a wonder, the missionaries were remembered in
a will of a benefactor in Mexico. He was Don Pedro Antonio
de Anteparaluceta, Canon of the Cathedral of Pueblo. In
his testament he bequeathed the sum of $500, which was to
be divided among the California Missions. The College Procurator at the Capital of Mexico accordingly purchased for
the Indians drygoods at the rate of $36 for each Mission, ex-
cept Soledad which received $40 worth, and Santa Cruz whose
share was $60 worth. Thus Fr. Pangua wrote from Mexico
under date of October 27, 1793, to Fr. Lasuén. (Santa Barbara Archives, No. 252).

In the Biennial Report at the end of 1796, Fr. Lasuén
writes that the church had been roofed and covered with tiles.
The workmen were finishing the whitewashing of the interior.
The flooring, the greater part of the vestry, and the top of the
tower (turrecito) were still wanting; nevertheless, the construction of the tower was so far advanced that the bells were
to be put up shortly. The church was blessed and dedicated
in September, 1797. Neither the Annual nor the Biennial
Report give the details of this ceremony. Four years later,
1801, however, it is stated that the walls of the church had
been raised one vara. They had not been built to stand this
added strain wherefore a stone buttress of about seven varas
was put up to strengthen the front wall which had bulged out
to the extent of four fingers' breadth.

Building activity was not confined to the church structure.
In 1796, a room, 20 by 3 varas was built with three troughs
for tanning; the walls were of adobe, the troughs of lime and
stone. Two years later an addition of four rooms was made
to the courtyard. Their dimensions were six varas; each had
an opening and were roofed with tiles. A wing was added to

---

[14] *Cal. Arch.*, *Prov. Rec.*, v, page 650.   Borica to Comandante de
Loreto, 1795.

the square or courtyard the following year. It was 107 varas long, six and a half varas high, with six openings, and the roof was of tiles. Four more rooms were built in 1800, like those described before.

Special attention was paid to the acquisition of church goods needed in the sanctuary. In 1795, of four albs which had been procured, three were of fine, the other of bramant linen. Six altar cloths of bramant linen were added. Three of these had lace, the others had no lace, because these latter ones were to be placed beneath the former. Six amices of bramant linen and three sets of corporals of fine white linen fabric were likewise supplied. Two new surplices are mentioned, the one of fine linen the other of bramant with lace however. Eighteen purificators and three finger towels for the sacristy completed the outfit. A black chasuble was procured in 1798.

Fr. Lasuén in his *Reply to Accusations*, June 19, 1801, writes: "There was an Indian at San Carlos in 1799 who at one sitting won more than $30 from two white men. So expert had Indians become at gambling."

Fathers Carnicer and Viñals write in 1802 of having procured a crown of gold and silver, three strings of pearls and some fine necklaces for the statue of Mary Most Pure. Likewise a canopy of figured silk stuff, tinged with a deep red color; a light bright green tabernacle veil of satin, and two girdles for use on the feast days of greater solemnity. The interesting remark is made that all, save the girdles, had been paid for from alms. Many implements for field and shop were also acquired.

Hermenegildo Sal, Lieutenant Commander of the Presidio of Monterey had this interesting note in connection with the work of construction at that place: "I certify in as far as I can and must that Toribio Ruiz, an artisan under contract, who came from the Presidio of San Diego to this of Monterey, has been employed in repairing the roof of the church and dug trenches and laid foundations for the living quarters of a detachment of volunteer troops, since the 16th of June last until today, December 31, 1797.[15] Four years later, however, March 11, 1801, Governor Arrillaga wrote to the viceroy from Loreto "I have to inform you that the church of the Presidio and other buildings are in ruins;[16] that the labor of twenty years of the troops, Indians and settlers in constructing and repairing, etc., is spoiled owing to the precipitation and fragility with which they were built. I believe it will be nec-

PARISH CHURCH AT MONTEREY.

[15] *Cal. Arch.*, vol. xxv, no. 384.

[16] That must refer to the structure on the hill; for the one below, now parish church, was erected five or six years previously and solidly too.

essary that the buildings of Monterey and San Diego be rebuilt and with more solidity."[17]

In 1800, the Presidio of Monterey lost by death its Lieut. Commander Hermenegildo Sal. For his last will and testament see the Burial Register.[18] Fr. Lasuén, the Presidente of the Missions, was called to his eternal reward three years later, Sunday afternoon, June 26, 1803. The details of the life and death of Fr. Lasuén, the successor of Fr. Palóu to the superiorship of all the Missions, will be given later. Besides exercising that office he had also been in charge of Mission San Carlos, and his death dealt a heavy blow to that Mission and to whole California. Before passing to his eternal reward, he declared in the presence of Fathers Bonaventure Sitjar, José Viadér, Francisco Gonzalez, Baltasar Carnicér, and José Viñals, that Fr. Estévan Tápis of Santa Barbara had been chosen by the Mother College to succeed to the office of Presidente of the Missions. Details on the life of Fr. Lasuén will be found in the second volume of *The Missions and Missionaries*. A short sketch of him will be reproduced in the chapter on the *Mission Registers*.[19] The new Fr. Presidente, Fr. Tápis, chose to have his headquarters at Mission Santa Barbara rather than at San Carlos. He remained there all through his three terms of office till 1812.

---

[17] *Cal. Arch., Prov. St. Pap.* vol. xxi, pp. 146-148; Bancroft, vol. ii, p. 143.

[18] *Libro de Difuntos* de la Mision San Carlos, no. 1342.

[19] Fr. Viñals to Fr. Estévan Tápis, June 26, 1803. *Santa Barbara Arch., The Missions*, vol. ii, end of chap. xi.

CHAPTER XII.

The Fathers, missionaries apostolic, members of the College of San Fernando de Mexico, in charge of this Mission of San Carlos of Monterey of Upper California, which was founded on the 3rd of June, Pentecost Day, 1770. Fr. José Señan, our Fr. Presidente, forwarded the list of questions to us; he had received it from His Excellency, the Bishop of Sonora. It had been sent out by the Most Excellent Sir, Don Ciriaco Gonzalez Carvacal, Secretary ad interim of the government of the dominion overseas. We were to obtain whatever information possible about each of the 35 articles contained in the questionnaire which had been gotten up very sagely. We shall give this information as extensively, clearly and accurately as possible.

We call to mind, in the first place, that we have charge of two churches, or congregations; the one is the chapel of the royal presidio of Monterey. The lord governor of the province resides at that place, as well as the officers, cavalrymen of the Leather-Jacket company, some retired soldiers and their families. These call themselves gente de razon in their own circle and in the entire province without any distinction of class or caste. They are looked upon as heroes in these new lands provided that they speak the Castilian tongue in some measure. Anyway we shall be excused for making a distinction of class and caste, notwithstanding that they do not believe in such distinctions, only looking upon themselves as gente de razon. The other church or congregation is the Mission of San Carlos commonly called Carmel, because it is in the plain of the Carmel River. The guard of five or six soldiers from the above mentioned company lives here together with their families. The remainder of the population consists of full blooded Indians, some but recently baptized, others born of neophytes, baptized at a very early period. We proceed to give an exact notion of them just as we have been able to procure it.—Answer to the article.

1. Seven tribes live at this Mission. They are the Excelen and Egeac, Rumsen, SargentRuc, Sarconeños, Guachirron, CalendaRuc. The first two are from the interior and have the same language or dialect which is wholly distinct from the other five; the latter speak the same tongue among themselves. At the beginning of the conquest the missionaries experienced difficulty in getting them to assemble for religious services, agricultural pursuits or any duty whatsoever. Today they have succeeded in making them associate together. This exclusiveness and slight friendly feeling were the reasons that, in paganism, they ordinarily lived in a state of war. The troops tried to counteract this condition from the beginning. Since all have become Christianized, they recognize the advantages of peace in which they live.

2. There are two dialects among the seven tribes; the one is *Rumsen*, the other *Excelen;* they differ entirely. Take an example in *Rumsen: "Muxina Muguianc jurriguing igest oyh laguan eje uti maigin;"* in *Excelen: "Egenoch lalucuimos talogpami ege salegua lottos, takeyapami lasalachis."* Translated these two sentences mean: "Men who are good bowmen are esteemed and well liked." But whilst they speak these dialects, the majority sufficiently understand and speak Spanish; the minority, though they can barely speak it, understand it somewhat. They have progressed so much in the Castilian tongue because the inhabitants of the presidio are near, as also the seaport. Communication with the Europeans is frequent; with them they play, buy, exchange, sell wood and other little things; and intercourse is one of the ways best suited to learn any language.

3. Generally speaking the menfolks love their wives. Whilst pagan conditions held sway, unfaithfulness of the women led to many wars and killings; wherefore self-restraint was observed. Since Christianity has been accepted by them

the missionaries are sorely put to it to bring about a recon-
ciliation between husband and wife who have become mutually
angry and who are childless. Admonitions and punishments
avail nothing in getting them reunited if they are living in
concubinage. The parents love their children dearly; but the
latter, upon reaching maturity, care little for their fathers
and mothers. The girls indeed are accustomed to assist their
mothers during their lifetime. The parents give their children
practically no education; they rather offer a bad example. At
most they instruct them in the use of the bow and arrow;
above all the boys learn idleness, for it is characteristic of the
Indian to shun labor. The women and girls naturally are
occupied with preparing food. The men possess aptness for
agriculture and the mechanical arts; but since they naturally
abhor work an overseer must be put in charge.

4. & 5. The conquest has made them recognize the superiority of the gente de razon. No distinction is made by them
between European and American; they respect, honor and
serve all alike. Because they are timid and pusillanimous,
when handled tenderly and compassionately, v. g., like a
child or one to be pitied, they prove themselves useful in
many ways. This article also includes the answer to the
fifth question.

6. & 7. We have not discovered even an attempt, let alone
a trace of any style of reading or writing. They are greatly
astonished at seeing how the Fathers communicate by letters
or read the missal. We have instructed boys and employ
them in all church functions for the time being; on account
of their limited mental ability they do not fix the mind upon
their reading and so have not advanced in it. Nevertheless,
the written characters help them to spell and so to understand and speak Spanish. This article likewise contains the
answer to the seventh.

8. The moral virtues manifested by them are charitable-
ness and a readiness to give food to anyone and sympathy
with those in distress. But they possess these virtues after
the fashion of mock colors, which fade at the first wetting. In

truth, at the first sign of anger, the Indians forget sympathy, etc.

9. Very few superstitious rites are in evidence, and these are rather the vagaries of old men and women. Of these, one gets the reputation of being a healer; the sick person calls and permits him to suck the ailing part, and soon the healer extracts a stone which he had hidden in his mouth and says: "Behold this stone has been the cause of your illness; this stone was within you!" They receive pay for this deception, but the patient does not recover. Others sing and dance in front of the sick person and for this service they are rewarded. Other old women maintain that they are the ones who give growth to the fruits and seeds and on this account they are favored with gifts. Should the year happen to be a barren one, the old woman pretends that she is angry and makes it known that she did not care to give harvests. Thus they see themselves compelled to favor her with more gifts to appease her anger so that she may give seed in the following year. If the harvest chances to be abundant the old woman is showered with joyful praises and all are pleased with her. Thanks be to God, however, these excesses are disappearing; the children as well as adolescents maintain that God alone produces the seed and fruits and all other things.

10. They are advancing day by day in a more complete understanding of the truths of religion since they receive religious instructions in their own tongue under the guidance of the missionaries and the Fr. Presidente of the Missions: according to the statues of the royal decree, relative to places not yet formed into parishes.

11, 18, 19 & 27. This sort of idolatry is practiced by them: at times they blow smoke to the sun, moon and some beings whom they fancy dwell in the skies. These words are uttered during the act of blowing: "Ay, this wisp of smoke is blown that you may give me a good (day) tomorrow." In like manner, they take pinole or flour of the seeds which they have gathered; and throwing a handful to the sun, moon or the heavens they say: "I send you this that you may give me greater abundance next year." Thus the sun and moon are looked upon as affecting their needs; likewise those beings in the skies who send what may be necessary. For this reason flour, seeds, and tobacco smoke are sent heavenwards. Now, however, these practices have been discontinued because the old folks who performed them have died. Due to the mode of their ancestors' lives, a wild carefree existence appeals to them rather than civilization (en poblado), and so they seek permission to live thus three weeks out of the year, and they rove about wheresoever they desire. This seems to them expedient for the well being of the body. At the conclusion of the harvesting of the seeds, the chiefs of each tribe are accustomed to give a feast, at which they eat, sing, and dance. We have asked them repeatedly if they have stories as to their origin. To this question all reply that they do not know. This ignorance should cause no surprise in view of the fact that these natives consider it the greatest dishonor (disrespect) to talk about their dead parents and relatives. Thus a boy whose parents have been buried when he was very small, has no one to tell him the names of his dead father, grandfather or kinsfolk. In the course of a quarrel, for greater vituperation, they exclaim: "Your father is dead!" and the flame of their fury grows greater. Thus the memory of their ancestors has been allowed to lapse into oblivion. When some one dies, his clothing and belongings are burned. If the possession be an animal, such as hens, dogs, a horse, they are killed; if they be plants, they are uprooted. Upon being asked the reason for such a proceedure, the answer is to obliterate the memory of the deceased. The 18th, 19th and 27th answers are included in this article.

12. Baby chicks wax more and more golden and each day become more pleasing to the sight during that period when they receive heat from the mother hen. The Indians fare similarly while they find themselves under the instructions of the missionaries. Daily progress has been made in moral and political enlightenment. Whereas twenty years ago the Fathers and veteran troops were compelled to make them

attend Mass and pray; nor would they submit either to subjection or government; today they assist at holy Mass, pray,
frequent the sacraments and wish to die as Christians. They
acknowledge the superiority of government and give evidence
of it. These changes are admitted by them and they maintain
that now it is different and they are a changed people; though,
they declare that two decades ago they often fled to the mountains, ate mares and deserved to be punished continually.

13. Matrimonial alliances are brought about in this fashion: The father, mother and nearest kin declare that they
have a marriageable son or daughter for so and so. Should the
parents and nearest kin of both sides reach an agreement, the
son or daughter is asked if he or she wishes to marry so and so.
Given an affirmative answer they go at once to see the kins-
folks and the intended. If the latter consents the contract is
concluded then and there, and the groom has the privilege of
eating in the house of the bride and he sees to it that he makes
her a gift of a blanket or some beads. But should the son or
daughter not care to contract matrimony with the one whom
their parents designate; and should their parents force or persuade them to marry or consent it happens that soon after
the marriage they hate one another, separate and it is rare
that they can be reunited. Worst of all, they live in concubinage; ordinarily this is an incurable evil in the Indian.

14. Natural remedies are used. They bind fast an aching
leg, arm, etc., and say that so the pain is alleviated somewhat.
One of the tribe knows a root, a remedy against bloody
dysentery. The root is beaten to powder and this is given with
a little water. Some have been cured and highly praise the
remedy. It has not been possible to learn the name of the
root. The Indian, who knows, does not care to tell where the
root is found, because in this way he gains a livelihood and so
guards his secret. Recently we ordered him to bring it from
the country and we saw that it is a root of a plant, large and
tender, like the parsnip. For blood-letting, a frequent practice, they gather very jagged flints; with these they puncture
the aching part, be it head, body, abdomen, chest, etc.; they

continue to scrape the wound so that much blood comes forth. This operation works wonders with them. Being plethoric, they suffer intensely in that part of the body which extends from the armpits to the hipbone (costado) and from copious vomiting of blood. These attacks usually take place during three seasons of the year. They are subject to very many other kinds of maladies at all times; the result is that this Mission is reduced in number by eight or ten every year. They are frequently and habitually indisposed because little attention is paid to their health by them. They eat, until they can eat no more, of meat and other victuals of the gente de razon. Wild foods, such as acorns and various other seeds, sea weed, oysters, etc., are esteemed all the more; they gorge themselves and so bring about ailments. It is futile to exhort them to moderation because of their principle: "Is there much to eat, let us eat much; when we are sick we will not eat." For emetics they use sea water, as also sap from the head of a plant like saffron, called by them "amole." (There is much of it in this region and it serves the purpose of soap). It is also a purgative and they drink it freely. The men have the daily custom of entering an underground oven, known as the "temescal." A fire is built within and when the oven has become heated sufficiently, the men enter undressed. They perspire so freely that, upon coming out they appear to have been bathing. It is understood that this is very beneficial for them. For a time the attempt was made to stop them, and as a result skin diseases and boils and other ailments appeared among the men. When they betook themselves to the "temescal" again, scarcely a man was found afflicted with the itch, a disease common to the women and children who do not make use of such baths. The women, but recently delivered, employ another method of perspiring. They dig a hole in their huts, put wood therein and set fire to it. Many stones weighing about sixteen ounces (pound weight) are put into the fire. When hot, these are covered with green herbs, which make a sort of mattress. The woman who was recently delivered lies upon this together with the baby. The mother sweats freely

INDIAN SWEAT-HOUSE.

and the baby is kept warm. This is done for a period of six or seven days, and thereafter they are as vigorous as if they had not given birth; this is the case although their broths and foods are poor indeed. The hot springs have never been made use of by them. Gossip had it that these springs would kill the people because they had seen, at a distance, birds, wolves, bears and other animals die from contact with the water. Small wonder at this, because the water is very hot. Now, however, they notice that the gente de razon temper it with cold water and bathe therein. They do likewise, drink it as well and experience the good effects; but the mischief is that they return to their evil habits, so the ailment returns.

15. Calendars were not used by these people. They speak only of the year as from "corn to corn," from "seed to seed," so that when it lacked four months to the harvest they would say: "There are still four moons until the acorns, etc." They neither know their ages nor how many years elapsed since the death of their grandfather, father or mother. These and similar questions were extremely displeasing to them and are so even to the present. They remembered some epochs, as when wars were waged, when the sea was very angry; (This according to their explanation and from signs which have been discovered must have been a terrible earthquake), when a ship arrived, etc.

16. As heathens they would eat whenever they desired; now, as Christians, they are given three meals: morning and night, atole, which is wheat and barley toasted and ground, dissolved in water and boiled. At noon their meal consists of peas, avas, pottage (pulse) beans, etc.; but they are free to eat in their huts, and so they eat day and night, and there is no way of making them use moderation. They eat rats, squirrels, moles, shell-fish and all living things, except frogs, toads, owls, which are the only animals of which they entertain fear.

17. Water was the only kind of drink among them, but it did not have to be pure. Now, however, they know how to drink wine, whiskey and mescal. They take to getting tipsy,

even intoxicated, by chewing tobacco; and this is very harmful for their chests.

18. This answer has been taken care of in article 11.

19. Article 11 contains the answer to this question.

20. As pagans the method of burial was to dig a large hole or pit; they threw the corpse therein; and, if it happened to be a mother with a very young child, as yet unweaned, it was buried with its dead mother, in case the father or relatives were not able to look after the child. All the relatives threw beads and seeds upon the dead in token of their love for the deceased. As Christians, they are buried according to the ritual of the Church. Nevertheless, in secret, they cling to the method of the time when they were heathens. As a sign of mourning, the father, mother, child, husband or wife, or brother and sisters cut off their hair; if shears are lacking they burn it bit by bit. Moreover, they strew ashes over their entire bodies, weep bitterly, fast, and the old women smear their faces with pitch. Since the effects of this remain for months, they seem to be Ethiopians. It is also their habit to go to the mountains to drown their sorrows.

21. Contracts are sacred to them at all times; non-fulfillment makes for loss of caste so that afterwards none care to deal with anyone who does not keep his word. Giving, lending and bargaining are done as amongst brothers and not strangers. Article 24 also treats of the natives' mode of life.

22. The old men maintain that duplicity or lies were not current among them. But now associating with Christians, they rarely tell the truth and deceit takes precedence. Though they be known to be guilty, so brazen is their duplicity that it does not make them blush. One must believe that though pusillanimous and timid, fear it is which protects and aids them in denying that which is evident.

23. The prevailing vices are stealing which they call "taking," no more; immorality which is destroying them; idleness which they crave in the extreme. It is the dominance of these vices which makes them gluttons, drinkers and gamblers and hinders graces, given them as Christians, from acts

of the love of God and holy things. They did not have so
many vices as pagans, because whoever practiced them paid
oftentimes with life itself. Idleness has held sway chiefly
among the men. They are prone to anger, but cowardice re-
strains them; perhaps the punishments which they mete out
among themselves also act as a check. Lasting feuds are due
to a spirit of vindicativeness which does not permit forget-
fulness of an injury done them. That which might be said
under article 26 belongs here.

24. Inasmuch as these Missions have been brought under
control only recently, earnest responsibility has not been
placed on individual shoulders. All work in common; all eat
and dress from the communal stores. This is entirely under
the supervision of the missionaries. They are instructed to
learn how to live as rational individuals. Besides the communal fields, a parcel of land for a kitchen garden is allotted
to some to get them accustomed to this kind of labor. But
the net result is that on some day the woman in a fit of anger
roots out the shoots of corn, squash, etc., saying that she has
planted them. Her husband does likewise. Therefore, in
these matters, they behave like children of eight or nine years,
who are as yet not of constant or steady disposition.

25. This article has its answer in No. 23.

26. That which might be said in answer here has been
put in article 23.

27. Article 11 contains the response to this number.

28. The entire savage population of this mission has become Christianized. No more information could be unearthed
as to sacrifices than which has been quoted in article 11; as
to burials no more than which has been explained in paragraph
20.

29. These natives are not known to be consumed by cupi-
dity, either as pagans or as Christians. They are a disinter-
ested people. He is considered a rich man who possesses a
kerchief for his head, though he be otherwise unclothed. The
goods of the Mission would be squandered in a week were it
not for the vigilance of the Fathers.

30. The prominent Indians are the captains or kings. There is one for each tribe. They command obedience and respect during their lifetime. This office is hereditary, or in default of an heir by direct descent, it goes to the closest relative. This chief alone among the pagans could retain or desert a plurality of wives, (unmarried women), but if he had children by one of them, she was held in higher esteem and he lived permanently with her. He retained the privilege of living with unmarried women whenever he so desired. The entire tribe rendered service (tribute) to him in the days when they were pagans as well as now that they are Christians. He led the van in battle, supplied the bows and arrows and encouraged his people. He was, as a rule, a very good archer. Even today they show more respect and submission to their chiefs than to the alcaldes who have been placed over them for their advancement as citizens. They (the chiefs) remain known at all times as governors of their tribe, even in the event that old age forces them to give the chieftainship over to a successor. They wear no distinctive mark of any kind. In the days of paganism, a cloak made from rabbit skins usually distinguished them. The missionaries strive to humor them, because the contentment of the Indian depends on this.

31. Brotherly love prevails among these natives. It is their great delight to be of mutual help, now collecting seeds from the ranges, now lending serviceable things. This holds good of the men as well as of the women. But if they become somewhat angry, charity ceases: they imitate a child of eight or nine years.

32. Musical instruments of native design are very crude. They consist of a hollow tube from an alder tree; this tube is a copy of the dulcet flute, but the imitation has not been very successful. They also use a split stick, like a distaff. It is used to beat time for their chants, which have the same tone, whether joyous or sad. For example, being in a merry mood, they chant and dance, while the names of the seeds or achievements are proclaimed; e. g., thus: "Acorn, a. a. Acorn," "much seed a. a. much seed." Should the chant

happen to be one of vengeance or of ill-feeling which is very rife and from which many feuds arise, they sing and dance to the same tones, shouting something disparaging of each tribe with whom they are at war. For example: "Thief e. e. Thief." "Maimed one e. e. maimed one," or other names and defects which they know of each tribe or personal enemy. The missionaries attempt to admonish and chastize them for this reason that they may not continue in disputes or feuds. And so their chants and dances are devoid of anything pleasant or melodious. They have been instructed in church music and plain song and acquit themselves creditably in all functions.

33. At the present time the natives of this Mission are so backward in reading and writing that there is no hope of progress, however much we attempt to instruct them in knowledge and letters, as has been noted in article 6. They are adepts in the use of bow and arrow, though deeds of prowess are related of none of their forebears, as has been explained in article 11. In the event that one of these natives slays a bear, lion or other wild beast, the hunter extracts a tooth, tusk or fang and suspends it around his neck in token of an heroic feat and bravery and thereafter he is respected.

34. They possessed a confused idea of eternity. It was their belief that after death they go to the west (where the sun sets); there a man received the dead; at times these returned to their relatives and visited them in their dreams; they were much affrighted at these visits. This is the lore of the elders. Now, however, they no longer converse of those matters. No trace could be discovered of an idea of reward or punishment final judgement, glory, purgatory or hell.

35. For the present, clothing of the following description is procured: for the men, a blanket, a garment of printed cotton or shirt of wool and "sendal," commonly called breechclout; for the women, a blanket, cotton chemise and woolen skirt; in this way all are clothed somewhat decently. Moreover, we manage to manufacture all wearing apparel. Then, too, the habiliments of the gente de razon are given to some, because they look after the property of the Mission. If all

valued wearing apparel much more would be given them, and in a short time we would have them going about as civilized beings. But they (that is the men) are not concerned whether they go about with or without clothing, inasmuch as they gamble away their wearing apparel; nothing is worn out of that which is given them; it is sold, exchanged, gambled or given away, then another garment older or newer is sought. They do, however, enter the church and Fathers' dwelling decently apparelled, because otherwise they would be reprimanded. Among the property of the Mission are lambs, not yet a year old, from which sufficient wool is sheared; this the Indians themselves spin and weave and a suit of clothes is given them each year.

All this information has been obtained with all possible clearness and exactness. The attempt has been made to put forth a true description of this nature-folk. It has not been our aim to make the natives seem lacking in understanding, although some of the paragraphs may create the impression of trying to belittle their mental ability. We merely wish to show that they are exceedingly lacking in civilization; even as new shoots which have but lately sprung out of the earth, so these people, placed in new soil, have given few signs of progress, though the attempt is being made to water them with the dew and warmth of teaching and example. Even though they listen, comprehend, and obey but feebly or like children in matters of life and health, nevertheless, in the hour of death all wish to die as Christians. And in that critical moment some have given manifestations which have been of much consolation to us.

We assert, moreover, that the better method for the advancement of these neophytes is to strive earnestly for the subjugation of the pagans; because the coarse, pagan customs, which do not merit even the name of superstitions, will decrease in proportion to the increase of those baptized. Would that there were on the go continually a company of fifty cavalrymen in this New California together with one or two missionaries who would continually visit and speak with the immense number of pagans! How many infants might be baptized, how many dying might gain eternal life! All this would prepare the way for the conversion of thousands and in a short time the Catholic Faith would extend over mountains and plains, where now countless souls perish! They are like the halt and the blind, inasmuch as they are weak of understanding; it is necessary to go in search of such, to importune them repeatedly and accompany them so that they may arrive at the waters of Baptism!

May God, Our Lord, give health and life to His Excellency, Señor Don Ciriaco Gonzalez de Carvacal, secretary ad interim of the government overseas, to this end that he may become a zealous promoter of this New California.
I am,

The servant of his apostolic majesty, whom I salute

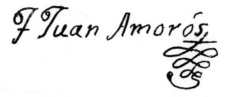

Mission of San Carlos of Monterey, February 3, 1814.

CHAPTER XIII.

Annual and Biennial Reports.—Reports from Year to Year.–The Memorias Cease to Arrive.—Drafts on Mexico not Paid.—Missions and Soldiers in Need.—Lament of Fr. Amorós.—Death of Governor J. J. Arrillaga.—Easter Duty.—Goods Obtained for Church.— Bouchard's Invasion.—Chólos Placed in the Mission.—Consequences. —Fr. Sarría Objects.—Viceroy Venadito's Remedy.—Fr. Luis Martinez on the Soldiers.—Bancroft's Generous Appreciation of the Missionaries.

Annual reports on the activites of the missionaries were demanded by the government of Mexico at an early date for the information of the Spanish king. Fr. Serra himself in September 1777, sent a formula to Mission San Antonio which was adopted by all the missionaries. It called for the information under the following heads: Name of Mission; Geographical Location; Distance from the next Mission; Names of the missionaries; Amount of Annual Stipend; Number of Baptisms, Marriages, Deaths, from the beginning; Number of Male and Female Neophytes at Mission—Livestock: Number of Cattle, Sheep, Goats, Horses, Mules, Swine.—Agriculture: Number of *fanegas* of Wheat, Barley, Corn, Beans, Peas, Lentils, Garbanzos (Chick-Peas).

The Fathers at each Mission filled out the blanks and returned them to the Fr. Presidente, who from these local reports compiled a general report: one for the governor of California for transmission to the viceroy; one for the College of San Fernando de Mexico; and the third for the Archives of the Fr. Presidente himself.

The first Annual Report, or "Informe Anual," was dated December 31, 1783. The Spanish sovereign wanted especially complete returns on the spiritual state of the Missions, such as the number of Baptisms administered annually. On this point the Fr. Guardian of the College urged the missionaries to be explicit; "for it is that which sounds best in the Court of Heaven as well as at the Court of Madrid."[1]

---

[1] Fr. Palou to Fr. Lasuén, July, 12, 1786.—S. B. A.—*Missions*, vol. ii, chap. iii.

A royal decree of March 21, 1787, in addition demanded Biennial Reports. In these the king wanted to be informed about the number of missionaries at each Mission; the amount of stipends received from the Pious Fund or from elsewhere; the number of male and female Indians and the total number of neophytes at each Mission. At the close of the report the difference between the preceding returns was to be stated. Furthermore, the number of boys and girls under nine years of age was to be noted.

The Fr. Presidente was also requested to draw up a summary, describing the newly-erected buildings and other improvements, and to note everything of interest at each Mission. This formula for the Biennial Report, however, failed to reach California until early in 1795. Thereafter the uniform reports were drawn up and signed by the missionaries at each Mission on the last day of the year 1795, and on the same date all subsequent years.

It would have made tiresome reading matter. We have therefore reduced all the annual reports to tabular form on three distinct Tables in the following order: Table of Spiritual Results; Table of Agricultural Results; and the Table on Live Stock. They will be found toward the end of the volume.

Besides succinct information on these three departments, only two other lines of activity remained to be considered in the prescribed reports, i. e., under the heading *Iglesia*—all that pertained to church goods, and under the heading *Fabrica* —all that concerned the building activities.

At San Carlos, no reports were made in either line, which would mean that nothing worth while had been acquired nor accomplished, in the last years of the eighteenth century and in the beginning of the nineteenth century down to the year 1805. In this year two silver chalices, one of them gold-plated, and a pair of silver cruets were acquired for the vestry. The Fathers, however, were not verbose; they used as many words as were necessary, nothing more.

In 1806 important work was done in the building line, when fifty-two dwellings or huts were raised for as many neophyte

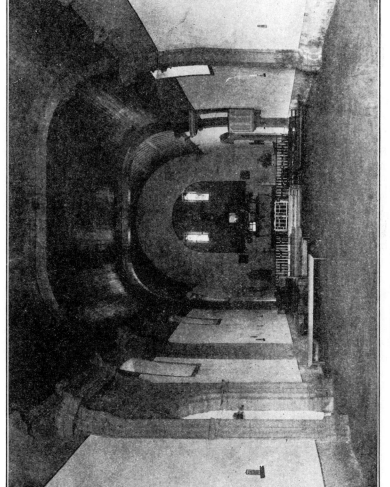

INTERIOR OF MISSION SAN CARLOS.

families. Various implements and tools for the fields and shops were also secured. In this year, too, the church was enriched with a pulpit which probably replaced an old one.

In the following year, May 16th, Fr. Presidente Estévan Tápis named San Carlos the Retreat Place whither the Fathers of the military district might retire to make the Annual Retreat by themselves.

In 1808 a silver processional Cross and a dozen candlesticks were obtained for the church; from where or from whom the report neglects to say.

On August 10, 1809, in accordance with the viceroyal orders, Governor José Joaquin Arrillaga appeared at Mission San Carlos at five o'clock in the afternoon. Before Fr. Presidente Estevan Tápis, in the presence of Fr. Vicente de Sarría, Fr. Juan Amorós, Surgeon Manuel Quijano, Ensign José Estrada, and others, he knelt before the Crucifix, placed one hand on the holy Gospels, and, with the other on the cross of his sword, swore allegiance to the new King Fernando VII, and obedience to the Junta Superior Gubernativa of Mexico.

In the same year, 1809, the images or statues of San Miguel, San Rafael, and San Antonio were placed in the church. They were carved from wood and nicely painted; but we are left ignorant of the details.

A most important acquisition for the year 1810 were two tower bells, one weighing 36 *arrobas* or 900 lbs., the other 27 *arrobas* or 675 lbs. The church was also enriched with the *Way of the Cross*, presumably new pictures were obtained.

Instead of the usual report issued on December 31, 1811, the Fathers explain that "all continues in the same status as in the previous year, minus what has been consumed in the workshops. No additions have been made because the ship bearing the *Memorias* (goods annually ordered from Mexico) has not arrived." This was to be attributed to the Hidalgo Revolt against Spanish authority over Mexico, for which the reader may consult *The Missions and Missionaries*, vol. ii. In consequence, the desired goods for the Missions ceased coming altogether with the year 1811. The soldiers, too, failed to receive their wages which were also paid in the form of goods. The troops became destitute with their families, so that the governor had to appeal to the Superior of the Missions for aid.

On July 13, 1812, the College of San Fernando de Mexico, created a new office for the Missions of California, by electing Fr. Vicente Francisco de Sarria, Commissary Prefect of the

Fr. Vicente Franco de Sarria

missionaries. On receiving the notification of his election about a year later by slow-going sailship, he issued his first Pastoral on July 2, 1813, from San Carlos which thus again became the headquarters of the Franciscans in California.

In 1813, the report has it that two apartments were set apart and supplied with everything necessary to serve as a hospital for the male and female sick respectively.

In 1814, the vaulted ceiling of the church was removed because it threatened to fall down, and a ceiling of planks was substituted. Twenty-two yards of wall were built toward closing up the Mission quadrangle. The remainder of the opening was closed by erecting fifty yards of wall in the following year. This year 1814 also witnessed the death of good Governor José Joaquin Arrillaga, "Papa Arrillaga," as he was affectionately called, which occurred at Mission Soledad July 25th. He was the staunch friend of the missionaries, and a true Catholic, whose every deed was influenced by the fear of God. More about him in chapter iv of Mission Soledad. He escaped the disagreeable consequences of the lack of means to maintain the soldiery. He would doubtless have compelled the idle soldiers to go to work and support their families without relying on the labor of the Indians at the Missions, as the viceroy later on directed.

Father Sarría in a circular of February 16, 1815, applied to the Fathers of the Monterey jurisdiction to provide what they could spare and charge it to the quartermaster of the presidio. Though there were poor prospects that the drafts would be paid in Mexico, owing to the Hidalgo Revolt, they willingly assented. Fr. Juan Amorós of Mission San Carlos, however, replied: "Mission San Carlos produces no more flour than it consumes. Some serapes will be furnished as we have done in past years, but there is not wool sufficient here to clothe the Indians."

Under date of March 17, 1816, good Father Amorós complained bitterly to Governor Solá about the depredations of which the soldiers were guilty. He wrote: "The soldier says everything belongs to the king, and so with a wide conscience he lassos and slaughters. The Indian is always poor; he is the one, then, that always kills the cattle, and to whomsoever he meets he is always bad, always the dog. If I should relate the damages known and unknown, which have been committed against the Mission in the last four years, I should never finish. This complaint may be more harmful than beneficial; yet I make it. When the soldiers see themselves accused they will commit other vexations. They will claim that this heifer or that one does not belong to the Mission or they will do other things which if done by defenseless Indians are regarded as altogether criminal. This being so, the neophytes do not carry out what is justly commanded them. They do not covet the goods of others; nay, they do not even attempt to preserve what is their own.

"Finally, Señor Governor, you know very well that we are mere administrators for charity's sake. We have no further interest in the property than the duty to manage what is for these poor a means for the propagation of the Faith. Without assistance from Your Honor we shall scarcely be able to preserve it for them. You know that our Indians go barefooted in order that they may provide shoes for the troops and many families. They eat their food without butter in order that the troops may have it. They do not taste beans in order to deliver them to the military store; and even the branding iron is put to the service of the military. To conclude, the whole Indian is for the whole Indian. The Indian will die, but he says, 'It is for that we have the Father!' Let what has been said suffice, Señor Governor. I believe I have not been moved by passion nor by self-interest, nor am I angered at any one; but I considered myself obliged to make this denunciation.''[2] Why the neophytes would run away under such conditions cannot be a puzzle.

As something extraordinary, the Annual Report for 1816 notes that three Anglo-Americans and one Chinaman were baptized at the Mission.

In 1817 a chapel was built contiguous to the church. No details were volunteered. Furthermore, a new chasuble, a frontal, and new *manteles* were procured for the church. All the reports from 1810 to this year, 1817 inclusive, were signed by Fathers Sarría and Amorós.

In the following December 31, 1818, Fr. Amorós alone reports that during the last twelve months 310 neophytes made their Easter Confession and that 130 neophytes had received holy Communion. The practice obtained here that those not intelligent enough were not permitted to receive holy Communion. The Holy Viaticum was given to eleven neophytes in their last illness.

For the church a new alb was obtained. Also a chapel was built and an altar, wood carved, and entirely painted placed therein.

This year, too, is notable for the arrival on November 22nd of South American insurgents under Hipolite Bouchard. They attacked Monterey and captured the presidio after Governor Solá and his much inferior force had retreated to the Rancho del Rey near the present town of Salinas. The enemies ruined the orchard and garden, seized goods to the value of about $5000, destroyed as much more which belonged to officers

---

[2] *The Missions, etc.* Vol. iii, pp. 18-19, 82-83.

and private persons, set fire to the buildings and reembarked on the fifth day, to repeat the depredations farther south. No harm was done to the Mission of San Carlos itself.

In September, 1819, one hundred infantrymen, under Captain José A. Navarrete, in two ships, *San Carlos and La Reina de los Angeles* arrived at Monterey. These men were better known as *Cholos*. "They were most emphatically a bad lot," says Bancroft.[3] "Such is the unanimous testimony of the governor comandantes, friars and citizens. They belonged to the criminal and vagabond classes; were taken for the most part from the jails or picked up by pressgangs in New Galicia; and they were altogether ignorant of military discipline or the use of arms. Of mixed race and worse than mixed character, they were vicious and quarrelsome. Their conduct inspired disgust, and was the origin of the subsequent bitter feelings between Californians[4] and Mexicans. They were small in stature, wearing the hair short in contrast with the presidial, drunkards, gamblers and thieves."

For once the harassed Governor Solá lost his head. He determined to lodge the rogues and moral lepers in the very Indian Mission of San Carlos, instead of keeping them under his eyes at Monterey. At the Mission there was no other habitation available than the storeroom. There the governor insisted the newcomers should take up their quarters contrary to all royal laws and common sense. Fr. Sarría, then in charge, at once turned over the keys of the Mission with the mild remark, "Here are the keys. We have obeyed whatever we were commanded. There is nothing left for us to do but to take up our staffs and hats, and go whither obedience destines us." The governor then tried to make it appear that Fr. Sarría was guilty of disrespect to royal authority. "What," he exclaimed, "will you not aid the troops of His Majesty!" The undaunted missionary meekly replied: "I have not said that; I have said that if Your Honor bring these men right here into the

---

[3] *California*, vol. ii, p. 255.

[4] Descendants of immigrants from Mexico, who had assumed the term *Californians*, hijos del pais—native sons, or paisanos for short.

Mission, here are the keys of the quarters. I will not actively participate in this transaction."[5]

The governor furthermore demanded *metates* and *comales*.[6] Fr. Sarría declared that so far as he knew there were no such articles for common use; that if any existed they belonged to the Indian women from whom he would not take, because they would need them for their own use. Solá, thereupon, ordered the Indian alcaldes to procure them. They did so, but regretted it next day, when they complained to Fr. Sarría that they feared these utensils would not be returned. In fact they were taken to the presidio at Monterey, and on the following day Comandante Estudillo came for some more. Reporting the matter to the Fr. Comisario Prefecto Mariano Payeras the amazed Fr. Sarría exclaimed: "Why were those utensils demanded from the unhappy Indians of San Carlos to whom they belonged, as the Mission possessed none for the common use after it had suffered in the Bouchard invasion! It seems to me that in such and similar cases they should have applied to other parties, such as the settlers and soldiers who have such articles. Why do not such people have to contribute in case of public necessity."[7]

Despite Fr. Sarría's objection and in violation of royal regulations, thirty men under one officer came out and took up their quarters right in the Mission, and lodged in the storeroom arranged for them. What was feared came to pass. "As I go through the Indian village," Fr. Sarría wrote to Fr. Payeras, "I find this one at the door of a neophyte's hut, and that one inside the hut of another. I have told the officer, who promised to stop it; but how is it possible to avoid everything. The words of Solorzano come to my mind: 'The scum of other races kills the Indians.'[8] ('Que el vaho de las otras gentes mata a los Indios').

[5] Fr. Sarría reporting to Fr. Payeras, Sept. 7, 1819. *Santa Barbara Arch.*
[6] The *metate* was a curved stone for crushing corn and making tortillas. The comal was an almost flat earthen plate for cooking maize.
[7] Fr. Sarría to Fr. Payeras Sept. 7 and 26, 1819.
[8] Ibid, Sept. 7, 1819.

Only two weeks later, the good Father with keen sorrow was compelled to report to the governor that the soldiers had seduced an Indian woman.[9] Fr. Prefecto Payeras on September 16, 1819, protested to Solá against quartering soldiers at the Mission, or letting them have anything to do with the neophytes. It is hard enough, he said, to manage the Indians with the best soldiers from the presidio as guards; but this kind of troops should be kept in the garrison. If some must be quartered at the Mission he would direct the missionaries to construct separate buildings for them. Fr. Payeras actually gave orders to that effect on October 8th. Meanwhile Solá

began to be troubled in conscience at sight of the grave disorders caused by his *Cholos*, and he promised Fr. Sarría that he would remove the objectionable men before the end of the month.[10]

Neither the *San Carlos* nor the *Reina de los Angeles* in September, 1819, had brought up any supplies and equipment for the troops, nor the *Memorias*, i. e., the usual goods requested by the missionaries for their annual allowance. Want accordingly prevailed in the presidios and among the Mission guards, and complaints never ceased. The governor could only express his sympathy, and echo the complaints in letters to the viceroy. The viceroy could send no relief because of the rebellion which consumed the income from custom duties. In reply to a letter of Governor Solá which appeared more than inconsiderate, Viceroy Venadito with much justice wrote: "Two vessels have been laden with supplies, and will

---

[9] Fr. Sarría to Solá, Sept. 21, 1819.
[10] Fr. Sarría to Fr. Payeras, Sept. 26, 1819. *Santa Barbara Arch.*

take away the product of the country and thus aid the people whom you say you have to feed. As to those settlers, let them go to work, as God and the king require. Let them develop the rich resources of their province and talk less. Thus will they live comfortably, and also be an aid rather than a burden to the govenment in such trying times as these." Instead "at the pueblos a large part of the settlers were content to be idle, giving the Indian laborers one-third or one-half the crop for tilling their lands and living on what remained."[11] Had the soldiers likewise heeded the advice of the viceroy little want would have existed in the territory. They too, preferred to idle away the days, go in rags, and depend for support upon the missionaries who, in consequence, had to suffer privations besides overworking themselves along with their neophytes.

Similarly other Missions at this time and later were burdened with demands from the idle soldiery, as a letter, dated September 19, 1819, three days later, from Fr. Martinez of San Luis Obispo to Governor Solá reveals. "Never before," he writes, "has so much watchfulness been necessary with regard to the soldiers. They have come to us without discipline and Religion. They have been taught to suffer many hardships, but never for God and for the king. They should be relegated to the presidios and an eye should be kept upon them. They should be given some occupation which is not useless and which is calculated to banish idleness, the mother of all vices."[12] Father Sarría only two days later, September 21st, notified the governor that a soldier at Mission San Carlos had seduced an Indian woman. Such cases were common at all the Missions. The distress of the missionaries may be imagined.

The missionary is expected to furnish shoes, boots and even gunsticks. They want him to be tailor, weaver, mason, carpenter and everything else without having learned it, and this too without support. Whence shall he obtain the infused

---

[11] Viceroy to Solá. December 15, 1819. Bancroft, vol. ii, pp. 257-258; 415.

[12] Sept. 17, 1819. Fr. Martinez to Governor Solá.

science? Then, how can a poor Indian be cheerful, who throughout the year is occupied at work in a Mission, when his labor procures for him nothing more than a poor suit of clothes and a blanket, since he must labor for others; (i. e., soldiers and their families). The soldiers would also kill Mission cattle, and claim they were animals running wild.

"The response of the missionaries," Bancroft acknowledges[13] "was most satisfactory and liberal; especially when we consider that there were now (at San Carlos) two hundred additional mouths to fill; that the loss of the Mission in connection with the Bouchard affairs had been quite considerable in time, labor and effects, besides the inconveniences naturally arising from the hasty abandonment of Monterey, and that the Padres made a direct contribution of about $3500 to supply losses sustained at Monterey, besides furnishing laborers and many articles to which no special value was given, etc. It is, indeed, surprising how cheerfully each Mission did its part either in voluntary gifts, in regularly assessed contributions, or in response to special local demands, and how rarely even slight misunderstandings arose in individual cases. Yet at times they were much discouraged at the prospect before them."

"There is little to be added," says Bancroft, "on the matter of mission supplies to the presidios. Upon the Franciscan establishments fell the whole burden of supporting the provincial government and the troops, and their dues for unpaid drafts amounted in 1820 to nearly half a million dollars. Not a dollar of stipend (annual allowance) was received by the friars during the whole decade; and not a single invoice of goods for the missions—goods usually bought with the proceeds of the habilitado's drafts and the friars' stipends—could be forwarded, except one or two of very small amount obtained from other sources. The fact that the stipend came from the Pious Fund, to which the royal treasury had no claim save as a kind of 'self-constituted' trustee for the missions; and the fact

---

[13] *California*, vol. ii, pp. 257-258.

that other missionaries were not so entirely neglected as those in California, made the situation all the more exasperating; yet the protests and complaints of the friars were neither so frequent nor so bitter as might be expected considering the legal rights that were being violated."[14]

---

[14] *The Missions*, vol. iii, pp. 67-70.

CHAPTER XIV.

The Decay of the Mission.—Further Reports.—Deliberations of the Junta.—Mexican Independence Celebrated.—The First Legislative Assembly.—Father Abella's Report on Mission Activities.—Scarcity of Laborers.—Conditions Grow Desperate.

During the eventful year 1819 the two Fathers Sarría and Amorós could do little more than keep everything in repair, and therefore reported nothing regarding church goods or building activities. The neophytes had been dwindling in numbers since the year 1795 when the Indian population had reached its highest point with 444 males and 434 females. At the close of 1819 San Carlos Mission consisted of only 219 males and 178 females, old and young. The Mission was already dying.

Fr. Ramon Abella took Father Amorós' place by the side of Fr. Sarría at the close of 1819.

In the Annual Report on December 31, 1820, both Fathers write: "There was purchased a stone tablet bearing the sculptured image of our Father St. Francis. Furthermore curtains have been placed on the windows of the church."

In the same year on October 30th, Governor Solá informed the Fathers that from the brigantine *El Señoriano y San Francisco Javier* the Franciscan Fathers Ibárra, Altimira, Esténaga and Ordáz had landed at Monterey.

For the year 1821 nothing more is noted than the following incident: Governor Solá, writing to the comandante of Monterey says: "I learned that Ramona has been happily delivered of a child. Shave her head with a razor, and on the first feastday let her be seated in a chair in the middle of the plaza, with her head uncovered so that the entire public may see her for two long hours before and after Mass."[1] If the seducer had been ordered pilloried for double the space of time in the same place followed with a flogging on the bare

---

[1] *Cal. Arch., Prov. State Papers, Indexes,* vol. xxiv, p. 619

VIEW OF SAN CARLOS CRUMBLING TO RUIN. ETCHING BY HY. CHAPMAN FORD.

back, the punishment would have been more fair, and liber-
tines would have been deterred more effectively.

In 1822 the Fathers report that two fine albs and two
amices were made, perhaps by the girls in the *monjerio*. In
addition four scarlet cassocks and eight linen surplices were
made for the altar boys.

Mexico at last became independent of Spain in 1821, but
the news of it failed to reach California till 1822. What took
place then will be learned from the official communications
of the time.

Governor Solá on April 8, 1822, informed Captain José
de la Guerra of Santa Barbara that on said day "there was
celebrated in the government house a junta or meeting, pre-
sided over by him, and at the request of the Rev. Canonigo
Agustin Fernandez de San Vicente prebendary of the Cathedral of Durango, commissioned by the Regency of the Mexican
Empire for both Californias. Those attending were Rev. Fr.
Mariano Payeras, Comisario Prefecto of the Franciscans
in the territory; Rev. Fr. Vicente Sarría, Rev. Fr. Estévan
Tápis; Luis Antonio Argüello, Comandante of the Presidio
of San Francisco, and José Ant. Navarrete, Captain of the
Auxiliary Infantry of San Blas, the Lieutenants Estudillo,
José Mariano Estrada, Manuel Gómez, and Alferez Francisco Haro, as Secretary. The discussion turned on the sub-
ject of establishing a Territorial Deputation or Assembly,
and on creating an Ayuntamiento or Town Council for San
José and for Los Angeles. The plan was finally adopted."[2]

The Independence of Mexico was accordingly celebrated
at Monterey in the following manner: "At the presidio of
Monterey, on April 9, 1822, the Military and Civil Governor
of this Province, Colonel Don Pablo Vicente de Solá, the Captains Comandantes of the presidios of Santa Barbara and
San Francisco, Don José Ant. de la Guerra y Noriega and
Don Luis Ant. Argüello; the Captains of the Militia Com-
panies of the Batallones de Tepíc and Mazatlán, Don José
Ant. Navarrete and Don Pablo de Portilla; Lieutenant José

---

[2] *Cal. Arch., Prov. Records,* vol. xi, pp. 316-318.

Maria Estudillo for the presidial company of San Diego; Lieutenant Don José Mariano Estrada for the garrison of the Monterey Presidio; Lieutenant of the Artillery, Don Manuel Gómez, Comandante of his company; the Rev. Fathers Mariano Payeras and Vicente Francisco de Sarría the former as Prelate of these Missions, the latter as substitute of the Rev. Fr. Presidente and Vicário Foráneo Fr. José Señan,— having assembled in virtue of previous citations in the *Sala* of the Government to hear of the happy inauguration of the Regency of the Empire and Soberano Junta Provisional Governativa at the Capital of Mexico from official letters and other documents which the before-mentioned Governor had read in full Assembly.

"Those present declared that for themselves and their subordinates they decided to fulfill the orders which the Supreme Government now indicated. They would at once recognize that this Province is solely dependent on the Imperial Government of Mexico and independent of Spanish domination, and of any other foreign power. In virtue of which they must now proceed to take the corresponding oath in the terms prescribed by the temporary Governing Regency, for which effect the opportune steps should be taken by the said military and civil governor, and the respective commanders of presidios. The Missionaries of the Missions will affirm their compliance by means of certificates which they will sign and remit with a copy of this Act to the Excellent Señor Minister concerned.

"Pablo Vicente de Solá, José de la Guerra y Noriega, Luis Argüello, José M. Estudillo, Manuel Gómez, Pablo de la Portilla, José M. Estrada, Fr. Vicente de Sarría and Fr. Mariano Payeras.—José M. Estudillo, Vocal and Secretary."[3]

The First Legislative Assembly.

The Assembly chosen in April, 1822, at last met in open session seven months later. The report of this memorable event reads as follows:

"At the presidio of Monterey in Alta California, on the 11th

---

[3] *Cal. Arch., Prov. State Papers*, vol. xvi, pp. 1-2.

day of the month of November in the year 1822, came together in the principal chamber of the governmental building, the Señor Colonel Don Pablo Vicente de Solá, Superior Civil and Military Judge of the Assembly, which consisted of the Electors Don Francisco de Ortega, Don José Aruz, Don José Palomares, Don Francisco Castro, and Don José Lopez for the purpose of choosing the individuals who are to be the members of the Provincial Deputation to be installed. . .

"The Comisionado for both Californias, Dr. Agustin Fernandez de San Vicente, Prebendary of the Cathedral Church of Durango, Mexico, being present, declared that the same Electors present might constitute themselves the Deputation by naming a Secretary from their own number. In consequence, they elected as Secretary Ensign Don Manuel de Otero of the Auxiliary Company of San Blas. At the same time they elected as *Diputados*—Don José Aruz, Don Francisco de Ortega, Don Francisco Castro, and Don José Antonio Carrillo, and as Substitutes—Don Antonio Castro and Don José Castro. These before the Political Judge took the oath to guard the Political Constitution of the Monarchy, observe the laws, be faithful to the Emperor, and fulfill religiously the obligations of their charge.

"Before they had assembled for the actions taken as related, a solemn High Mass preceded at which an exhortation in keeping with the occasion was delivered by the Rev. Fr. Mariano Payeras, Commissary Prefect of the Missions. Afterwards the *Te Deum* was sung, and the *salvos* of the artillery by the troops of the Auxiliary Company of Infantry from San Blas concluded the installation of the Assembly. The witnesses present at the signing of the names were Captain Don José Ant. Navarrete, Ensign Don Francisco de Haro as Secretary and Don José Joaquin de la Torre."[4]

During the Sessions it was officially reported that in the whole province of California the population consisted of 21,196 Indian neophytes in the twenty Missions, 2,994 settlers and their families, besides the soldiers and their families

---

[4] *Cal. Arch., State Papers, Naturalization*, vol. cxciv, pp. 1-2.

at San Diego, Santa Barbara, Monterey, and San Francisco.

Whatever the benefits that came to Mexico in consequence of the Hidalgo Revolt and of the Declaration of Independence,[5] for the California Indian Missions the Mexican struggle brought on nothing but distress and final ruin.

The change of government in California with its first Assembly so solemnly introduced afforded no relief to the harassed Indian neophytes and their spiritual guides from the forced contributions in behalf of the shiftless soldiers and their numerous families.

Governor Solá resigned and went as delegate for California to the Mexican Congress. Captain Luis Ant. Argüello, on November 11, 1822, succeeded him as temporary governor.

Resuming the report on such activities as were still possible in the Mission of San Carlos, owing to the scarcity of able and willing hands, we find on December 31, 1823, Fr. Abella informing his Superior that for the vestry a white chasuble of damask and a frontal for the main altar of the same material but of red color had been procured; and that a frontal of red color had also been secured for each of the three altars. Portions of the garden wall had been ruined, and it was not possible to make repairs because the reduced number of Indians were occupied in planting grain, taking care of the livestock and working in the weaving rooms. The Mission family at this date consisted of only 317 neophytes, 170 males and 147 females.

The Mission this year had harvested 500 fanégas of wheat, 600 of barley, 140 of beans, and 131 of peas, or in all 1371 of grain and vegetables, or 2285 bushels. If the Mission could have retained all it raised the Indians needed not to suffer; but the soldiers had to be considered and for what the Mission supplied it received nothing from them in return. The livestock at the end of 1823 consisted of 2240 cattle, 5000 sheep,

---

[5] Let the readers examine the facts on the origin, struggle and results of Independence as brought out in *The Missions and Missionaries*, vol. i, sec. iv, chaps. ix and x; and in vol. iii, chap. vii. They will conclude that Independence has proved a curse rather than a blessing for Mexico.

16 goats, 20 pigs, 16 mules and 400 horses, or in all 7964 animals of all kinds.

In the same year 1823, Bancroft claims, "The Padres received from the Santa Barbara presidio $1,802, which had been due since 1804. (Vol. ii, p. 616). The troops might have helped themselves to a great extent and thus made it easier for the missionaries and Indians. They possessed cattle and might have cultivated some patches of land for gardening vegetables. Yet, the new governor, Luis Argüello, on February 13, 1823, had to write to Fr. Prefecto Payeras: "Since I have arrived here at this presidio of Monterey in January, there have been nothing but lamentations on account of the great scarcity of *soap* from which every individual of this company is suffering."[6] Of course the Missions were to supply the desired article and much more.

A month after this plaint, at the request of the same Governor Argüello, Fr. Payeras sent a list of goods and other articles which each Mission, *except San Carlos*, (which was unable to contribute) donated outright. The goods included clothing, shoes, hats, blankets, stockings, grain, peas, beans, *soap*, and mules with their saddles and bridles. San Fernando instead donated $200. Purisima, Fr. Payeras' own Mission, gave $500.[7]

The first legislative assembly was composed of the following six members: José Aruz, José A. Carrillo, Carlos Castro, Francisco Castro, Francisco Ortega, and José Palomares. They seemed to have possessed a lofty conception of their powers, inasmuch as they attempted to legislate on matters that pertained to the Missions. For instance, this assembly proposed the suppression of Mission San Carlos and Mission Santa Cruz. The Missions were ecclesiastical institutes, *under the protection* of the territorial government, but they were not government establishments. Fr. Sarría quieted timid souls with the remark that the decrees of the assembly had no binding force until approved by the Supreme Mexican Govern-

---

[6] *The Missions*, etc., vol. iii, p. 167.
[7] *The Missions*, etc., vol. iii, pp. 167-168.

ment. However, the six assemblymen could not agree on the subject, and so the proposition for the time being failed to pass.[8]

In 1824 the dwelling of the missionaries and the workshops were reroofed and efforts were made to restore the walls around the Mission garden.

For the Mission church a large Crucifix was secured. In addition four large statues of wood were acquired, it is not said how or from whom they came. They represented "Our Father San Francisco," Santa Clara, Santo Domingo and San Buenaventura.

At the close of the year 1825, in the Annual Reports, Father Abella informed the Superior and the governor that the "adobe garden walls have fallen down. It is not possible to rebuild them on account of the lack of hands. Those able to work are engaged at planting grain and in the weaving rooms."

For the vestry a black cope and two frontals of the same color were obtained.

In 1826 some dwellings were reroofed. Other work had to be postponed owing to the scarcity of laborers.

In 1827 conditions grew desperate when twenty-three Indians of the Mission quite legally severed their connection with the Mission in order to hire themselves out to neighboring ranchos, some even as far as the Pajaro River. Others found employment at the presidio of Monterey. Doubtless these were able-bodied men with their families. Fr. Abella offers no particulars nor any explanation for this remarkable action of so many neophytes at a time when laborers were in demand at the Mission. It will come to light when we reach the last annual report made by good Father Abella in 1832.

---

[8] *The Missions*, etc., vol. iii, p. 176.

CHAPTER XV.

Meanwhile startling news had come from Mexico. General Agustin Iturbide, who had on May 21, 1822, taken the oath as Emperor of Mexico under the name of Agustin I, found it wise to abdicate in a special session of Congress on the night of March 19, 1823, and to leave the country lest his presence occasion more trouble. In the following year, April 28, 1824, the clique that controlled Congress persuaded a majority to declare the real Liberator of Mexico, the magnanimous Iturbide, an outlaw and an enemy of the State if he should set foot on Mexican soil. Not aware of this decree, Iturbide, for the purpose of offering his services to the Mexican Government in case of war, which he had heard was planned against his native country, landed at Vera Cruz on July 15th, and was arrested. The hostile Congress on July 18th voted his death. Next day he was informed and told to prepare for death at sunset. He made his confession and asked to have the execution postponed till next day so that he could hear holy Mass and receive holy Communion. This reasonable request was refused, which of itself makes it clear that the majority of the Congress consisted of rabid elements quite capable of concocting a Constitution on October 4th, of the same year 1824, to which the missionaries in California would not subscribe.

Iturbide with unfaltering step walked to the place of execution. A platoon of soldiers fired and killed him instantly on said July 19, 1824, scarcely forty-one years of age.[1] On the following morning his body, vested in a Franciscan habit,

---

[1] Bancroft, *Mexico*, vol. iv, page 811, says: "His execution was an unjust proceeding."

was buried in the old, roofless church of Padilla. There it remained till October 24, 1838, when a less rabid Congress had it removed and interred with solemn obsequies in the Cathedral of Mexico. Furthermore, in later years, Iturbide's services in accomplishing the Independence of Mexico were officially recognized. In 1853, the title of *Liberador* was bestowed upon him, and in 1855, the anniversary of his death was declared a public holiday.[2]

On October 4, 1824, less than three months after the execution of Iturbide, the Congress so-called, adopted and promulgated a Constitution. The Provisional Executive Power in control thus far, on the same day issued a decree which read as follows: "The individual or individuals comprehended in the articles of this decree who in any manner shall refuse to take the prescribed oath on the Constitution, will be banished from the territory of the Republic, if, after they have been once called upon by the Government or corresponding authority, they shall persist in their determination."

The first President, Guadalupe Victoria, was chosen six days later, October 10, 1824. In the provinces, hence in California, Victoria directed that the oath should be taken within nine days after the reception of the Constitution and decrees.[3]

Governor Luis Argüello received the documents in February, 1825. He at once summoned the legislative assembly to meet at Monterey. At the same time he notified Fr. Prefecto Sarría that he was expected to comply and take the oath on the Constitution on Sunday, February 13, 1825.

The venerable Comisário Prefecto on February 11th replied in substance as follows: "Having reflected on the oath demanded of us, I have concluded that I cannot take it without violating prior obligations of justice and fidelity. . . . .I should wish to give an example of submission as I have done

---

[2] Bancroft, *Mexico*, vol. iv, pp. 810-811;—*The Missions and Missionaries*, vol. i, section iv, chap. ix.

[3] *The Missions and Missionaries*, vol. iii, p. 213, where see references.

heretofore; yet I am now unable, because my conscience forbids. For the same reason I will not influence the other Fathers to take said oath, or to sanction it by celebrating holy Mass and singing the *Te Deum*, as is ordered in your communication of the 3rd instant (i. e. February 3, 1825). I am aware that we are threatened with exile, but I will undergo all, along with the crushing sorrow and many tears which the much beloved flock entrusted to my care will cause me, and will bear it for God's sake."[4]

Although Fr. Sarría would not direct the Fathers to swear allegiance to the Constitution, he wrote to Governor Argüello under date of March 30, 1825: "I assure you that so far as my subjects are concerned, I have left them entirely at liberty to do in this particular what they may judge proper before God; nor did I in the Circular to them give the motives of my refusal."[5]

On Saturday, March 26, 1825, two-thirds of the delegates to the Assembly responded to their names, that is to say, Governor Luis Argüello, Francisco Castro, Carlos Castro, Antonio Castro, José Castro, and the Secretary, José de la Torre. The southern members were detained by rainfalls. The Constitution of Mexico was read and ratified by the same members of the Assembly. The document was then read at the foot of the flag in the garrison to the officers, soldiers and settlers, who all took the oath. The new order of things was thus inaugurated with triple salutes from the artillery, and amid joyous shouts and the ringing of bells for three days. "Only the Solemn Mass and the Te Deum were wanting because the Rev. Fr. Prefecto Vicente Francisco Sarría would not take the oath, much less call upon his subjects to do so," as Secretary De la Torre noted in the minutes of the session.[6]

However, José Maria Estudillo on July 7, 1825, in a letter to Governor Argüello corroborated the statement that the missionary Fathers by Circular from Fr. Sarría were left free

---

[4] Fr. Sarría to Argüello, Febr. 11, 1825.—Archb. Arch. no. 1724.

[5] Fr. Sarría to Argüello, March 30, 1825. *Archb. Arch.* no. 1725.

[6] *Missions and Missionaries*, vol. iii, p. 215.

in the matter. As proof there is recorded the fact that at the San Francisco presidio, according to Comandante Ignacio Martinez, "on Sunday, April 24, 1825, the soldiers marched into the chapel of the presidio where Rev. Tomás Esténaga sang the High Mass and preached the sermon. At the close of the holy Mass the *Te Deum* was intoned."[7]

When the news reached Mexico that Fr. Prefecto Sarría had refused to take the oath in the Constitution, President Victoria in June, 1825, despatched an order to California for the arrest of Fr. Sarría and for his deportation to Mexico. Fr. Sarría in October was accordingly arrested, but that was as far as the new governor, José M. Echeandia, appointed February 1st, 1825, dared to proceed. Sarría was but nominally under arrest, yet it prevented him from leaving Monterey or the Mission and from making the periodical canonical visitations. In October, 1825, through the respective military comandantes Echeandia requested all the missionaries to take the oath of allegiance to the Mexican Constitution. Fr. Ramon Abella of San Carlos replied that he would not swear; that he had come to the territory for God's sake, and for God's sake he would depart, if they wanted to eject him; but that he would serve in matters spiritual and temporal with the fidelity corresponding to his sacred character. Twenty other Franciscans similarly refused to swear allegiance to the Constitution; five Fathers offered to take the oath with the clause, "so far as is compatible with my ministry or religious profession," "or in everything not contrary to my conscience." Father Barona's name does not appear in the record. He doubtless would have replied in the terms of the others. Only two offered to swear without clause—Fr. Antonio Peyri and Fr. Francisco Suñer, who later regretted their action.

In truth, the Fathers had sworn to the Mexican Independence, and therefore deemed the second oath quite superfluous, especially as a deeper study of the text made them

---

[7] *The Missions and Missionaries*, vol. iii, pp. 215-216. At San Diego, on the other hand, the missionaries refused to participate in the solemn ratification of allegiance to the Constitution.

hesitate to commit themselves to a document which savored of Voltairianism.

Fr. Durán doubtless voiced the sentiments of all the Franciscans when he replied: "I am not inclined to take more oaths, *not from disaffection for the Independence,* nor for any other odious passion; for I am of the political opinion that Independence is of more benefit to Spain than to America; but because it seems that *oaths have become playthings.*"[8] Thereafter Echeandia thought wise to let the devoted Franciscans alone.

Meanwhile Mexican politicians were chafing because their demand for Fr. Sarría's expulsion was not gratified. Ramon Arizpe, the Minister of Justice and Ecclesiastical Affairs, again directed Echeandia to send Father Sarría out of the territory of California. The Governor on November 4, 1828, replied as follows: "Most Excellent Sir,—This reply to your Superior Order of March 26th, with which Your Excellency was pleased to instruct me, offers me the motive for manifesting to Your Excellency that the said Prefect is Fr. Vicente Francisco de Sarría, the same to whom the Supreme Government extended the passport for departure from the Mexican Republic, because he had not wanted to take the oath on our Constitution. He has not left the country for the reason that, since he has not completed his term of office of Commissary Prefect, he could not deliver the office to the Fr. Presidente so long as he himself remained in the country.

"If the departure of the said Commissary Prefect should come to pass, the rest of the disaffected Religious, who form the greater number, would also leave. Under such circumstances, the departure of the Fr. Prefect and of many Religious who would follow him, in my judgement would occasion much disquietude in the territory which I have always tried to preserve in best order.

"The lack of missionaries would cause disorder in the establishments of the neophytes who are in their charge, and which they have been able to preserve in the same state. I have,

---

[8] *The Missions and Missionaries,* vol. iii, pp. 213-223.

therefore, not urged the quick departure of Fr. Sarría until the time when a sufficient number of missionaries might relieve those, who by reason of the law must leave the Republic.

MISSION SAN CARLOS IN RUINS.

Nor have I urged the departure of the old and infirm, who by reason of infirmities deserve to be relieved of their burdens.

"Your Excellency, being informed of all, will direct me if, notwithstanding these obstacles, I should carry out the banishment of Fr. Sarría, or in view of them the Exmo. President shall be pleased to resolve to decide what he judges more expedient.—"Dios y Libertad."—San Diego, November 4, 1828.—José M. Echeandia.[9]

Father Sarría, already sixty-two years old, then offered to leave the country for the Sandwich Islands in order to preach the Gospel to the Kanaks, and thus relieve the governor of his embarrassment; but these far-off islands were situated too near to California to satisfy the spiteful politicians of Mexico. The Supreme Government rejected the proposition, and instead directed Echeandia to give the proscribed missionary his passport for Europe. The governor assured the Minister of Justice that the Father Prefect should be put on board the first ship bound for Europe or the United States.[10]

On March 20, 1829, the Unchristian Government of Mexico manifested its insane bitterness against the mother country by publishing a decree of exile against all Spaniards residing in California, New Mexico, and other territories. Spanish settlers were directed to leave the country within a month and the Republic within three months after publication of the law. Governor Echeandia published the iniquitous measure on July 6, 1829; "but, in accordance with his previously expressed opinion," says Hittéll,[11] "he had little expectation that it could be, or in fact ought to be, any more rigidly enforced than the other. There was in fact, among the people, a very strong opposition to it in so far as it affected the missionaries, and especially those that had taken the oath. In the pueblo of San José this feeling was apparently unanimous. The ayuntamiento or town council of that place met (on August 25, 1829,) and in the name of the whole people protested against its execution. . . .It was apparent that there would be very great difficulty in attempting to carry out either the letter or the spirit of the law; and during Echeandia's administration, with the exception of expelling a few persons of little consideration, nothing of importance was done in relation

---

[9] *Cal. Arch., Dept. Rec.*, vol. i pp. 215-216.
[10] See *Missions and Missionaries*, vol. iii, chap. xvi, for details and references.
[11] Hittell, vol. ii, pp. 87-88.

to it." At any rate Fathers Sarría and Abella were at San Carlos and were not molested in their work of saving the Indians.

No distinction seems to have been made in favor of those who had taken the oath, so that the friars would have sworn in vain had they complied. They were Spaniards; that was their crime; therefore they would have to depart, oath or no oath. Truly, the Mexicans in power had a singular conception of liberty. Just about as much as the rabid Mexicans in power regarding the liberty of conscience of the citizens of Mexico at this writing.

The Town Council of Monterey went further than the Ayuntamiento of San José. On September 22, 1829, it addressed a noble protest to the President of Mexico, which is too long for reproduction here. The few extracts given will reveal the spirit of the document and of the petitioners. "Most Illustrious Sir:—The Ayuntamiento of this port in the name of the whole community addresses Your Excellency in order to place before you with candor the spiritual desolation to which it will be reduced if—what is incredible—the expulsion of the Missionary Fathers is carried out. The Council implores your piety that, as first magistrate of such a Christian(!) Republic, you cast a compassionate glance at our unhappy condition and provide a suitable remedy. This territory, Most Excellent Sir, receives its spiritual nourishment from the Missionary Fathers of these Missions. There are twenty-one situated along a stretch of more than two hundred leagues, and there are twenty-eight missionaries of whom twenty-five are Spaniards. Besides the Missions, they are in charge of the souls of four presidios with their adjoining settlers of three pueblos and a considerable number of ranchos scattered throughout the territory. If the Government should fully execute aforesaid law, in the vast territory only three Religious would remain to attend to the spiritual needs of the inhabitants. . .This Ayuntamiento shudders when it contemplates the bereavement in which the inhabitants would be left without the meritorious laborers of the Gospel. . .This

Ayuntamiento cannot convince itself that the Supreme Government, which watches so much over the happiness of its subjects, should overlook the foundation, which is the preservation of our beloved Religion, and should leave the country without a proportionate number of priests.[12] This Ayuntamiento faithfully observes our wise Constitution, and punctually obeys the Laws; but it believes that it would fail of its duty, if it passed over in silence the eminent merit won by the Spanish Religious and Missionaries, who are at present in the territory and discharge their obligations. As men, truly apostolic, they have continually given us an example of most eminent virtues; and inasmuch as their civil conduct has been so peaceful and they are the first in obedience to the laws, it is but right that this Ayuntamiento should regard itself bound to beseech the Supreme Government to urge Congress to make an exception in favor of said Religious."—Port of Monterey, September 22, 1829.—José Tiburcio Castro, Francisco Soria, Feliciano Soberanes, Santiago Moreno, and José Ant. Gajiola, Secretary.[13]

No action seems to have been taken concerning this Protest and Petition; but Henry Virmond, a German merchant, who conducted a lucrative trade with California, wrote from Mexico on October 12, 1829, that the President had not the slightest intention of expelling the Friars from California.[14] No, but he changed his tactics; for, on the same day on which the decree of expulsion was issued, March 20, 1829, Minister Juan de Cañedo wrote to Governor Echeandia "that the Apostolic College of Zacatecas would replace the fugitive and other Franciscan Friars."[15] This Missionary College was entirely composed of Mexicans. As we shall see in time, Fr. Ramon Abella, accordingly had to withdraw from San Carlos

---

[12] What sort of reception would such a Protest and Petition receive at the hands of the infidel Mexican Government of today?

[13] *See, The Missions* vol. iii, pp. 275-277, for the references.

[14] *The Missions, etc.,* vol. iii, p. 277.

[15] "El Collegio Apostolico de Zacatecas proveerá á reemplazarlos."
—*The Missions, etc.,* vol. iii, p. 277.

and give way to a Zacatecan or Mexican Franciscan missionary.

At this time, about September, 1827, other more agreeable
news reached California. Fr. Juan Cortés, who had served in
California at Santa Barbara and now acted as Procurator,
under date of May 31, 1827, communicated a circular informing the missionaries that the administrator of the Pious Fund
had been allowed to pay the annual stipends for the three
years—1820-1822. Payment had also been made for the year
1819, but the Sindico Escalante, a layman, had been unfaith-
ful, and so the money for 1819 was lost.[16] These stipends were
the annual allowance for every missionary in California. The
annual stipend amounted to $400 for the Fathers who instead
would receive the Memórias or goods desired in behalf of their
respective Mission. They had ceased coming since 1811.
What was being paid now reached the sum of $42,680.50.
Father Abella as his share would accordingly receive in goods
as much as $1200. In 1827 we have no further details on the
subject. Fr. Abella, doubtless, procured such goods as would
be of use to his poor neophytes. In his Annual Reports for
this and subsequent years, he makes no mention of having
received anything, which is good evidence that nothing came
to Mission San Carlos. Had anything been contributed, it
is certain that the neophytes who had severed their connection
with the beloved Mission, would have remained at San Carlos
under the fatherly care of Fr. Ramon Abella.

---

[16] *The Missions, etc.*, vol. iii, p. 248.

CHAPTER XVI.

Echeandia Demands Description of The Mission Lands.—Fathers Sarría
and Abella Supply the Governor's Demands in Detail.—The Num-
ber of Cattle and Sheep, and Other Livestock.—The Neophyte
Population.—Many Leave The Mission to Serve in White Ranchos.
—Causes of Withdrawal.—Mrs. W. H. McKee Describes Life at The
Mission.

On October 7, 1827, from his headquarters at San Diego,[1]
Governor José M. Echeandia issued a proclamation ordering
every Mission in California to report on the extent and chief
features of the land occupied. Whatever the motive of this
unfriendly official, the information elicited proved in time
most valuable to the historian. It also served to disprove the
assertions of the greedy paisano chiefs and their henchmen
that the missionaries occupied all the lands capable of cultivation from one Mission to another, so that industrious settlers could not acquire land suitable for raising grain or for
the pasturing of live stock. The charge was false, as Governor
José Figueroa wrote to the President of Mexico on October 5,
1833, just a century ago at this writing. "There are extensive
tracts which need settlers," he assured the President. "There
the foreigners may obtain for cultivation the land which they
lack in their own country."[2] Those clamoring for land and
more land could have had these tracts. They could have made
them productive as the missionaries had made thousands of
barren acres productive with the aid of the neophytes. That
involved labor and the sacrifice of ease so dear to the class of
people who coveted the cultivated lands of the industrious
Indian converts. The reader will obtain details on the subject
in our volumes iii, and iv.

We now present a translation of the answer which the
Fathers at San Carlos returned to Echeandia. It reads as
follows:

---

[1] Echeandia would not reside at Monterey.
[2] *The Missions and Missionaries*, vol. iii, p. 500.

Viva Jesus Maria y José!

"Description of the lands which this Mission of San Carlos de Monterey occupies and which was requested by the Superior Government of the Territory in the Proclamation of October 7, 1827.

"This Mission of San Carlos adjoins the territorial Capital of the Province. The distance between them from north to south is scarcely two leagues. Assuming the middle of this distance to be the dividing line there will be one league for this side. To the westward a league reaches the ocean. From east to south are hills and along the road up to the Mission are pinegroves and tule thickets.

"A lesser drawback in this stretch of land is the place called 'El Pescadero;' wherefore they keep there some young milk cows and often some sheep when they have dwindled in numbers owing to various accidental causes. Once, even, they did some planting there, but it was not worth the labor as the soil is not good for planting grain.

"The Cañada of the Mission begins at the beach commonly called Rio del Carmelo. It runs from northeast to west-south-west; it is more or less wide and about two and a half leagues in length up to the so-called Corral de Padillo. In some parts it is as much as fifteen hundred paces wide, in others it is one thousand paces wide and in others it is very narrow. On reaching said corral, it meets the river, which is enclosed between two ridges of craggy rocks. Following the sierra on the north (because the southern ridge is rather inaccessible), one comes upon timbers, laurels, chupines and tularisitos. This is true also of the hills on the other side, which, from the mouth of the Rio Carmelo, to the Cañada of the Tularisitos, may measure about six leagues. It must be noted, however, that in this entire stretch of land there are no more than three *ridges* (cerros): high mountains up to the Corral de Padillo, which is the near valley of the river; the Cerro de las Laurelos, and the Cerro de los Tularisitos. The remainder on either side is precipices, crags covered with brushwood or tules. In a word, the land is useless so far as cattle are concerned. Nevertheless, the horses and mares of the National Service have grazed in years of drought in the locality from the valley christened "La Segunda" even up to the one called "Palo Escrito," which the other pasture for the horses of the National Service is termed.

"Immediately in front of the Mission building one can see that the land contains fields, flocks, the river, hills, and plains from San Francisco to San Clemente; and it is the usual place for the tamed horses. There are no neighboring ranchos in all the places which have been named; there is nothing save the high sierras some of which stop at the ocean, others at Arroyo Seco, others at Sanjones, others at Buena Vista, and at Toro; but the topography is one made by nature, and the thickets and ravines do not inconvenience us.

"The Mission keeps a flock of sheep, 2200 head, in the lands which have been described; other sheep, 3300 head more or less, have been brought from Salinas in time of scarcity of pasturage; this might have been done every year; if not, it is because the nation has a small cattle herd in the National Rancho. In those years they have allowed, for the summer seasons, the flocks to go to graze in the National Ranch and that of Don Joaquin de las Flores which are in front of the Pass of the Carretas, as it is termed.

"In the above-mentioned places of the river valley there are also 450 head of mares, old and young, 200 head of a tamed cattle herd, 40 yoke of oxen, 200 horses good and bad, and about 16 or 20 mules; and as we are adjoining the Presidio, in the summer, on account of water in the river some herds and horses come of themselves and are almost always there.

"In consideration of the dryness of the region, the government has been requested to give permission to move the ranch of the larger flock to a place called the Rancho de San Bernardino, also known throughout the territory as Los Sanjones; this is the native place of the greater part of the neophytes living at this Mission and it is recognized as theirs. This was in the year 1801, and in the language of the Indians of this Mission is called Ensen. The width of this ranch from hill to hill would be about two leagues, in length two leagues and a half; for neighboring places there are: Soledad Mission, the ranch of Don Mariano Estrada from Buena Vista, the ranch of the nation, which is in the hills, and a sheep ranch of Soledad Mission. For the same reasons an agreement has been reached with the government to put a ranch of lambs, not yet a year old, at the place named Las Salinas. This is the native place of many of the Indians now living at this Mission. This was in the year 1798. This ranch would be about one league and a half in length from and including the place commonly known as El Tucho up to the ocean. In width the land that would be of any use, would be about three quarters of a league. The soil is very sandy. The Monterey River separates it from the national domain and from the ranch of Don Joaquin de la Torre, from the ocean and the reed thickets. Consequently, a flock of sheep of 3300 head cannot possibly be kept there throughout the year without driving them to the other side, or taking them to the valley of the Tularisitos, as has been done in various years; moreover, the flock of the Sanjones has of necessity grazed at Los Tularisitos.

"The Mission has 1800 head of cattle, more or less, in the ranch of Los Sanjones; in that of Las Salinas 3300 head of sheep. The principal watering places for these flocks are: the Rio Monterey, Rio Carmelo, the lake of the Tularisitos, the San Franciscito Springs, and in some spots, some swamps; but these are few and of small consideration.

"There is no land irrigated; nor can it be; for the San Franciscito Springs merely form a brook. The place itself is not suitable for summer planting, because sufficient heat is lacking during the day. Each night of the year, be it San Juan, Santiago, etc., there is hoar-frost. Consequently, the corn and beans freeze. The reason is obvious; the altitude of the place is very high, and the mist is entirely in the valley of the Rio Carmelo and that of San José; the wind passes through and above the mist and lessens the night fog, and as early as seven o'clock in the morning the corn has been dried up. This has been our experience in various years. Water cannot be led from the Rio Carmelo and Rio Monterey, for the soil is not suitable, their beds are narrow and the currents not swift enough for proper leading of water.

"Useful timber is at hand. There are red-woods, or larch-trees, pines and some oaks; all the rest is serviceable for fuel; but there is an abundance of that, for which thanks be to God! The mark or brand of this Mission of Monterey will be sent also, but under separate cover. January 22, 1828.—"

Fr. Vicente de Sarría—Fr. Ramon Abella.[3]

We have once more to take up the narrative of the inner life and activities of Mission San Carlos. We may liken it with a death scene. Good Fr. Ramon Abella's heart must have ached at sight of the havoc wrought amid his decreasing flock. Yef he could do nothing to arrest the fast approaching doom. By the end of the year 1827 he with Fr. Sarría signed the usual *Informe Anual*. They could only report 153 male and 122 female Indians living at San Carlos. The noble Ex-Prefecto, still under nominal arrest, once more signed with Fr. Abella on December 31, 1828. The population consisted of 134 male neophytes and 100 Indian women and girls. Thereafter Fr. Abella managed alone for both the Indians at the Mission and for the white congregation at Monterey.

The year 1829 remained almost steady with 134 male and 99 female Indians.

No building activities or acquisitions were reported in 1829 and 1831. At the close of the year, 1832, Fr. Abella, as did the missionaries at all California Missions, signed the last Annual Report for his Mission. We can imagine with what emotions he penned the following lines along with the report on the spiritual and material state of the Mission in 1832: "The neophytes have decreased in the years 1831 and 1832 by as many as forty persons, old and young. It is not that they died, but because they have left, because they obtain no help, aid or advantage. I have tired myself representing the matter to the government. They always gave me words of

---

[3] This cattle brand appears to be lost.

"THE DEATH SCENE" OF MISSION SAN CARLOS.

hope, but nothing came of it. Finally, those that wanted to leave I allowed to do what they wished. I had no means to attract them. More than seventy individuals have thus gone away; those who had the license of the government, and some without it."[4]

Fr. Ramon Abella

On July 12, 1830, Mariano Soberanes listed the population of Monterey and adjacent Ranches as follows for 1829:

Population of Monterey...............502 souls.
"   of the Ranchos adjacent.... 365 souls.
                                     ———
                                      867

The Ranchos mentioned here are: *Buenavista, Sausal, Alisal, Salinas, Tucho, Pilarcitos, Moro Cojo, San Cajetan, Pájaro, Escarpin, Navidad.*

Governor Echeandia, one year after his arrival in California, that is to say on July 25, 1826, from his headquarters at San Diego, issued a Proclamation, without warrant from the Supreme Government in Mexico, which emancipated from Mission tutelage all such neophytes as might be found qualified to become Mexican citizens. This entitled the neophyte and his family to go withersoever he pleased after having received a written permit from the missionary.[5]

"The natural result of movements in behalf of the Indians," says Hittéll, "was to make them restive and more or less disorderly."[6] "The neophytes," Beechey remarks,[7] "soon fell into excesses, gambled away their property and were compelled to beg or steal."

Fr. Abella failed to reveal the cause of the withdrawal of

⁴ Report of Fr. Abella, at the close of year, 1832.
⁵ *The Missions, etc.*, vol. iii, p. 240.
⁶ Hittéll, *California*, vol. ii, p. 92.
⁷ Beechey, *"Voyage,"* vol. ii, p. 320.

so many neophytes. For this we must look to Governor Echeandia, who, on July 25, 1826, issued a decree emancipating from Mission tutelage all such Indians within the military districts of San Diego, Santa Barbara and Monterey as might be found qualified to become Mexican citizens. In virtue of this decree the neophyte who wished to leave the Mission might apply to the commander of the presidio of his jurisdiction. If the applicant had been a Christian from childhood, or for fifteen years, was married, or at least not a minor, and had some means of gaining a livelihood, and if the respective missionary's report was favorable, the commander was to issue a written permit through the missionary. This entitled the neophyte and his family to go whithersoever he pleased, and his name was then erased from the Mission *padron* or list. The provisions of this decree were in 1828 extended to the military district of San Francisco, exclusive of San Rafael and San Francisco Solano.

With regard to the neophytes who remained at the Missions, the same decree restricted punishments to mere correction, such as is allowed to fathers of families in the case of their children. Unmarried male Indians under age were to receive no more than fifteen blows in a week, and faults requiring severer penalties were to be referred to military officials.

Mrs. M. Ord, a daughter of José de la Guerra, in her *"Ocurrencias,"* 52-54, according to Bancroft, vol. iii, page 104, relates that the ideas instilled into the minds of the neophytes by the *gefe politico* (Governor Echeandia) made a great change in them. They were not as contented nor as obedient as before. For further details see *The Missions and Missionaries*, vol. iii, page 239-241.

We close this chapter with some notes regarding the inner life of Mission San Carlos in charge of Father Ramon Abella. Mrs. W. H. McKee, daughter of Estevan Munras, a well-known Spaniard of Monterey, who was well acquainted with Fr. Abella, communicated this important information to us in April, 1907, while we occasionally assisted at the parish church of Monterey. The lady, though quite old, had a bright mind and a good memory, which render her description entirely reliable.

"Padre Abella," said Mrs. McKee, "on Sundays used to come to Monterey on horseback with a little Indian boy from the Mission to celebrate holy Mass. The Indians from the Mission, bringing their rations along, also came to do the singing at High Mass. They used a triangle to measure the time, as there was no organ. They had good voices. There was no house for the priest near the church at Monterey, wherefore Father Abella and his attendant would take meals at our house (house of her father, Mr. Munras). At times he would stop over night there for special services in the evening. The Indians would return to the Mission after their noon meal. There were in those days only big tenement quarters for the officers, men, and others in the town or presidio.

"Father Abella would have his sleeve pocket full of apples for the children.

"The monjerio at the Mission was in charge of trusted Indian women. No little girls were kept there, but only from the age when there was danger, fourteen years old or more. This monjerio was kept like an orphanage or academy. The girls were not permitted out alone all day. Some were hired out in single families for a time. The Indian alcalde had charge of all. He did the whipping of the boys. The girls slept on mats or hides.

"La Pozolera was the big kettle or iron pot in which the food was cooked. The Pozolero was the cook.

"If the Indian wanted a wife, he would go to the priest. The priest went with him to the monjerio. The Indian would point out the girl he desired. If she was willing, the priest regulated the rest.

"There were no women in chains. The young men had more liberty. The Indian men were hired out as cooks. They received pay for which they purchased clothing.

"As pagans the Indians were brutes. The priest labored hard to remodel them and civilize them. About twenty

Tulareños in breech cloth would every year come to help Mr. Munras, my father, to fish.

"There was no drunkenness before secularization among the Indians in charge of the Mission Fathers; but after that there was much drunkenness, because the Indians were abandoned. They would be employed at chores, etc., and then they would get drunk.

"In the early Mission times the Indian men would let their hair grow to the waist. They cultivated it, plumed it, and were proud of it.

"Figueroa had a married brother in Los Angeles. He himself had a wife in Mexico. He looked like an Indian, which he was pretty much. He was very civil and had nothing to say against the Fathers."

Mrs. McKee's description shows that Fr. Abella to the last conducted the affairs of Mission San Carlos in conformity with the Regulations and in keeping with the fatherly customs of all the missionaries.

CHAPTER XVII.

Echeandia had now rendered himself obnoxious to the Supreme Government. Some of his acts embarrassed President Atanasio Bustamente, who did not belong to the infidel administration that sent Echeandia to California. On March 8, 1830, Bustamente appointed Colonel Manuel Victoria governor of Upper California.

From Loreto, Lower California, he wrote Echeandia that he desired a meeting at San Diego, Echeandia's headquarters. Arriving in December or possibly early in November, Victoria was much disappointed at not finding Echeandia there. He therefore despatched a courier to the territorial capital, with the information that the incumbent (Echeandia) should transfer his office at Santa Barbara. On reaching Santa Barbara, instead of Echeandia, to his amazement, a proclamation arrived which declared all the Missions of California "secularized." It had been issued at Monterey on January 6, 1831, long after the notification from the Supreme Government in Mexico to turn the office of governor over to his successor, who was indeed already in the territory!

"Echeandia's act," says Bancroft, "was wholly illegal, uncalled for, and unwise. It was simply a trick, and an absurd one."[1] Thus it is clear that Echeandia with Padrés and a clique of young Californians had determined to carry out the confiscation[2] of the Missions against the wishes of the Indians,

---

[1] Bancroft, *California*, vol. iii, pp. 184-185.
[2] Bancroft, *California*, vol. iii, p. 303.

without the consent of the Federal Government, and despite
the presence of the newly-appointed governor, and therefore
"it was a most absurd and aimless scheme" as Bancroft
affirms.

Convinced that Echeandia would not surrender the office
at Santa Barbara, the new governor went to Monterey, after
endeavoring to prevent the publication of the audacious proclamation in the south, and on January 19th, reporting the
situation to the Supreme Government in Mexico. There on
January 31, 1831, he took the oath and assumed control of the
government.

Victoria's first administrative act was a proclamation,
published on February 1, 1831, in which he declared that he
suspended the execution of Echeandia's decree of "secularization" because it was not in accordance with the will of the
Supreme Government.[3]

"As soon as Victoria received the command from Echeandia,"
writes Alfred Robinson an eye-witness, "his first step was to
counteract the ruinous effects of the imprudence of his pre-
decessor, and to restore the Missions to their former state."[4]

The new governor honestly strove to promote the welfare
of the territory, and he desired to be guided in his efforts by
the Supreme Government, and therefore kept the President
of Mexico informed of every step he took. "All Victoria's
official papers read well. He handled the pen with ability,"
says Hittéll.[5] "All this officer's communications were brief
and to the point, showing the writer to be more of a soldier
than a politician, and lacking of the usual Mexican bombast,"
as Bancroft has it.[6]

Governor Victoria investigated the charges against the
missionaries. The result was that he, on February 7, 1831, informed the Supreme Government that he had seen Fr. Vicente
de Sarría; that he had received from him an exposition of the

---

[3] *The Missions and Missionaries*, vol. iii, p. 354.
[4] Robinson, *Life in California*, p. 108.
[5] Hittéll, *California*, vol. ii, p. 134.
[6] Bancroft, *California*, vol. iii, p. 185.

prelate's acts and the reason for his conduct, and that he considered the Father entirely exonorated. Fr. Sarría had grown old and was a man of great intelligence, honesty, culture and incapable of sedition. It was not he nor the missionaries who had caused trouble, but Padrés and his evil-minded confederates, etc.[7]—The missionaries might well rest satisfied with this splendid vindication, which for all that is in strict accordance with the facts.

The rage of J. M. Padrés and his *paisano* confederates at finding themselves baffled in their designs on the Mission temporalities may be imagined. Echeandia, instead of leaving the territory, on the ground that he was still military commander subject to the civil governor, had remained at San Diego. He declared that the devil had prompted Victoria to prevent the publication of the decree of secularization in the south, and afterwards to nullify it in the north. What added fuel to the hatred which the Padrés conspirators had enkindled among the *paisanos* against the governor was Victoria's strict ideas of discipline.[8]

Bancroft writes concerning the new governor: "Victoria was personally brave, honest, energetic, straightforward, and devoted to what he deemed the best interest of the territory; but the trick that was attempted by Padrés and Echeandia and formidable opposition, forced him to a more arbitrary(?) policy than he would otehwise have shown. . . .The Californians (young paisanos rather) have weakened their unfounded and exaggerated attacks on Victoria's personal character. The foreign residents were silent. David Spence

---

[7] The Carrillos, Osios, Vallejos, Picos, Alvarados, Bandinis, named by Bancroft, vol. iii, pp. 184-185. They called themselves *Californians* with an air of superiority. They were young upstarts, who came to the surface when the Mexican clique issued the decree of expulsion of Spaniards. They had tasted of the swill of Voltaire and Rousseau, and on that ground they imagined themselves filled with superior wisdom. They were later called paisanos, and by that term we quote them as they have nothing else to recommend them.

[8] *The Missions and Missionaries*, vol. iii, p. 358. Bancroft, vol. iii, pp. 189-190.

merely says that Victoria was energetic and made every one respect order and law, which did not please a certain class; but I suspect that their views were more favorable to the governor than they cared to admit generally to the strong element opposing him."[9]

"Interested parties," says Fr. Narciso Durán, "among whom were some members of the territorial assembly, sure of their prey, were disappointed and disappointment turned into hatred for the equitable Victoria. Never had they forgiven this just governor for having rescued the booty already within their grasp. They sought to force him to convene the assembly, in order that with a semblance of legality they might accomplish their designs, ungrateful for the sacrifices of the poor Indians; but Victoria never consented. In November they proclaimed a plan of attack."[10]

Here in a nutshell, as it were, the Fr. Presidente of the Missions exposes the true inwardness of the young paisano chiefs to Governor Victoria. The Mission temporalities were the real bone of contention. The Padrés and Pico clique had stood so near the coveted prize that it exasperated them beyond bounds to see the governor manfully placing himself in the way. Hence it was that on one November night at San Diego, Pio Pico, his brother-in-law, José Ant. Carrillo, and Juan Bandini, resolved on rebellion. At their request the unprincipled Echeandia put himself at the head. The soldiers of the presidio joined readily, but the officers yielded reluctantly. The three arch-plotters on November 29, 1831, drew up a Pronunciamento to the Mexican citizens. It was signed by Pio Pico, Juan Bandini, and José Ant. Carrillo. On December 1st, a supplement was added to justify the treacherous conduct of the San Diego troops, and José Echeandia, Captain Pablo de la Portilla, and Santiago Argüello; it was signed by

[9] *The Missions, etc.*, vol. iii, pp. 359-360; Bancroft, vol. iii, pp. 198-200; 212. The reader is recommended to consult our larger volume for details. In the local histories we quote only what concerns the respective mission.

[10] Fr. Durán, *Epilogue* to his *Notas*, December 31, 1831. See *The Missions, etc.*, vol. iii, p. 361.

Carrillo, José Ramirez, Ignacio del Valle, José Rocha, Andres Cervantes and the three principals.[11]

"The reader who may have the patience to examine this state paper," Bancroft contemptuously remarks, "will find in it a good many words. It was apparently the production of Bandini."[12] As it is mostly bombast, worthy of the overgrown boys who concocted it, we shall touch but two points which sufficiently reveal the animus.

Meanwhile Governor Victoria had been warned that a revolt was brewing against him in the south. He therefore set out from Monterey in company of Ensign Rodrigo del Pliego and only ten or twenty men. At Santa Barbara, José de la Guerra and Captain Romualdo Pacheco persuaded the fearless Victoria to increase his force. Pacheco and a dozen men were at last permitted to join him, so that his entire command consisted of only thirty men. Victoria here committed a grave error in that, knowing the character of the conspirators, he expected no fight. He had not heard of the treachery of the Comandante Pablo de Portilla of San Diego on whose aid he had counted. Portilla with one hundred and fifty men left Los Angeles on December 5th, and met the governor's little troop outside the town. Not heeding the overwhelming numbers, Victoria, followed by the faithful Pacheco and his men, rushed upon the revolters. In the encounter Pacheco was killed, and the governor received several dangerous wounds which disabled him. On the side of the rebels José M. Avila was killed and a few men were wounded. Thereupon the faithless Portilla and his valiant men ran away. Pico, Echeandia, and Bandini took no part in the struggle. Victoria's men bore the wounded governor to Mission San Gabriel. Had it not been for his wounds, Bancroft remarks, the governor would have retaken Los Angeles without difficulty, and it was by no means unlikely that he would have crushed the rebellion altogether. As it was, Victoria lay at San Gabriel in

---

[11] *The Missions, etc.*, vol. iii, pp. 360-361; Bancroft, vol. iii, pp. 200-204; Hittéll, vol. ii, p. 139.

[12] Bancroft, vol. iii, pp. 203-204.

danger of death attended by Surgeon Joseph Chapman, whilst with two or three exceptions his men deserted him. There was no possibility of further resistance. When out of danger Victoria sent for Echeandia, who under Mexico held the title of military commander, and after an interview with him on December 9, 1831, resigned his command. About December 20th, sufficiently restored to make the trip, he departed for Mission San Luis Rey, and on January 17, 1832, he sailed for Mexico in the American ship *Pocahontas*.[13]

Echeandia, on December 9, 1831, convoked the legislative assembly. The members Pio Pico, Mariano Vallejo, Antonio Osio, and Santiago Argüello met at Los Angeles on January 10, 1832, and were next day joined by José J. Ortega and Tomás Yorba. J. B. Alvarado acted as secretary.

Pio Pico, the senior member according to the law of May 6, 1822, was elected temporary *gefe-politico* or civil governor of California. The military command was left with Echeandia. For about twenty days the arch-plotter, Pio Pico, was recognized by four members of the legislature, but after February 16th, Pico laid no claims to the office. Captain Agustin V. Zamorano of Monterey, as ranking officer, pretended to represent the Supreme Government in California. To avoid blood-shed, Echeandia was allowed to rule from San Gabriel southward and Zamorano was recognized in the north until a new governor should be appointed in Mexico and arrive in California.[14]

On May 9, 1832, the Mexican Government appointed General José Figueroa governor of California. He sailed from Acapulco to San Blas, in order to take on board ten native Mexican Franciscans. These were sent by the Missionary College of Guadalupe, Zacatecas, at the request of the Mexican Government, in order to take charge of the Indian Missions in northern California, ceded to them by the Missionaries of San Fernando College in the City of Mexico, who were mostly Spaniards, and named Fernandinos to distinguish them from the newcomers who were styled Zacatecanos.

[13] *The Missions and Missionaries*, vol. iii, pp. 361-365.
[14] *The Missions and Missionaries*, vol. iii, pp. 365-367.

These missionaries, all priests and native Mexicans, were Francisco Garcia Diego y Moreno, the Commissary or Superior, Rafael Moreno, Bernardino Perez, José Maria Gutierrez, J. M. Mercado, José Maria Gonzalez Rubio, Lorenzo Quijas, Antonio Reál and José Maria Reál.[15]

"These friars," says Alexander Forbes,[16] "were for some time detained at Tepic, a town near San Blas, waiting for a vessel, where I had an opportunity of seeing them. They were fresh from a convent at Zacatecas (Guadalupe) where the rules were very strict. They all wore a habit of coarsest grey[17] woolen cloth, their crown shaven and sandals on their feet. . . .It was impossible not to feel respect for their character and a degree of veneration mixed with pity on thinking on their destiny and observing their very pious, humble and meek demeanor."

After many difficulties[18] Figueroa with the missionaries at last landed at Monterey on Tuesday, January 15, 1833. The Zacatecans were heartily welcomed at Mission San Carlos by Fr. Ramon Abella, and on the following Sunday, January 20th, by direction of the new governor, a solemn High Mass was offered up in thanksgiving for the safe arrival.

On January 18th, Figueroa notified Echeandia that he had come as governor and comandante-general. This left the arch-plotter without an occupation and without any excuse for tarrying in California.[19]

On the 19th Figueroa officially announced his appointment to the office of governor and military-inspector to Fr. Presidente Durán.

The Zacatecanos were assigned to the northern Missions from San Carlos to San Francisco Solano at Sonoma. Their

---

[15] *The Missions, etc.*, vol. iii, p. 442.

[16] Alexander Forbes, *California*, pp. 138-139.

[17] This color prevailed over nearly all the Spanish-speaking countries. Some in Mexico and in Peru wore a bluish habit, who were therefore known as Los Frailes Azules. The regulation color everywhere now is brown, because Pope Leo xiii directed all Franciscans to wear that color. See p. 262.

[18] See *The Missions, etc.*, vol. iii, sec. ii, chap. ix.

[19] *The Missions, etc.*, vol. iii, pp. 445-447.

THE LANDING OF THE ZACATECAN FRANCISCANS

Fr. Presidente, Fr. Rafael Moreno, was given charge of Mission San Carlos by their Commissary Prefect, Fr. Francisco Garcia Diego. There was not much to do at the Mission, but the incumbent had also to care for the spiritual affairs of the presidio of Monterey. It was not an agreeable position as may be imagined. Fr. Ramon Abella, on the other hand, was transferred to Mission San Luis Obispo.

At San Carlos the situation was more deplorable than at other Missions. It had exhausted its resources so that scarcely anything in the nature of supplies could be furnished to the military. Writing to Governor Figueroa on June 14, 1833, Fr. Moreno complains as follows: "Your Honor knows how very few Indians[20] this Mission contains, and half of these are invalids by age or infirmity. Moreover, some have run away and others, the majority, will not work even if they are chastized."[21]

---

[20] There were at the end of 1832 only 185 Indians, men, women, and children, at Mission San Carlos.

[21] Father Moreno to Figueroa. *Archbishop's Archives*, no. 2138. By consulting the Tables the reader will learn what Fr. Moreno and later Fathers succeeded in accomplishing. *The Missions, etc.*, vol. iii, pp. 460-461.

CHAPTER XVIII.

Figueroa's Secularization Decree.—Inventory of Mission San Carlos.—
Governor Figueroa's Last Illness, Death, and Burial.—The Fulsome
Laudation of the Assembly and of the Town Council.—Funeral,
Procession and Burial at Santa Barbara.—Body Discovered August
24, 1911.—High School at Monterey.—First Book Printed at Monte-
rey.

On August 9, 1834, yielding to the threats of the anti-
Mission clique[1] and against his convictions, as expressed the
year before,[2] Governor Figueroa by means of a printed *Bando*
or Proclamation promulgated the *Reglamento Provisional* as
the assembly's secularization decree was called. Supplemen-
tary regulations followed on November 4, 1834.

"Figueroa," writes Bancroft, "in 1834 was in a position
similar to that of Echeandia in 1831. Each desired to advance
the scheme of secularization, each expected the arrival of a
successor, each had the support of the Diputacion (Assembly).
*Both knew perfectly well that they had strictly no legal right to
act in the matter;* yet both chose to assume the responsibility
of such action. Figueroa's act, if somewhat less arbitrary and
uncalled for than that of Echeandia, was none the less a
trick."[3]

Inventories were accordingly drawn up of all movable and
immovable property of the Missions by so-called commissioners. The inventory of Mission San Carlos Borromeo, or
Carmelo was drawn up by commissioner José Joaquin Gomez,
assisted as witness by the Rev. Fr. José Reál, a Zacatecan,
who had arrived in the preceding year and was now in charge.
The Inventorio covers thirty-nine pages and was dated December 10, 1834. The valuation of the Mission, including the live

---

[1] See for details *The Missions and Missionaries*, vol. iv, pp. 7; 109.

[2] *The Missions and Missionaries*, vol. iii, pp. 496-501.

[3] *The Missions, etc.*, vol. iii, pp. 522-523. Figueroa and Echeandia knew
perfectly well that they had strictly no legal right to act in the matter.
That is the one item upon which Figueroa agreed with Echeandia. Figueroa was intimidated however. The rest is Bancroft's opinion.

stock, was stated as $46,922, 7 reales, 10 granos. In this amount the church building is appraised at $10,000; the church's sacred vessels, vestments, etc., and the library were valued at $10,217, 7 reales and 4 granos.[4]

Old San Carlos Mission was now managed by seculars. Details are lacking entirely save that the first Administrator was José Joaquin Gomez. He turned over the charge to José Antonio Roméro.

Less than a year after the promulgation of the illegal secularization decree, poor Governor Figueroa, who had been ailing a long time, took to his bed on September 6, 1835. On September 22nd he resigned the office of governor and in accordance with the National Law of May 6, 1822, directed that the Senior member at the assembly sessions, José Castro, should succeed him as civil governor. At the same time he summoned Lieutenant-Colonel Nicolas Gutierrez, the ranking officer in California, to the capital (Monterey) to assume the position of comandante-general and military commander.

On September 27th Figueroa made his last will. It contained the following instructions: "In the first place I commend my soul to God, its Creator and Redeemer, and the body to the earth as the common mother of all mortals. Nevertheless, I wish my body to be deposited, if it shall be possible, in the church of Santa Barbara Mission, and I solicit its better conservation through the care of the San Fernandino Religious, whom it may please to do me this charity and also to preserve my ashes if the Supreme Government, to which an account shall be sent at the first opportunity, does not direct otherwise."[5]

---

[4] *The Missions, etc.*, vol. iii, p. 534.
[5] *The Missions and Missionaries*, vol. iii, p. 598.

Thus it came to pass that the man who had deprived the penniless and unselfish missionaries of the homes they had reared for themselves with the aid of their neophytes, in his last moments begged his victims to grant his body the narrow resting-place at Santa Barbara Mission among the departed priests in token of forgiveness. It looks very much like retribution. At all events Figueroa's dying request was granted. After all, Figueroa had acquiesced in the wicked confiscation plan through fear of having to suffer the fate of the noble Governor Victoria.

When he saw his end approaching, the dying governor called for the Last Sacraments of the Catholic Church, the consolations of the believing soul the world over when about to meet its Creator and Judge. He wished that the Very Rev. Father Commissary Prefect, Fr. Francisco Garcia Diego, would come from Santa Clara to prepare him for the last journey. Father Francisco Garcia Diego, however, failed to arrive in the time expected, wherefore Father José Reál, the priest in charge of Mission San Carlos and Monterey, at the request of the dying governor, administered all the Sacraments, except the Viaticum or last Holy Communion. The Viaticum was not administered because Figueroa was suffering from a spell of vomiting. Fr. Garcia Diego at last arrived just as the sufferer was about to breathe his last between four and five o'clock in the afternoon of September 29, 1835.

The funeral services were held on October 2, 1835, with all the pomp and solemnity due the dignity of Don José Figueroa, Brigadier-General and Governor of the Territory. Five squads of soldiers marched ahead, then the remains were deposited temporarily in the vacant room fronting the sacristy on the Gospel side.[6] It was the intention of the officials to transfer the remains of the deceased governor to Mexico when the orders to that effect should arrive. Meanwhile, October 10th, the Territorial Assembly met at Monterey. On the 13th the resolutions were adopted in keeping with the pompous style customary among the Mexican leaders of those days, but

---

[6] This vacant room has long since disappeared.

altogether too exaggerated to be sincere. They are repeated here to complete the record.

After a long preamble of fulsome praise, Juan B. Alvarado closed as follows: "Let us immortalize his glory and our gratitude and encircle his brow with a crown of *siempre viva!*' Yes, Most Excellent Sirs, listen and please approve of the following proposition or resolutions:

1st. "The portrait of General Don José Figueroa shall be placed in the Hall of the Sessions of this *Excelentisima Diputacion* in proof of the esteem they bear for his distinguished merit.

2nd. "To perpetuate his memory and the gratitude of this Corporation, a durable monument shall be erected, with an appropriate inscription, in one of the most unoccupied sites in the capital (Monterey); and to fulfill which the *Ilustre Ayuntamiento* shall be authorized to have its sole direction and care.

3rd. "Three copies of these proceedings shall be drawn up. One shall be delivered to the executors of our beloved deceased General and Chief, another copy shall be transmitted to the widow and his children; and the third shall be passed to the printer that it may be annexed to the *Manifiesto of said General*, which is now in course of publication."

These resolutions were adopted, whereupon Manuel Jimeno on October 14th offered two others, which read as follows:

1st. "That the three resolutions of Senor Alvarado shall be put into execution immediately.

2nd. "That at the bottom of the portrait of the Señor General Don José Figueroa shall be affixed the title of 'Bienhechor del Territorio de la Alta California.' "

The high-minded town council of Monterey now took the matter in hand and in turn resolved to place upon the monument the following inscription: "The Provincial Diputacion and the Town Council of Monterey, at Public Cost, in Proof of Gratitude, Dedicates This Monument to the Eternal Memory of GENERAL DON JOSÉ FIGUEROA, Military and Political Governor of Alta California, The Father of the

Country, Who Died at This Capital September 29, A. D. 1835, Aged Forty Three Years.[7]

The remains of the deceased governor, in charge of Captain Juan Antonio Muñoz, were at length placed on board the brig *Avon*, which on October 19th set sail for Santa Barbara where it dropped anchor on October 27th. Next day the coffin was taken ashore by Captain Muñoz, and under orders from the military commander of California, Nicolas Gutierrez, received by Comandante Juan M. Ibárra of the Santa Barbara presidio. With all the pomp possible the coffin with the remains was taken to the presidio chapel of the town, and deposited in a room for the night. Next morning, Thursday, October 28th, the funeral procession formed again and wended its way to the Mission where the burial ceremonies took place. Strange enough no interesting details about the last rites or who performed them are on the records of either the presidio or the Mission books.

We relate the circumstances of Governor Figueroa's death and funeral somewhat minutely for the sake of true history. All the writers on the subject, Bancroft included, are at sea on the subject, especially with regard to the burial place. With the documents before us it is possible to remove all doubts once for all.

The body was never taken from the crypt where it had been deposited on the date specified. On August 24, 1911, all the niches in the vault beneath the sanctuary, which had been walled up years before, were opened by a stone-mason. It was found that one of them contained a well-preserved wooden coffin. On removing the lid it was discovered that it held the remains of a military officer of highest rank. The uniform was rich and, though water-soaked, in good condition. The shoulder straps appeared to be of silver. The chapeau lay

---

[7] *The Missions and Missionaries*, vol. iii, pp. 598-601. "Days! Months!! Year!!!" Alfred Robinson exclaims in his *California*, p. 180, "have rolled away and yet naught has been done to perpetuate the memory of this exalted man! the country's loss! This serves to show a want of sincerity in those *who deeply deplored his death*, and the instability of their character."

over the abdomen. The sword lay on the left side of the person but had rusted away to within about eight inches of the hilt. On the right side of the person lay a gold-headed cane. The body itself had decayed as the uniform lay flat and shriveled. The skull was still covered with a strong growth of long dark hair. It was very small and corresponded with the size of the corpse which measured not more than five feet, or at most about five feet two inches.

With several other members of the community, besides two laborers, the author viewed the contents of the coffin so that there might be no doubts with regard to the whereabouts of Governor Figueroa's remains and his last resting-place. A record was drawn up of the contents of the several niches and then they were walled up by the two stone-masons mentioned before.[8]

A notable event happened during the administration of the late Governor Figueroa at Monterey. On December 10, 1833, William Edward P. Hartnell published an announcement to the effect that he and the Rev. Patrick Short would with the favor of God open a school at the beginning of the year 1834. He wished to ascertain how many children could be expected. They would be educated in the following branches: Reading, Writing, Spanish, Grammar, French, English, German and Latin Grammars, Book-Keeping, Arithmetic, Mathematics and Philosophy. Particular care would also be taken to instruct the young in the Christian Doctrine, and a watch would be insured over their morals and manners. The conditions would be that each pupil for his maintenance, washing of clothes and education pay annually $200.00, half of which was to be paid in advance. Each pupil was to bring along at least for himself "four changes of underwear and two suits (exterior), his own bedding, a pair of towels, napkins and one cubierto (set of table service?). He was also to have books, paper, pens, etc., or the price for them."[9]

[8] *The Missions and Missionaries*, vol. iii, p. 601.

[9] Archives of Clerk's Office, San José. Vol. iv, pp. 25-26. Bancroft Collection.

Figueroa himself while governor of the Territory wrote and published various works on questions of the day. The most complete was his *Manifiesto* A La Republica Mejicana, Que hace el General de Brigada JOSÉ FIGUEROA, Comandante General Y Gefe Politico de la ALTA CALIFORNIA, Sobre su conducta y la de los Senores D. José Maria de Hijar y D. José Maria Padrés, como Directores de Colonization en 1834 y 1835.—Imprenta Del. C. Agustin V. Zamorano.

It was the first book of any value in size and contents printed in California. It is exceedingly scarce. The text printed on common paper and with ordinary letters measures 3 by 4½ inches on 184 pages besides the title page. The Santa Barbara Mission Archives contains a copy in good condition.

When the Mexican Government learned that Governor Figueroa had died, Mariano Chico, congressman from Guanajuato was appointed in April, 1835, to succeed him. Chico proved such an erratic official and had made himself so obnoxious to all classes in California, that he reluctantly left the country before the lapse of four months. During that period he interested himself in behalf of Mission San Carlos to the extent of addressing a letter on May 14, 1836, to the administrator of the Mission, José Antonio Romero, in these laconic words: "I have written to the missionary of San Carlos (Fr. José Reál) that the establishment is going to ruin; that you are removed; and that he will take charge of the property."[10]

Lieutenant-Colonel Nicolas Gutierrez, as ranking officer, succeeded the luckless Chico. He reached Monterey on September 6, 1836. On November 11, 1836, he found himself sailing out of the harbor of Monterey for Mexico. The paisano clique had become experts in the occupation of expelling undesirable governors. In this case, however, the conspirators performed a praiseworthy deed; for Gutierrez's very name was despised.[11] As before, the Mexican Government dared not attempt to punish the rebels.

[10] See *The Missions, etc.*, vol. iv, chap. ii, and vi.
[11] *The Missions, etc.*, vol. iv, pp. 51-59.

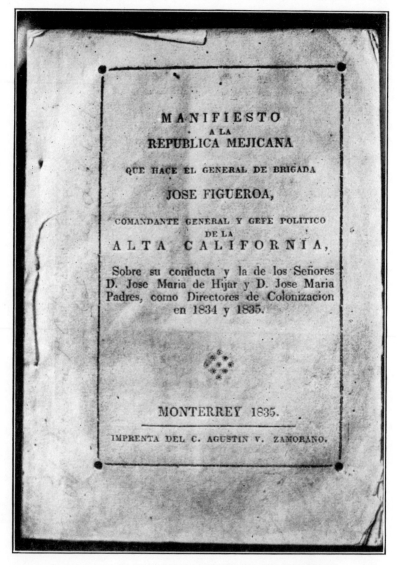

TITLE PAGE OF GOVERNOR FIGUEROA'S "MANIFIESTO."

On December 7, 1836, Juan Bautista Alvarado, the first native Californian, was declared governor by the assembly on December 20, 1836. The Government could do nothing to prevent it. We find nothing worthwhile to report in favor of Alvarado in connection with Mission San Carlos, though he ruled for six years till Mexico could make its power felt.

CHAPTER XIX.

Manuel Micheltorena Appointed Governor of California.—Arrival at San Diego Harbor.—His Wretched Troops.—Received with Enthusiasm at Los Angeles.—Issues Decree Restoring the Missions to the Franciscans.—Text of the Decree.—Micheltorena's Manly Religious Convictions.—Bancroft's View of the Decree.—Mission San Carlos.—The First Bishop to be Enthusiastically Received at Monterey.—Micheltorena Invites Bishop Garcia Diego.—The Bishop's Beautiful Reply.—Received at Monterey.—Confirms.

The Mexican Government, in the person of General Antonio Lopez de Santa Anna, the President, at last terminated the disgraceful reign of plunder engineered by Juan Bautista Alvarado. A good and capable man for the office of governor of California was found in the person of Brigadier-General José Manuel Micheltorena. He received the appointment on January 22, 1842. The general with about three hundred men, besides the officers, sailed from Mazatlán in four ships during the month of July, 1842. The new governor's ship cast her anchor in the harbor of San Diego on August 25th. The others arrived within ten days later.[1]

"I saw them land," writes Alfred Robinson,[2] "and to me they presented a state of wretchedness and misery unequalled. Not one individual among them possessed a jacket or pantaloons; but naked, like savage Indians, they concealed their nudity with dirty, miserable blankets. They appeared like convicts; and, indeed, the greater portion of them had been charged with the crime of either murder or theft. . . I had an opportunity of seeing them all afterwards at the pueblo (Los Angeles) when on their route to Monterey. They mustered three hundred and fifty men, and their general (while at San Diego) had given them a neat uniform of white linen."

Late in September, 1842, Micheltorena set out from San Diego with the whole expedition, and was received with enthusiasm at Los Angeles. The ceremony of taking the oath

[1] *The Missions and Missionaries*, vol. iv, pp. 269-270.
[2] *The Missions, etc.*, vol. iv, p. 270.

by the new governor took place on December 31st, in the presence of the town council, a portion of the legislators, and of the most prominent citizens. Speeches were delivered; salutes were fired; and the city was illuminated for three evenings.[3]

It was while the new governor tarried at Los Angeles that he issued the memorable decree of March 29, 1843, which restored the management of the former Indian Missions, or what was left of them, to the Franciscan missionaries. Micheltorena thereby merely executed the law which a Mexican Congress had passed eight years previously, but which the paisano chiefs headed by Pio Pico and Juan B. Alvarado had disregarded. The decree which is worth while reproducing in this particular volume reads as follows:

"Manuel Micheltorena, Brigadier-General of the Army of the Republic, Adjutant-General of the Staff of the same Army, Governor, Comandante-General and Inspector of Both Californias.

"Inasmuch as one of the complete instructions with which the undersigned general and governor finds himself charged is to examine the situation surrounding all the Missions under his jurisdiction, their prospects and their resources for stability, as well as to regulate them; and inasmuch as the Supreme National Government has transmitted to him all its powers, as is clear from the Supreme Order dated February 11, 1842; therefore, in accord and with the consent of the Very Rev. Fathers José Joaquin Jimeno and José Maria de Jesus Gonzalez Rubio, whom I had appear before this government as Presidentes of the other missionaries, and in the name of and as representatives of the Very Rev. Fr. Presidente and Vicar Forane, Fr. Narciso Durán, being well informed of everything necessary, and considering:

"That the vast and immense stretches of land, formerly the property of the Missions, have been allotted to individuals,

---

[3] *The Missions, etc.*, vol. iv, p. 271.

this having been done at a period when the exigencies of the country required it;[4]

"That these pious establishments, so beneficial to social order as well as to Religion for having converted the savages to Catholicity and brought them to lead an agricultural and civilized life are reduced to the gardens and to the plots on which stand the churches and other structures;

"That the Very Rev. Fathers have no other means of subsistence than what is given them, and that Divine Worship without prospering is barely sustained;

"That owing to their natural indolence, too heavy labor, the scarcity of nourishment and want of clothing, those Indians who have not any particular accommodation, or who are not in the Missions, prefer to return to the mountains and die in the wilderness rather than drag out a life of slavery full of privations and without any social pleasure;[5]

"That this continual emigration of the natives from the service of individuals to the Mission and from the Missions to individual employers, or to the woods, retards agriculture more and frightens away the Gentiles instead of attracting them to the bosom of our holy Religion;

"That in the administration of the Missions there have been committed some notorious frauds and extravagances which every inhabitant of the country laments;

"That, inasmuch as there is no other means to reanimate the skeleton of a giant, such as is the remnant of the ancient Missions, than to return to the practice of the past and uphold it by means of the civil and ecclesiastical powers, having considered and weighed all this well, I have deemed it well to decree the following articles:

1. "The Government of this department (California) will command that to the Very Rev. Fathers, who shall be named for each Mission by the respective prelate, be surrendered the Missions of San Diego, San Luis Rey, San Juan Capistrano, San Gabriel, San Fernando, San Buenaventura, Santa Bar-

---

[4] Micheltorena refrains from angering the paisano chiefs for the present.
[5] A sharp but just arraignment of the administrator period.

bara, Santa Inés, La Purisima, San Antonio, Santa Clara and San José, which shall hereafter be administered by the Very Rev. Fathers as guardians of the Indians in the same manner as they managed them before.

2. "As much as policy regards what has been done until now to be irrevocable, the Missions cannot reclaim any lands that have been thus far ceded; but they may collect the livestock, implements and tools which the Rev. Curators or administrators may have loaned, observing harmoniously time and manner as regards the debtors and holders.

3. "They shall likewise carefully collect the scattered neophytes, excepting, firstly, those legally exempt from tutorship by the Supreme Departmental Government; secondly, those who on the date of this decree are in the service of private individuals, it being understood, however, that if any of either class voluntarily desire and prefer to return to their Mission, they shall be admitted and received after having obtained the consent of their employers and of the Rev. Missionaries.

4. "The Territorial Government, in whose possession the Missions have been till now, in virtue of the most ample powers with which it is invested, and referring to the aforesaid considerations, authorizes the Rev. Missionaries to provide from the Mission products for the indespensable expenses of conversions, food, clothing, and other temporal needs of the Indians; and also to take from the same fund the moderate portion which they need for their own sustenance, for the economical salary of the majordomo, and for the maintenance of Divine Worship, on condition that they shall be obliged upon their honor and conscience to pay to the treasury, the Rev. Fathers having previously received an explicit order in writing signed by the governor, the military commander and inspector, for the sustenance and clothing of the troops and the needs of civil officials, one-eighth part of the total annual produce and revenue of every kind, taking care to present through their prelates an exact and truthful report at the end of each year regarding the number of neophytes, the movable and im-

movable property and of all kinds of fruits or their corresponding value, pertaining to the Mission.

5. "The Departmental Government, taking pride in being religious as well as wholly Californian, and as such interested in the same manner as all and every inhabitant of both Californias in the progress of the holy Catholic Faith, and in the prosperity of the country, offers to do all in its power to aid the Missions, and as Commander-General of the military to guard, defend, and sustain them, in the same way as it protects the rights and guarantees of private individuals, in the possession and conservation of the land which they hold at this date; promising, however, to make no new grants whatever without a report from the respective local authorities and from the Rev. Missionaries, or in case of notorious non-occupation and non-cultivation or necessity.

"Given in the City of Los Angeles, March 26, 1843.— Manuel Micheltorena. Francisco Arce, Provisional Secretary."[6]

What a manly profession of his Catholic Faith by Governor Micheltorena! There is nothing like it in the writings or speeches of the paisano upstarts. There is much in the written and vocal utterances of the paisano chiefs altogether out of

---

[6] *The Missions, etc.*, vol. iv, pp. 272-276.

accord with Catholic Faith and very much in accord with
Mexican-Voltairian swill. Hence, their animosity to the Mission Fathers and their greed for the Indian property!

"Under the regulation just cited," (Micheltorena's) Bancroft observes,[7] "the padres became independent of the administrators, with whom as a rule their relations had not been
friendly. They were enabled to protect from injury and loss
certain property in the shape of buildings and gardens, which
in the natural order of things would revert to the church.
With the small remnant of cattle and implements left from
the general wreck, with the few Indians whom past changes
had left in the communities and with the temporary use of
such poor lands as had not yet been granted to private ownership, the friars might now toil to support themselves. . . . .They
hoped by the change to avoid at least certain personal humili-
ations and annoying complications with local and departmental
authorities. On the other hand, the act was doubtless a wise
one on the part of Micheltorena. So completely had the Missions been stripped, in one way or another of all that was
valuable, that revenues could no longer be depended on."[8]

The new Governor with his wife Doña Josefa at last
reached Monterey by August 13, 1843, after making a stop at
Santa Barbara on July 29th. We know next to nothing about
what may have happened at the Mission of San Carlos, or as
Bancroft declares: "There is extant neither record of secularization or other events, nor statistical information for any part
of the decade. There was but little mission property left in
1834 and none at all except the ruined buildings in 1840."
William Hartnell on January 19, 1839, had been appointed
Inspector of the Missions by Alvarado and his salary was
fixed at $2000.00 to be paid pro rata by all the Missions save
San Carlos, Soledad and San Antonio. Therefore Hartnell
was excused from visiting our poor San Carlos where nothing
was left but ruins.

However, a notable event from a religious point of view

---

[7] *California*, vol. iv, pp. 370.

[8] *California*, vol. iv, pp. 370-371.

deserves to be recorded. It happened the year after the governor's arrival and caused much excitement especially at Monterey, because the governor himself participated. A great reception was planned. The Town Council was convoked by the chairman for May 14, 1844, in order to consider the invitation of the Rev. Fr. José Reál, pastor of both the Ex-Mission and the residents of Monterey, who dwelt at that capital, that all would cooperate with him in receiving the first Bishop of California in a worthy manner. It was resolved to vote the necessary expenses for that purpose. Invitations were sent out to the inhabitants to illuminate their homes for the period of three days after the arrival of the Bishop.[9]

The reception of Bishop Francisco Diego by the governor and citizens at Monterey was hardly less enthusiastic than at Santa Barbara. Bishop Francisco G. Diego arrived on May 26, 1844, just in time to celebrate the feast of Pentecost, and a few days later to add to the solemnities of Corpus Christi Day on June 6th. In the meantime His Lordship on various days administered the Sacrament of Confirmation to as many as two hundred and ninety-four persons at the parish church in the city of Monterey.

On August 27, 1844, Governor Micheltorena seriously addressed Most Rev. Francisco Diego as follows:

Ilmo. Senor Obispo: "I have the honor to transmit the original communication of the Il. Ayuntamiento of this city (Monterey), and also the original letter of the Rev. Fr. Antonio Reál that you might be pleased to take notice of the contents. These venture to remind Your Lordship that for many years the Rev. Fr. José Maria Suárez del Reál performed here the duties of the sacred ministry with truly apostolic zeal, inasmuch as he subsisted and served with affability, promptness, and careful attention in this city and jurisdiction without fixed emoluments. He depended on the piety of the faithful. It was observed that he used in the church for Divine Worship the little he acquired without burdening any one. He was much beloved and respected for his eminent qualities by this

[9] *The Missions*, vol. iv, p. 264.

population of a thousand souls together with 300 military men, who threatened with the probability of war are not able to exist without a priest. Some have already died without the aid of the priest. Some have already died without the aids of Holy Religion. Even this very day three have been mortally wounded in a quarrel and are now begging for the chance of making their confession; but no priest is around.

"The government (Micheltorena) in keeping with its duty makes everything clear to Your Lordship by stating the extraordinary effect of the situation here. We have had to patiently endure some Sundays without hearing holy Mass, as we could not explain to ourselves the motive of Your Lordship (i. e., for leaving us without a priest).

"I await Your Lordship's reply while I ease my conscience with this respectful manifestation, be it what it may please you to dispose concerning what has been said." Micheltorena.[10]

To the Señor Governor and Comandante-General under date of September 6, 1844.

Excellent Sir:

"By Your Excellency's official note of August 27th, I understand that the commendable citizenry of Monterey have stood in need of and actually lack a priest, and, as a necessary consequence, that succor so important in spiritual needs. I was forced to remove Fr. José M. Reál (from San Carlos) to meet greater needs. I placed him, a charitable and hard-working priest, to succor and minister in S. José Guadalupe, Santa Clara, San Francisco, Mission San José (the pastor of which can no longer officiate due to his infirmities) and at times to visit S. Solano. The curacy of these places is certainly difficult on account of the many ranches and the distances which are well known to Your Excellency. Formerly, four missionaries had charge; yet they could hardly perform that duty which is now given to one. In these arrangements I had not forgotten my esteemed people of the Capital. I had, therefore, determined to recommend to Rev. Fr. Presidente, Fr. José Ant. Anzar, the care of the people in Santa

---

10 *Cal. Arch., State Papers, Monterey,* vol. iv, pp. 264-265.

Cruz and the neighboring ranches, and to leave those towns which happen to be without a priest to my concern. I then determined to place Fr. Ant. Reál at Monterey convinced that there, even like his brother, he would bear with the miseries and poor living hoping to find a good welcome in that religious neighborhood, which having made known its needs, would give him an equitable and fitting means of subsistence.

"But I have learned that when he had arrived to fulfill his duties, he found himself without a house in which to live and without the necessary help to subsist. And the Bishop conscious of this fact, what course shall he pursue? What providential course shall he take? Shall I oblige my priests to go and suffer or die from hunger, or expose themselves to begging, ill-becoming their state? Shall I constrain them to. . . . .but enough; Your Excellency knows well that I can neither compel them to such sacrifices nor must they obey rules which are unjust and contrary to natural right."

(Then the Bishop goes on to say that everywhere they ask for *ministros* but that most do not wish to do and offer anything for their subsistence).

"When the support of the clergy and Divine Worship were regulated according to the Mission System, the missionaries had no need to burden the faithful with their support; now that the system is almost non-existant what course shall be employed? How will the obligations of the faithful be met? Ah, Most Excellent Sir, I can think of no other way than that which has been and is in vogue among all peoples, even non-Catholic nations, to wit, that the children of the Church support her priests in such a manner as befits their station; that they look upon the fulfillment of this obligation as an honor for themselves, glorying to be distinguished in it, and placing it above all other obligations.

"The said obligation, for this it is and a most serious one from every angle, is of divine right, which is patent to everyone, and has been sanctioned at all times by the law of nations, as is sufficiently clear to Your Excellency. All nations, all communities, even idolotrous peoples have honored, supported and reverenced their priests. All have erected magnificent places of worship to their divinities, as they conceived them. All have allocated sumptuous outlays and have increased them; they have made united efforts, according to their means, to establish the splendor and glory of their Maker and Benefactor who has given them that which they possess.

"My diocese alone has never complied with this sacred obligation; indeed, the few churches which exist are due to the courage and perseverance of the Religious Founders and to the labor of the unhappy neophytes who now are reduced to extreme misery, dispersed and scattered from the establishments which had been built for them. Hence, let Monterey and all the people of my diocese be undeceived and let them be convinced that if they desire to have religious service; if they long for one to guide them and in whom they may confide and one who may assist them in the hour of death; if they wish one to be at hand to administer the Blessed Sacraments to them and aid them to live as they should, then it is necessary to comply with that obligation which has been imposed by God. It behooves them to make some sacrifices of the goods which the same Lord has bestowed on them. It is obligatory that they revere their priests and support them in a decent manner.

"As a Catholic, by reason of your station, the protection of the Church in California is the duty of Your Excellency. In fulfilling your obligations, Your Excellency must use every possible endeavor to make your subjects comply with their duty and the outcome for Your Excellency interests me and I will recommend it exceedingly to Our Lord Jesus Christ.

"In short I shall take under advisement the matter which has been treated above, perhaps to appoint a priest for that parish of souls; and if he has not wherewith to subsist decently then what shall I do? I will tell him to save himself and leave the Pueblo which does not desire a priest indeed because it does not see to his subsistence. And by acting thus, I will be doing nothing else than to conform myself to the precepts of the Lord and the honorable laws of the Church.

"I ask Your Excellency and intensely entreat you to convoke a general meeting of the district and command these lines to be read. Let Your Excellency tell the people to consider the means which may be less onerous to assure a decent living for the priest who is destined for them. I can impose a tax upon the parishes since that method is according to the practice of all dioceses; but I do not care to do this. This is what I desire and wish: that the Montereyans themselves find a plan and let me know what is more agreeable, to approve it or not to approve it; let them bear in mind that it is to affect this (whole) population; if it is just I will make it apply to both the Californias, because it would be contrary to the stated order of things that uniformity should be wanting in one and the same diocese.

"I have the honor to acknowledge Your Excellency's note, which did not come by special delivery as you stated, and to renew my appreciation and consideration." Dios, etc.[11]

Notwithstanding Governor Micheltorena's kindness and solicitude in religious matters also, the paisano chiefs conspired against him. Briefly, he followed them with an insufficient force down to the vicinity of Mission San Fernando. There, as was the case with Governor Victoria, he was betrayed in that the troops enlisted withdrew and left Micheltorena to the paisano troopers. As he had been wounded and saw the futility of gratifying his enemies save by leaving California, the noble governor offered to resign. The treaty was signed in camp near Mission San Fernando on Saturday, February 22, 1845. The last article permitted "Micheltorena's division to march with all the honors of war, with music, flying colors and three pieces of artillery, the flag to be saluted by Castro's drummer, but the guns and appurtenances to be given up at San Pedro."[12]

---

[11] Libro Borrador, 1844.
[12] *The Missions, etc.*, vol. iv, p. 329.

MOST REV. FRANCISCO GARCIA DIEGO, FIRST BISHOP OF CALIFORNIA.

CHAPTER XX.

Although Governor Micheltorena's personal kindness towards everybody, his ability to govern, his clean moral life,
his marked solicitude for the religious well-being of the inhabitants, especially of the Indian neophytes, could not be
denied, the paisano clique, headed by Pio Pico, Alvarado and
other unscrupulous upstarts, would not forgive him that he,
at the request of the Federal Government, had returned the
management of the Indian Missions to the unselfish Franciscan Fathers. They accordingly resolved to drive the governor out of the territory on the ground that the presence of the
battalion commonly nicknamed *Cholos* was sufficient reason
for their animosity to his continuance in office and for deliver-
ing the country from the *Cholos*.

"The reader is aware," says Bancroft however, "that this
battalion was composed chiefly of criminals, a large part of
them having been taken from jails in Mexico and Jalisco. Yet
it must be admitted that the conduct of the *Cholos* was wonderfully good when compared with what might be expected
from their antecedents, from the outrages committed by men
of similar class, in different parts of Mexico, from their desti-
tution, and from the bitterly prejudiced through which nearly
all the testimony extant against them has come down to us. . .
The statement of Alvarado and other Californians representing the stay of the *Cholos* at Monterey as causing a reign of
terror in which vice, robbery, outrage and murder were ram-

pant, *must be regarded as the exaggerations of men in search
of justification for later revolt.*[1]

We may, in explanation, add the remark that the historical
documents extant contain no complaints from missionaries
against the troops that came from Mexico with the governor;
but we do find that the missionaries complained bitterly about
the conduct of the "soldiers" under the rule of the paisano
chiefs.[2]

Eventually Juan B. Alvarado and José Castro, at San Juan
Bautista, the latter's home town, began to collect their par-
tisans and marched south to the vicinity of Mission San Fernando, where they intended to make a stand. Governor
Micheltorena with an insufficient force followed and engaged
them in combat, with the result as noted in the preceding
chapter. Micheltorena returned to Monterey by ship in
order to take along his wife, Doña Josefa Fuentes.[3]

Thus terminated the disgraceful affair, disgraceful for the
young would-be rulers. General Micheltorena in his official
capacity as well as in private life was a consistent Christian
who like every true Christian regulated his conduct in conformity with Christ's double command: "Keep the Com-
mandments."[4] "Hear the Church."[5]

The same cannot be said of the young paisano chiefs, who
came into public notice when Mexico decreed that Spaniards
could not hold office within its dominions. Their whole life
was in opposition to Christ's double injunction. Greed, disregard for the rights of the neophytes, irreverence for Religion
and its representatives were the most conspicuous features of
their activity. Let us judge them in reference to their dealings
with the Indian Missions.

At the present time various religious denominations annu-

---

[1] Bancroft, *California*, vol. iv, pp. 363-366; *The Missions and Missionaries*, vol. iv, 331. Italics are ours.

[2] Pa-i-sa-nos or native sons of Mexican extraction.

[3] See Appendix, B.

[4] Mathew, xix, 17; John, xiv, 15.

[5] Mathew, xviii, 17.

ally collect millions of dollars from Christian peoples throughout the world for the purpose of establishing and maintaining
Missions among the heathens whose conversion is sought. It
has never entered the head of any right-minded Christian to
thwart such missionary endeavor. On the contrary, the laity
always have regarded this kind of work as one to be fostered,
since it allows them to share in the fulfillment of Christ's important command to His Apostles and their successors: "Going
therefore teach ye all nations baptizing them in the name of
Father and of the Son and of the Holy Ghost."[6] Now let
us see how the Missions in California were brought into being,
how they progressed and what they accomplished.

Father Serra and his Brother Franciscans were sent to a
people who lived like brutes. The Indians raised nothing,
wore nothing, and subsisted on anything that either the earth
produced of itself or that crawled over the soil. All this was
devoured uncooked. They hated labor and considered it
undignified for men.

Father Serra at once comprehended that the savage Indians
would have to be taught first how to live. The missionaries
selected the most suitable spot where they immediately planted the Cross and later the chapel as a center of population. The
Fathers at every Mission received $1000 from the Pious Fund
in Mexico.[7] But this amount was paid in goods, such as agricultural implements, mechanical tools, etc; especially two
small tower bells which would call the people to worship, to
work and even to diversion. From the same fund the two
Fathers each received $400 worth of goods such as they de-
sired; these were generally used as church goods and as gifts
to attract the pagans and retain prospective converts. Then
they gently taught the Indians to work, clothe themselves and
by degrees to produce all that was consumed and worn.

---

[6] Mathew, xxviii, 19.

[7] Pious Fund. Wealthy individuals in Mexico had given large sums of
money for missionary work. Estates had been bought with this money.
With the proceeds from the sale of the estates' products were bought the
goods necessary to found a Mission.

THEY PLANTED THE CROSS.

Cattle, sheep, goats, horses and mules were introduced gradually and increased wonderfully so that no outside assistance was needed. Thus the suspicious, sullen, lazy, and ignorant savages under the gentle and patient guidance of the missionaries produced everything needed in the material line. They not only supported themselves and cost the government nothing; but moreover, due to the situation arising from the Mexican revolt, they maintained almost alone the whole military and civil departments of California from 1811. For this the Mission Indians received nothing in return but the ingratitude of the beneficiaries. The buildings still left and the ruins of others tell a story of their own. They were the products of the once lazy Indians.

No reports were demanded concerning the mechanical arts exercised at the Missions and the products of the orchards and vineyards. Nevertheless, the reader is forced to the conclusion that, in every material department and spiritual line, the Missions proved their worth as no training school in this or any other country, when we repeat that the neophytes produced everything they wore or consumed; exchanged much for other goods with the skippers of vessels; and met moreover the demands of the insatiable, inconsiderate soldiers and their numerous families.

It was a wonderful picture of the patriarchal life. The missionary held the post of Father and was so designated by the Spanish Government itself. The Missions were moreover genuine industrial beehives, as a writer in Lummis' *Out West* summarizes them from his own knowledge of the documentary history of those wonderful establishments. The converted Indians were brought as much as possible within the walls and taught the arts of civilization. They became aiders of the Padres in farming and in horticulture; in raising cattle, sheep and horses; in curing hides and drying tallow; in tending vineyards and pressing wine; in carpentry and masonry; in tailoring and shoe-making. They were sharers not only in the labor but in its fruits.

The reports (at end of book) will show the reader that the

brutally destroyed California Missions were in their system and results the most wonderful the world has seen anywhere, and that it was indeed the Crime of the 19th Century to wipe them out as Pio Pico determined he would do from sheer heartless greed.

Pio Pico, as senior member, called the territorial assembly and assumed the governorship ad interim when Micheltorena had been ousted by the treachery of the paisanos. The Mission estates or what remained of them occupied the temporary governor's attention from the *very first weeks* of his rule. He gave evidence very soon how they would fare at his hands. It is enough to say that *three weeks after* the sessions opened the Missions were discussed and it was decided that they must be sold (or rented first) to pay the debts of the Missions which however *had not been contracted by the Indians or Fathers, but by free-booting paisanos in office.* This topic has been treated at length in *The Missions and Missionaries*, vol. iv.

It was to the interest of the paisano government to have the Missions appear as wealthy as possible. The officials found a receptive listener for their story in Walter Colton, a sectarian minister, who had come with the U. S. troops in 1846 and at Monterey held the office of alcalde or justice of the peace. His published report greatly exaggerates the material wealth of these establishments, in particular that of Mission San Carlos. "This Mission," he writes, "in 1825 branded 2,300 calves, had 87,600 head of cattle, 1800 horses and mares, 365 yoke of oxen, nine sheep-farms with an average of about 6,000 sheep on each, a large assortment of merchandise and $40,000 *in specie*, which was buried on the report of a piratical cruiser on the coast." Fancy the Monterey paisano chiefs knowing that there were locked up in the mission "coffers" $40,000 in cash! It is not likely that the Fathers in 1825 had on hand $400.00 with which to meet current expenses! According to the official report for that year there belonged to this Mission only 1,500 cattle, 570 horses and mares, 18 mules, 10 goats, 9 swine, and 5,450 sheep. Mofras, an otherwise honest writer, was also taken in by the exaggerated reports made by the paisano chiefs of the wealth of Mission San Carlos. According to him, this Mission in 1834, had 7,000 cattle, 1,200 horses, and 9,000 sheep. The inventories and the official reports show nothing of such herds at any period. In that year the Mission owned 312 cattle, 491 horses and 9 mules. Other items are not mentioned, a sign that there was nothing else to report.[8]

Mission San Carlos having been excluded from the jurisdiction of the inspector it was not visited by Hartnell in 1839 and 1840. Bancroft, however, confesses "there was little mission property left in 1834 and none at all in 1840, except the ruined buildings."[9]

It will be remembered that Bishop Diego found himself forced to transfer Fr. José M. Reál from Monterey to a field where greater need existed. Upon Governor Micheltorena's representation he sent Fr. Antonio Reál to replace his priest brother at Monterey and took occasion to remind the people of their duty to support their pastor. His words seem to have gone unheeded. Fr. Antonio found it imperative to write to the acting governor on May 3, 1845, with regard to the maintenance of the Church and its minister at Monterey. He proposed that a subscription of the citizens be taken for the purpose of supporting Divine Worship and the priest in accordance with an agreement which had been reached between Bishop Diego and Governor Micheltorena. Pico noted on the margin that the judge at Monterey assemble the people in order that they give a contribution in favor of Fr. Antonio Reál. On May 23rd, however, the same missionary wrote at the foot of the document that he asked nothing for his own person, but for the church and minister; that therefore the decree should read in favor of the churches of the department and not for his person.[10] Nothing seems to have come of the move. Fr. Antonio Reál wrote to the acting governor, Pio Pico, on May 28th, 1845, that as he found no justice in Monte-

[8] *Missions and Missionaries*, vol. iii, pp. 632-633.
[9] Bancroft, *California*, vol. iii, p. 680; *Missions, etc.*, vol. iv, p. 152.
[10] Dept. St. Pap., vol. vi, pp. 291-293.

rey, he asked that all the priests agree to accept fees for baptisms, marriages, burials in accord with the arancel (list) of the bishop when he would issue it.[11]

Fr. Antonio Reál was transferred to Mission Santa Cruz, leaving Monterey without a priest. It seems that José Castro, military commander of Monterey, applied for the return of Fr. José M. Reál to Monterey. To this request the Bishop replied on February 6, 1846: "Today I received the official note which Your Honor was pleased to send me under date of December 3rd last. Therein you interested yourself in behalf of Rev. Fr. José M. Reál that he return to the church at Monterey and take charge of the spiritual administration. I cannot explain to Your Honor how painful it was for me that, owing to the lack of priests, your town has been without one since last November. However, by the favor of God, I have succeeded in ordaining three priests, whom I have destined for your towns in the north; on the 10th of this month I shall name the priest, Don Dorotéo Ambrís, minister of Monterey. Rev. Fr. Reál has made repeated petitions for his removal from the ministry. For this reason and inasmuch as he is only waiting for passage in a ship in order to return to his College, I cannot count on that religious; nor can I destine him for your parish at Monterey or for any other. Nevertheless, since the chief desires of Your Honor are not the return of Fr. Reál to Monterey, but that your place may be attended by some priest, and Rev. Fr. Ambrís being one, the good wishes of Your Honor must be considered gratified and your town relieved of the need which it has suffered for a little while.— Fr. Francisco Garcia Diego, Obispo.[12]

Like the other Missions, San Carlos was first confiscated by the secularization decree of the Assembly of August 9, 1834, and completed by Figueroa's decree of November 3, 1834.[13]

The inventory drawn up by José Joaquin Gomez with Fr.

[11] Dept. St. Pap., vol. vi, p. 399.
[12] *Libro Borrador.*
[13] *Missions and Missionaries*, vol. iii, pp. 530-531.

José Reál and dated December 10, 1834, valued the Mission, including the livestock, at $46,022, 7 reales and 10 granos. In this amount the church building is appraised at $10,000; the church furniture, sacred vessels, vestments, etc., and the library were valued at $10,217, 7 reales, and 4 granos.[14] It is to be noted that even Church goods, such as vestments and sacred vessels, were listed and evaluated like everything else, as though these articles used at Divine Worship came under the jurisdiction of the unchristian paisano officials. The depth of their religious sentiments may be inferred from this irreverent action alone. "Quidquid semel fuerit Domino consecratum, Sanctum Sanctorum erit Domino," Father Narciso Durán on February 19, 1836, rubbed into Nicolas Gutierrez, temporary governor; that is to say: "Whatever has once been consecrated to the Lord, shall be Holy of Holies to the Lord." (Leviticus, cap. xxvii, verse 28). See The Missions, etc., vol. iv, page 48.

The Mission was now in secular hands. Pio Pico, however, was not satisfied. In 1845, therefore, he went ahead to secure the fulfillment of the wish fathered by him for a long time. He caused the church and appurtenances of Mission Carmel to be separated from the remainder of the premises. These last together with the edifices on them were to be sold at public auction on January 2, 3, 4, 1846. Thus he effected what he had in mind for the last fifteen years: the annihilation of the benevolent and once prosperous Indian Missions of Upper California. The Avenging Angel, however, was already standing at the door, for which see Chapter XXII.

---

[14] *S. B. Archives.* The inventory covers 39 folio pages, and is signed by Fr. José S. Reál and José Joaquin Gómez.

CHAPTER XXI.

We have yet to chronicle the final dispositions made of the San Carlos Mission property. Pio Pico, his henchmen assenting, had sold sixteen of the twenty-one Missions when the U. S. troops took possession of Monterey. San Carlos remained unsold, probably because no one offered anything for it. At any rate there is nothing on record to prove that Father Serra's Mission suffered the disgrace of having come

MISSION SAN CARLOS HAD BEEN BLED TO DEATH BY THOSE IN POWER.

under the hammer. It had been bled to death by those in power.

United States officers quite early suspected that Pico had exceeded his power in disposing of the Mission property. United States authorities accordingly, on taking possession of the country in 1846, constituted themselves watchful guardians of the property formerly belonging to the Missions. Squatters were ejected, and those claiming ownership were directed to present legal evidence. The churches, the dwellings of the priests, cemeteries, orchards, and gardens were left in charge of the priests until the United States Courts should decide otherwise.

As soon as the Most Rev. Joseph S. Alemany, O. P., the second Bishop of California and the first Archbishop of San Francisco, arrived from the East and had acquainted himself with his diocese, he put in his claims for the Mission property before the Land Commission appointed by the United States Congress empowered to determine all kinds of land claims. After the Commissioners had heard all the witnesses and had weighed the evidence, the Chairman, Alpheus Felch, on December 18, 1855, announced the decision and the reasons therefore in favor of the Bishop. The Patent for the property of Mission San Carlos was accordingly issued by James Buchanan under date of October 19th, 1859, and it is reproduced herewith entire.

To All To Whom These Presents Shall Come, Greeting:

Whereas it appears from a duly authenticated transcript filed in the General Land Office of the United States that pursuant to the provisions of the Act of Congress approved the third day of March, one thousand eight hundred and fifty-one entitled "An Act to ascertain and settle the Private Land Claims in the State of California," Joseph Sadoc Alemany, Roman Catholic Bishop of the Diocese of Monterey, in the State of California, as claimant, filed his petition on the 19th day of February, 1853, with the Commissioners to ascertain and settle the Private Land Claims in the State of California sitting as a board in the City of San Francisco, in which petition he claimed the confirmation to him and his successors of the title to certain church property in California, "to be held by him and them in trust for the religious purposes and uses to which the same have been respectively appropriated," said property consisting of "church edifices, houses, for the use of the clergy and those employed in the service of the church, church yards, burial grounds, gardens, orchards, and vineyards with the necessary buildings thereon and appurtenances," the same having been recognized as the property of said church by the laws of Mexico in force at the time of the cession of California to the United States, and whereas, the Board of Land Commissioners, aforesaid, on the 18th of December, 1855, rendered a decree of confirmation, in favor of the Petitioner, for certain lands described therein, to be held, "in the same capacity and for the uses set forth in his petition," the lands at the Mission of "El Carmelo," being described in said decree as follows: "The Church and the buildings adjoining the same erected on three sides of a quadrangle, being the same known as the Church and Mission Buildings of the Mission of El Carmelo situated in Monterey County, together with the land on which the same are erected and curtelage and appurtenances thereto belonging and also the Cemetery adjoining the same, with the limits fixed and defined by the stone wall enclosing the same. Also the garden of said Mission which is situated about southeast from said Church, with the limits as the same is enclosed by the hedge of willows surrounding it, being the same premises marked "Orchard" on map numbered 14 in the Atlas before referred to." "And whereas, it further appears from a certified transcript, filed in the General Land Office, that an appeal from said decree or decision of the Commissioners having been taken on behalf of the United States to the District Court of the United States for the Southern District of California, and it being shown to the Court that it was not the intention of the United States to prosecute further said appeal, the said District Court on the 15th of March, 1858, at the regular term "ordered that said appeal be dismissed and said appellee have leave to proceed under the decree of the said Land Commissioners in his favor as a final decree." "And whereas, under the 13th section of said Act of 3rd of March, 1851, there have been presented to the Commissioner of the General Land Office a plat and certificate of the survey of the tract of land confirmed as aforesaid, authenticated on the 19th day of May, 1859, by the signature of the Surveyor General of the public lands in California, which plat and certificate are in the words and figures following, to wit:

"United States Surveyor General's Office,

San Francisco, California.

"Under and by virtue of the provisions of the 13th section "of the Act of Congress of the 3rd of March, 1851, entitled An "Act to ascertain and settle Private Land Claims in the State "of California, and of the 12th section of the Act of Congress "approved on the 31st of August, 1852, entitled An Act "making appropriations for the Civil and Diplomatic expenses "of the Government for the year ending the thirtieth of June, "eighteen hundred and fifty-three and for the purposes, and in "consequence of a certificate of the United States District "Court for the Southern District of California, of which a "copy is annexed having been filed in this office, whereby it "appears that the Attorney General of the United States "having given notice that it was not the intention of the "United States to prosecute the appeal from the decision of "the United States Board of Land Commissioners appointed "under the said Act of March 3rd, 1851, by which it recognized "and confirmed the title and claim of Joseph S. Alemany, "Bishop, etc., to the tracts of land designed as "Mission of "El Carmelo," the said appeal has been vacated, and thereby "the said decision in favor of said Joseph S. Alemany, Bishop, "etc., has become final.

"The said tract has been surveyed in conformity with the "grant thereof and the said decision, and I do hereby certify "the annexed Map to be a true and accurate plat of the said "tracts of land, as appears by the field notes of the survey "thereof, made by James E. Terrell, Deputy Surveyor, in the "month of December, 1858, under the directions of this office,

SURVEY OF LAND RESTORED TO THE CATHOLIC CHURCH
BY THE UNITED STATES GOVERNMENT.

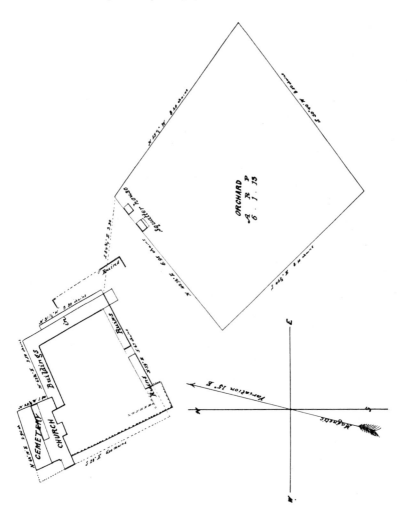

"which, having been examined and approved, are now on "file therein.

"And I do further certify, that under and by virtue of the "said confirmation and survey, the said Joseph S. Alemany, "Bishop, etc., is entitled to a patent from the United States, "upon the presentation hereof to the General Land Office for "the said tract of land, the same being bounded and described "as follows, to wit:

"Beginning at a stake, marked "A, 1," at the north east corner of the Cemetery.

"Thence, according to the true meridian, the variation of the magnetic needle being fifteen degrees East, South, twenty-eight degrees, forty-five minutes East, ninety-five links to the corner of the Church buildings, one chain and forty links to Station, at the angle formed by the Church and adjoining buildings.—

"Thence, along the line of buildings North, sixty-three degrees, forty-five minutes East, two chains and sixty-five links to Station, at a corner of the buildings.—

"Thence, South, thirty-one degrees, thirty minutes East, one chain and sixty links to Station, at corner as above.—

"Thence, North, fifty-eight degrees, thirty minutes East, fifteen links to Station, at corner as above.—

"Thence, South, thirty-one degrees, thirty minutes East, two chains to Station, at corner as above.—

"Thence, South, fifty-eight degrees, thirty minutes West, fifteen links to Station, at corner as above.—

"Thence, South, thirty-one degrees, thirty minutes East, seventy-four links to Station, at corner as above.—

"Thence, South, fifty-eight degrees, thirty minutes West, thirty links to Station, at corner as above.—

"Thence, North, thirty-one degrees, thirty minutes West, forty-one links to Station, at old adobe wall.—

"Thence, along the ruins of an old adobe wall, South, fifty-nine degrees West, five chains and eighteen links to a post marked "A," Station.—

"Thence, North, thirty-one degrees West, four chains and

forty-four links to Station, at point of intersection of old wall, with the row of Church buildings.—

"Thence, along the line of Church buildings South, sixty degrees, forty-five minutes West, thirty-six links to Station, at corner of buildings.—

"Thence, North, thirty degrees, thirty minutes West, fifty-one links to Station, at corner of buildings.—

"Thence, North, fifty-seven degrees East, sixty links to Station at corner of buildings.—

"Thence, North, twenty-six degrees, fifteen minutes West, at forty links leaves the line of Church buildings, and along the ruins of the old adobe wall of the Cemetery, one chain and ten links to a post, marked "A," at Station.—

"Thence, along the north boundary of the Cemetery, North, sixty-eight degrees, fifteen minutes, East, two chains and fifty-one links to the point of beginning. Containing two acres and seventy-five hundredths of an acre, being the tract containing the Mission buildings and the Cemetery, and being designated upon the plats of the public surveys as Lot numbered Thirty-eight, in Township Sixteen, South, of Range One West, of the Mount Diablo Meridian.—

"A tract of land designated as the "Orchard" of the "Mission Carmelo," and bounded and described as follows, to wit:

"Beginning at a post marked "A, I," at the north corner of the Orchard, from which, Station, "No. 7" of the tract containing the Mission buildings and Cemetery, bears North, eighty-four degrees, forty-five minutes West, distant three chains and fifty links.—

"Thence, according to the true meridian, the variation of the magnetic needle being fifteen degrees East, along the hedge of fruit trees, South, fifty-five degrees, thirty minutes East, eight chains and twenty links to a post marked "A, 2," at the corner of an old ditch, Station, from which the corner to Sections Seven, Twelve, Thirteen and Eighteen, Township Sixteen South, of Ranges one East and one West, bears North, fifty-two degrees, fifteen minutes East, distant fifty-seven chains and twenty-six links.—

"Thence, along the old ditch, South, forty-seven degrees, forty-five minutes West, eight chains and eighty-one links to a post marked "A, 3," Station.—

"Thence, along line of fruit trees, and old ditch, North, forty degrees, thirty minutes West, eight chains and ten links to a post marked "A, 4," Station, and—

"Thence, North, forty-eight degrees, thirty minutes East, at six chains a Squatter's house is about fifty links to the right of the line, six chains and seventy-five links to the point of beginning, containing six acres and twenty-five hundredths of an acre, and being designated upon the plats of the public surveys as Lot numbered thirty-nine, in Township Sixteen South, of Range one West, of the Mount Diablo Meridian."

"In witness whereof, I have hereunto signed my "name, and caused the Seal of the said Office to be "affixed, at the City of San Francisco, this Nine- (L. S.)   "teenth day of May, A. D., 1859."

"J. W. Mandeville,"

"U. S. Surveyor General, California."

"And whereas there has been deposited in the General "Land Office of the United States a certificate dated May 19th, "1859, from the Clerk of the United States District Court for "the Southern District of California, showing that in the "cause entitled "J. S. Alemany et al Appellees ads. the United "States appellants," due notice by publication in manner and "form as required by the law has been made by the Surveyor "General of the United States for California in the matter of "the approved survey of the Mission "El Carmelo," confirmed to the claimant and Appellee in the above entitled cause of "J. S. Alemany vs. The United States," and "that the full "period of six months from and after the completion of said "publication has elapsed and no objection thereto having "been made or filed, the said approved survey has become "final, and the claimant and Appellee entitled to a Patent," "for the said Mission,

NOW KNOW YE,

That the United States of America, in consideration of the premises and pursuant to the provisions of the Act of Congress aforesaid of 3rd of March, 1851, HAVE GIVEN AND GRANTED, and by these presents DO GIVE AND GRANT, unto the said Joseph S. Alemany, Bishop of Monterey and to his successors, "in trust for the religious purposes and uses to which the same have been respectively appropriated," the tracts of land embraced and described in the foregoing survey, but with the stipulation that in virtue of the 15th section of the said Act, the confirmation of this said claim and this patent "shall not affect the interests of third persons."

To Have and To Hold the said tracts of lands with the appurtenances, and with the stipulation aforesaid unto the said Joseph S. Alemany, Bishop of Monterey, and to his successors, in trust for the purposes as aforesaid.

"In testimony whereof, I, James Buchanan, President of "the United States, have caused these letters to be made "patent, and the Seal of the General Land Office to be "thereunto affixed.

"Given under my hand, at the City of Washington, "this nineteenth day of October, in the year of "Our Lord, one thousand eight hundred and fifty-
(Seal) "nine, and of the Independence of the United "States the Eighty-fourth.

James Buchanan

"By the President: James Buchanan,
By J. B. Leonard, Secretary.

J. N. Granger, Recorder of the General Land Office.
Recorded Vol. 2, Pages 304 to 311, inclusive.
"Recorded at the request of Father Cassanova, July "27th, 1874, at 50 minutes past 9 o'clock, A. M., in "Liber A of Patents, page 432, etc., following of Records "of Monterey County.

Herbert Mills, County Recorder.

CHAPTER XXII.

The Mission Registers.—The Baptismal Register of San Carlos.—Noted Converts from Foreign Nations.—The Confirmation Register.—The Marriage Register.—The Burial Register.—Burial of Fr. Juan Crespi.—Burial of Fr. Julian Lopez.—Burial of Fr. Presidente Junipero Serra.—Interment of Fr. Presidente Fermin Francisco de Lasuén.—The Burials of Other Noted Individuals.—Epidemic.— Death and Burial of the Very Rev. Angelus Delphinus Casanova, Pastor of Monterey Parish.

The Mission Registers were uniformly bound in flexible leather; one side of the cover overlapped the other, where it was fastened with two leather strings or two leather buttons. The paper page measured about 8 by 11¼ inches. The College of San Fernando de Mexico supplied these books to the Missions under its jurisdiction. By order of the same College every Mission had to keep, besides the local account books:— 1. Baptismal Register.—2. Confirmation Register.—3. Marriage Register.—4. Burial Register.—5. Libro de Patentes in which were transcribed the Circular Letters of the Higher Superiors.—6. *The Padron*, or Census Roll, in which were kept the names of the father, mother and children according to date of birth, baptism and origin, or native village, of the families. Separate lists for widows and widowers were added in the rear pages.

The Baptismal Registers commonly have a title page with data peculiar to each Mission. The one of Mission San Carlos informs us that the entries contained in the first book are those of converts from paganism as well as of those who were born of Christian parents. There is further information to the effect that the spiritual care of the Mission was in the hands of Franciscan missionaries of the Apostolic College de Propaganda Fide of San Fernando in Mexico; that the expense of the founding was borne by King Carlos III, Monarch of all Spain;* that Señor Don Carlos Francisco de Croix, Marquis

---

* That is to say: The king reserved to himself the credit of permitting the Pious Fund to contribute the $1000 needed for the founding, and $400 annually for each missionary as his personal stipend. Only goods were sent, and the freighting was charged to the Fathers.

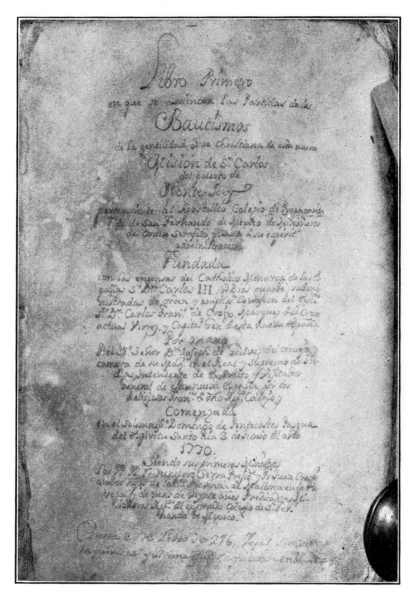

TITLE PAGE OF BAPTISMAL RECORD OF MISSION SAN CARLOS.

de Croix, actual Viceroy and Captain General of New Spain ordered and commissioned the supplies; that Señor Don Joseph de Galvez, Councillor and Chamberlain of His Majesty in the realm and the highest in the Indies, Lieutenant in the Army, Visitor General of New Spain for the Religious of the Apostolic College aided the work. It is noted that the Mission was started on Pentecost Sunday, June 3, 1770. Fr. Serra and Fr. Crespi were the first appointees. The first book contains 276 pages not counting the first and the last ones. The second book began with Baptism, No. 3167, April 15, 1820.

Subsequent entries reveal a story proper to San Carlos alone. The pages of the Register relate that Fr. Serra baptized three male children of pagan parents, with the consent of the latter, by the end of 1770, more than six months after the founding of the Mission. Fr. Juan Crespi baptized No. 4 on New Year's day, 1771. Then, until the end of the year, both Fathers alternated. Their efforts added twenty-three names to the list. It was not a brilliant success as to numbers; but at San Diego the Indians had been even more backward. The converts increased rapidly with the year 1773. Fr. Francisco Palóu, the earliest historian of Upper California and the Missions, and Fr. Serra's biographer, entered his first Baptism (No. 1074) on August 20, 1784, eight days before Fr. Serra's death. He had resided here before, having come from Lower California in 1773. Fr. Fermín Francisco de Lasuén was the regular successor of Fr. Serra in the superiorship of the Missions. He came to San Carlos from San Diego in 1785 and entered his first baptism (No. 1198) at this place on January 22, 1786.

On January 7, 1773, Fr. Juan Crespi baptized a very sick girl, aged fifteen years, of pagan parents, at the rancheria of *Santa Teresa*, situated about a league from the Mission up the Rio Carmelo. She recovered; wherefore he supplied the ceremonies at the Mission on February 22nd. The rancheria of *San Miguel* is mentioned at the end of 1774; that of San Francisco (Chilat) in 1780.

Two children, Leoncio Francisco from the rancheria of

San Carlos (Achasta) and Estefana Francisca from that of *Santa Clara*, were the last to be baptized by Fr. Serra. He entered their names on the same date, August 2, 1784, only twenty-six days before his death. Fr. Crespi had entered his last one (No. 656) on the twenty-fifth of the same month, three years earlier.

Occasionally, Baptisms of persons other than Indians were administered at the Mission. José Antonio, twenty-eight years old, was baptized on June 2, 1817. He was an Anglo-American, having been born at Malden, two leagues from Boston. His parents were Samuel Grover and Rachel Grover. Fr. Sarría performed the ceremony. The same priest also baptized an Englishman on February 5, 1825, and a native of the Sandwich Islands on December 5, 1826. The former was Felipe Duckenort, 25 years old, a native of Manchester; the latter, Juan Andres, also twenty-five years of age, had the queer name "Peg" as a pagan; he had been baptized as a child by a Protestant clergyman. There was also baptized at the Mission Cornelio Andriason, fifty-eight years of age, a Lutheran from Cilaufer, a Danish possession.

The Capilla del Real Presidio de Monterey (chapel of the royal presidio of Monterey) was the place of Baptisms at times. There is the interesting case of Diego Mariano. His father, Julian Balduan (Baldwin?), he thought, was a native of England, his mother, Sarah Balduan, of the parish of Ostre, in the province of Worwicyer (Warwickshire?). He came from Islyngton, about two miles from the city of London. He received the requisite instructions, abjured his errors and was baptized on November 12, 1814, by Fr. Vicente de Sarría, the first Comisário Prefecto of the Missions. There were baptized six Russians, all men ranging from nineteen to forty years of age. Diligent inquiry made it plain that their former baptism had been invalidly administered. Fr. Juan Amorós, therefore, gave them the sacrament conditionally on June 29, 1819. These were his last entries. Fr. Ramon Abella baptized a child in the presidio chapel on February 5, 1826. Its father was William Edward Hartnell, a native of Hackbarrow, England; later he became prominent in California history.

In the middle of February, 1833, Fr. Rafael Moreno, a Zacatecan, administered the Sacrament of Baptism; Fr. Ramon Abella, the last Fernandino, on April 21, 1833. Fr. Garcia Diego, later first Bishop of California, baptized in the presidio chapel on March 3, 1833. With November 13, 1834, Fr. José Reál begins to use the term "in this pueblo of San Carlos," when making baptismal entries. Very probably he moved to Monterey. In the next year, November, he writes: "in the church of this Mission of San Carlos of Monterey," also, "in the church of Monterey," then again, "chapel of Monterey," or "chapel of the presidio," the latter presumably for Monterey fort. Fr. Antonio Reál (November 21, 1844) has "in the church of Monterey."

A few Baptisms continued to be given at the Mission all along, also at the chapel of Monterey. Among those baptized were very few children. On December 22, 1839, an adult Hawaian (Canaca) (No. 4423) was baptized. It was the only one at the Mission since June 29th of the same year.

The *Confirmation Register* was begun on the Feast of Saints Peter and Paul, June 29, 1778, as the title page indicates. Fr. Serra is careful to note therein that he began the administration of this sacrament after having been duly authorized by the faculty from the Holy See. The document is reproduced entirely in the pages of the register which preceed the entries. Fr. Serra confirmed thirty-one persons at San Carlos on various occasions from December 19, 1779, up to June 6, 1881. Fr. Serra's last entry is No. 938 and was made on July 6, 1784. On that occasion he confirmed a boy only a few months old and a girl; both were from the rancho of SargentaRuc.

The *Marriage Register's* title page, like that of the other books gives the information that the Franciscan missionaries of the Regular Observance from the oft-named College of San Fernando in Mexico had spiritual charge of the Mission of San Carlos. There is mention of the fact that the expenses of the founding were met by Carlos III, King of all Spain. The supplies were made available by His Excellency, Señor Don Carlos Francisco de Croix. Señor Don Joseph Galvez also lent his efforts to the work. It is also noted that the date of the founding of the Mission was Pentecost Sunday, June 3, 1770. It tells us that Fr. Junipero Serra, Presidente, and Fr. Juan Crespi were the first in charge of the Mission. It adds that both were from the Holy Province of Mallorca in Europe; but that they had been missionaries of the Apostolic College more than ten years.

According to the entries, Fernando Malaleta and Catharina Maria, two young people, were married on November 10, 1772; they were the first to receive this Sacrament in the church of the Mission del Rio del Carmelo. This was more than two years after the founding of the Mission and is proof that the missionaries were not wont to administer the Sacraments to the neophytes before the latter were sufficiently grounded in their newly accepted Faith. The records numbered 1062 entries at the end of 1834. The last Franciscan to make an entry (No. 1193) was Fr. Anzar November 30, 1845.

The title page of the *Burial Register* is similar in form to those of the other books. Fr. Serra, however, penned, these texts on the reverse side:

"We all die; and like waters that return no more we fall down into the earth." (II. Kings, xiv, 14).

"Blessed are the dead, who die in the Lord." (Apoc. xiv, 13).

"He that believeth in Me [said Christ] although he be dead, shall live." (St. John, xi, 25).

The first entry is worthy of reproduction because of its priority and also because of an explanatory note. "Ecclesiastical burial was given to the body of Alexis Viño, an adult from Acapulco, in this new Mission of San Carlos de Monterey on June 3, 1770. He was interred at the foot of the large Cross which was planted and blessed in front of the (temporary) chapel and altar, the same day that preparations were under way to celebrate the first holy Mass near the shore of this port."

Fr. Juan Crespi entered the burial of a child (No. 235) on October 22, 1781. Fr. Serra penned the obituary notice of this faithful worker in the Lord's vineyard about ten weeks later. Fr. Serra wrote that he gave ecclesiastical burial to the body of the Rev. Predicador Fr. Juan Crespi, Priest, on the 2nd of January, 1782, in the Mission church of San Carlos of Monterey. He further noted that the body was interred near the main altar on the Gospel side; that the interment was preceded by the chanting of the Office for the dead and a Requiem Mass which was also sung. All the rubrics were carried out as prescribed for the burial of a Religious by the Franciscan Ritual. Fr. Juan Crespi resided at this Mission since its founding, as can be ascertained from the title pages of this and the rest of the books of records. He was a member of the Holy Province of Mallorca from which he set forth in 1749 to convert the pagans. He had papers of incorporation with the Apostolic Missionary College of San Fernando in Mexico under the jurisdiction of Propaganda de Fide. 1750 was the year of his arrival at the College. He received the Sacraments of Penance, Eucharist and Extreme Unction on the last of December. Fortified by these, and with the comforting presence of two companions of the same province (Mallorca), he died on January 1, 1782, at about six o'clock in the morning with all the signs of a true Religious. He was sixty years and ten months of age and had worn the religious habit forty-four years.

On July 30, 1784, Fr. Serra entered the burial record of an adult Indian. About four weeks later the Presidente's own death was recorded by Fr. Palóu. It is No. 381. The original entry, in Father Palóu's handwriting, covers three pages in the Register. A translation is reproduced here in full.

"On the 29th of August in the church of this Mission of San Carlos de Monterey in the sanctuary on the Gospel side in front of the altar of Our Lady of Sorrows I gave ecclesiastical burial to the body of the Rev. Fr. Lector, Junipero Serra, the

Presidente of these Missions and the Founder, as appears
from the first page of this book and from the rest of the parochial registers of these Missions. I was assisted by the Priest,
Señor Don Carlos Diaz, Chaplain of the packetboat *San
Carlos* which rode at anchor in this port. The Rev. Fr. Bonaventure Sitjar, missionary in charge of Mission San Antonio
and Fr. Mathias de Santa Catalina also were present. The
burial service was preceded by the Divine Office and a High
Mass of Requiem. The Office was chanted as the Manual of
the Order prescribes for the interment of a Religious.

"He was a member of the Holy Province of Mallorca where
he took the habit on the 14th of September, 1730. At the time
he was nineteen years, nine months and twenty-six days of
age, and he persevered in his vocation with all the signs of a
true Religious and wise man. As a Religious he taught the
course of Philosophy which met with much approbation, and
I had the good fortune of being one of his pupils. Upon the
completion of the course, the University of the Isle of Mallorca
elected him Professor Extraordinary of Sacred Theology. He
was honored with the doctor's cap by the faculty because he
acquitted himself as a teacher to the satisfaction of the University and of the Holy Province. All regarded him as very
learned and no less capable in the pulpit. He held the attention in both sermons and lectures by limiting himself to dis-
courses about more important matters. Whilst at the pinnacle
of fame, he was touched by the grace of God and became undeceived. He forsook all the honors he had or might receive,
and resolved to employ the talents with which God had en-
dowed him in the conversion of pagan Indians.

"In the year 1749, he obtained permission and the letters
of obedience to join the Mission (band) at Cádiz, for the
Apostolic College of Propaganda de Fide of San Fernando in
Mexico. The first of January, 1750, found him at this College
where he remained until the beginning of June of the same
year. Then he was transferred to the Sierra Gorda Missions
which had been established six years previously. He labored
there most zealously and exemplarily for nine years. There-

upon his Superior called him to establish the Missions on the
Rio of San Saba. This was delayed by the death of the Viceroy
who had promoted that conquest. He remained at the College
and busied himself in giving missions to the faithful and in
the affairs of the Holy Tribunal of Faith, which constituted
him one of its commissioners. He discharged his duties to the
satisfaction of this holy Tribunal. Whilst giving a mission to
the faithful in June, 1767, the R. P. Guardian summoned and
named him Presidente of the sixteen missionaries who went
to take charge of the fifteen Missions of Lower California,
which had been in the hands of the Jesuit Fathers. One whole
year was spent in Lower California with headquarters at the
Mission of Loreto. In that period he made occasional journeys
to visit these Missions both north and south. He left Loreto
in April, 1769, with the Expedition which had as object the
discovery of this port and that of San Diego. Upon arriving
at the frontiers of Lower California, in passing, he founded the
Mission of San Fernando de Vellicatá and came to the Port
of San Diego. He established the Mission of San Diego whilst
the expedition sought the Port of Monterey. In the year
1770 he sailed to discover this port and immediately gave his
hand to the founding of this Mission; and as occasion offered,
he established all the others which have been founded up to
the present time, as is patent from the parochial books.

"Many journeys were made by him during the fourteen
years; one to Mexico to hasten the supplies for this conquest,
the others to visit the Missions for the sake of inspiring his
subjects with his own holy zeal and prudence. These tours
took place, more or less, after he had obtained the faculty to
confirm, which his zeal made him solicit. He managed to confirm 5307 whilst the faculty lasted. (It expired on the 10th
of last July). His Reverence yielded his soul to his Creator
one month and a half after the expiration of said faculty. His
life's span was seventy years, nine months less four days. He
had been a Religious for fifty-three years, eleven months and
four days and an apostolic missionary for thirty-five years,
four months and a half.

"He made ready for death by repeating the general confession which had been made a number of times. The pain in his chest became much worse. On the 27th of this month fever set in. On that date he walked unsupported to the church to receive the Holy Sacrament as Viaticum, after having recited the Divine Office up to Tierce inclusively. I gave Holy Viaticum to him with the ceremonies which the Roman Seraphic

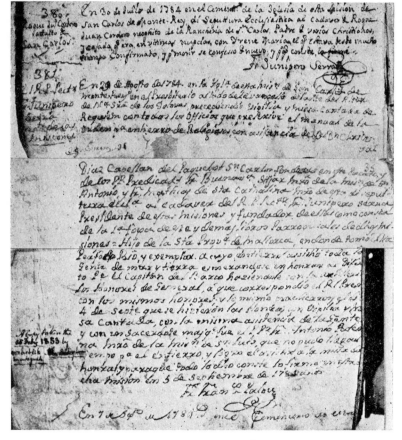

OPENING AND CLOSING LINES OF FR. PALÓU'S ENTRY IN BURIAL REGISTER, RECORDING FR. SERRA'S DEATH.

Ritual prescribes. He received it on his knees to the edifi-
cation of the whole pueblo and many people who were present.
At the beginning of the ceremony, the Presidente, who knelt
as if he were not seriously ill, intoned the verse *Tantum Ergo*
with his sonorous voice. This affected us so much that we
were unable to accompany him. He received the most Holy
Sacrament with burning devotion and in the same posture
gave thanks to God; then he retired to his cell. That night
he begged for Extreme Unction. He prayed the Penitential
Psalms and the Litany with us. The remainder of the night
was spent in giving thanks to God. At times he knelt, and at
other times he sat on the floor, but did not go to bed. He
kept on his habit and mantle all the time. At dawn he besought me to apply the Plenary Indulgence. In preparation
for its reception he knelt and reconciled himself to God by
renewing the general confession. On the morning of the 28th,
the ship's captain, Don José Canizares and the Rev. Chaplain
came to visit him. He received them graciously and welcomed
them by giving a familiar embrace to the Chaplain and saying
to both: 'Thanks be to God that you have come to cast a
little earth on my grave after so great a journey.'

"After the lapse of some time he remarked that a certain
dread had taken possession of him, wherefore the recommendation of the soul should be read in a loud voice. I did as he
requested; he gave the responses as if he were not sick. At
the conclusion, he exclaimed joyfully: 'Thanks be to God, I
am no longer fearful; I am no longer full of anxiety; I feel
better now. I will take a little broth.' I went to procure it,
and he sat at the table. After partaking of the broth, he desired to go to rest. He retired without removing more than
his mantle and thus he fell asleep in the Lord. Indeed, without
the least commotion he surrendered his soul to his Creator a
little before two o'clock in the afternoon of the 28th, the feast
of St. Augustine, Doctor of the Church.

"The whole pueblo was deeply affected at the tolling of the
passing bell. The Indians wept at the death of their beloved
Padre, as did all the *gente de razon*, in the countryside and on

the ship in the bay. They begged for a precious bit of cloth of the deceased Padre's habit which he had worn. So eager were they that even in church they cut some pieces from the habit in which he died. It had not been changed or taken from him. He was placed in the coffin with the same habit in which he had died. The deceased Father, unbeknown to us, had called the carpenter of the Presidio some time before and had given him orders to make the coffin which was to receive his corpse. I promised the people that if they would restrain themselves I would give them a tunic of the Rev. dead Padre from which they could fashion scapulars which they did. Notwithstanding the guard around the body in church, some of the hair was cut. Everybody was touched by the fame of the pious and exemplary Presidente.

"All the *gente de razon*, those of the district and of the ship in the harbor, assisted at the interment of the deceased. They took great pains to pay honor to the dead Padre. The Captain gave him the salute of a general with the ship's artillery; the Royal Presidio replied with a like salute. The same was done on the 4th of September when the Office and Mass of the dead were chanted. All the people assisted again and one more missionary, Fr. Antonio Paterna, of Mission San Luis. He was unable to arrive in time for the interment but succeeded in being present at the Mass of Honor. All the above is true as I affirm at this said Mission on September 5, 1784."

To Fr. Francisco Pujol fell the duty of entering the death notice of Fr. Julian Lopez. The translation of this entry is as follows: "I gave ecclesiastical burial to the body of the Rev. Predicador and apostolic missionary, Fr. Julian Lopez, on July 16, 1797, in this church of the Mission of San Carlos de Monterey. He was interred on the Gospel side, close to the wall. The deceased was a member of the Apostolic College of Propaganda Fide of San Fernando in Mexico; before, he belonged to the Holy Province of Purisima Concepcion in Castille. He was thirty-five years of age, two of which had been spent as missionary. The Holy Sacraments of the Eucharist and Extreme Unction were received by him in preparation for death; he received them with all the signs of a true and perfect religious and a faithful son of Our Holy Father, St Francis."—

The Death Register of Mission Carmel contains the burial record of another remarkable character of the Mission period. We read "On June 27, 1803, (26th has been erased) in the sanctuary of this Mission of San Carlos Borromeo de Monterey of New California, on the Gospel side and in a grave of rock, right close to the high altar, I gave ecclesiastical burial to the body of Rev. Fr. Fermin Francisco de Lasuén, a Religious of the Franciscan Observants, Apostolic missionary, universally approved de Propaganda Fide, Vicar Forane of the Bishop of Sonora, Commissioner of the Holy Institute of the Inquisition of Mexico, and Presidente of these Missions in Upper California. He was a native of the city of Victoria in the province of Alaba, a member of the holy province of Cantabria. He joined the Apostolic Missionary College de Propaganda Fide of San Fernando in Mexico. The holy Sacraments of Penance, Eucharist and Extreme Unction were administered to him. In proof of this I sign."—Fr. Baltasar Carnicer.

Names of famous Californians are also found in the Register. William Edward Hartnell died at Monterey and was buried on February 2, 1854, by Fr. Vilarosa, O. P., who had given him the Last Sacraments. Esteban Munrás aged sixty-one, died from apoplexy at Monterey and was buried September 3, 1850. He was the artist who painted the church of Mission San Miguel.

Governor Roméu's entry reads: "On April 10, 1794, in

the church of this Mission of Monterey, I gave ecclesiastical burial to the body of Señor Don Joseph Antonio de Roméu, a native of Valencia, Lieutenant-Colonel in the Royal Army, Governor and Comandante Inspector of this province of California. He was the husband of Señora Doña Josepha Sandoval, who came from Cádiz. The Sacraments of Penance, Eucharist and Extreme Unction were administered to him. In proof of this I sign."—Fr. Fermín Francisco de Lasuén.

The Biennial Reports for certain years throw considerable light on entries in the Register. The one of December 31, 1804, contains the information that the Mission suffered from a pest at the end of 1801 and the beginning of 1802. During that time some of the Indians betook themselves to the sierras. There the ravages of the epidemic became very great and eighty-six people died. The names of the deceased could not be entered because it was difficult to know their identity. "But since certain knowledge is at hand of the death of those who are now missing, eighty-six entries must be added to the number of deceased for 1803. Eleven more deaths have resulted in the past two years. Add these last to the foregoing eighty-six and the result will be ninety-seven, the total decrease in the population for these years."

The Biennial Report for 1806 gives notice of the deaths of some pagan children who were being brought up in the mountain fastnesses, as also of some adults whose whereabouts had been a mystery. The number of these adults and children amounted to twenty-four. Therefore this number was added to the report because it helped to account for the total of forty-one, by which number the Mission had decreased during these two years.

The Burial Entry of Very Rev. Fr. Casanova deserves a place here because this priest labored indefatigably to restore Mission San Carlos. The record, signed by Very Rev. Ramon Mestres reads: "Very Rev. Angelus Delphinus Casanova, Pastor of the Church of Saint Charles, Monterey, California, and Vicar Foraneo of the Diocese of Monterey and Los

Angelus, fortified with the Sacraments of the Roman Catholic Church, died in the Lord on the 11th of March of the year of Our Lord, 1893. He was buried in the Church of St. Charles of Monterey on the 15th of the same month and year."

MISSION SAN CARLOS RESTORED.

APPENDIX

A

SAINT CHARLES BORROMEO, ARCHBISHOP OF MILAN

Fr. Junipero Serra established the second Indian Mission in California under the title "San Carlos Borromeo." St. Charles was born at Arona, Italy, on October 2, 1538. Count Giberto Borromeo and Margherita de' Medici were his parents; Pope Pius IV, his uncle.

The child's inclination to piety and ecclesiastical functions caused his parents to look upon him as destined for the clerical state. It was his usual amusement to build little chapels, adorn altars and chant the Divine Office. He received the clerical tonsure at the age of twelve. Shortly afterwards he was made titular abbot of the Benedictine Abbey which Julius Caesar Borromeo, his uncle, had turned over to him.

Upon being elected to the Papacy, Pius IV lost no time in summoning Charles to Rome. The cardinalate was bestowed upon the young man, twenty-two years of age. To him was entrusted the administration of the Papal States. Moreover, he was made Legate of Bologna, Romagna and of the March of Ancona, and the Protector of the Kingdom of Portugal, Lower Germany and the Catholic cantons of Switzerland. The Orders of St. Francis, the Humiliati, and the Canons Regular of the Holy Cross of Christ in Portugal were also placed under his protection.

Charles had matriculated at the University of Pavia in 1552 and he received the doctorate in civil and canon laws seven years later. He proved himself to be a great patron of learning, and established the Vatican Academy for literary work at Rome and other institutions of learning. Above all however, he labored with signal success for the reassembling of the Council of Trent which convened again in 1562 and was particularly zealous in enforcing the reforms, instituted by the Council, and in composing the Roman Catechism, embodying its teachings.

Pope Pius IV had nominated him Archbishop of Milan on February 8, 1560. It was not until 1562, however, that Charles secretly took Holy Orders and was consecrated Bishop in the following year. One more year elapsed before he could obtain permission to retire from his manifold duties at the Roman court and take up his residence in his episcopal city. Charles found Milan in a state of great disorder. But he immediately began the work of reforming his diocese and labored with signal success at this task for the remainder of his life. Visitations were held regularly, parishes were created and monasteries were established. In consequence, the deplorable conditions of the diocese disappeared; and the simplicity, piety, generosity and self-sacrifice of St. Charles endeared him to his flock.

The zealous Archbishop was taken sick in October, 1584. He arrived at Milan from Arona on November 2nd and scrupulously followed the directions of the ablest physicians who had been called to treat him. They despaired of being able to resist the advance of the fever. Wherefore, he received Viaticum and Extreme Unction with great devotion. He expired in the forepart of the night between the 3rd and 4th of November, 1584, with these words on his lips: "Ecce venio"—Behold I come.

His sacred remains lie deposited in a rich underground chapel just under the cupola of the great church of Milan. Near the burial vault which contained his holy body until it was removed to the place where it now rests, there is a small marble stone with this inscription: "Charles, Cardinal of the title of St. Praxedes, Archbishop of Milan, desiring to be recommended to the frequent prayers of the clergy, people, and the devout sex, living chose for himself the monument." The addition follows: "He lived forty-six years, one month, and one day; governed this church twenty-four years, eight months, twenty-four days, and died November 4, 1584."

B

SPIRITUAL RESULTS.
(Whites)

Year	Baptisms	Marriages	Deaths
1770			1
1775		3	
1795		5	5
1797	18		
1798	27	9	7
1799	32	11	10
1800	50	15	15
1801	62	19	17
1802	76	21	29
1803	89	22	36
1804	92	23	
1805	103	28	40
1806	118		46
1808	124	31	50
1809	136	32	53
1810	153	33	60
1811	175	40	65
1812	190	43	73
1813	210	47	79
1814	220	49	84
1815	236	52	92
1816	255	59	96
1817	276	67	106
1818	294	69	125
1819	306	73	127
1820	330	74	139
1821	353	80	149
1822	369	84	161
1823	397	87	168
1824	417	93	174
1825	454	99	192
1826	489	108	203
1827	541	115	217
1828	577	120	241
1829	623	125	268
1830	672	134	285
1831	719	145	295
1832	758	154	313

SPIRITUAL RESULTS.
(Indians)

Year	Baptisms	Marriages	Burials	Existant	Male	Female	Confessions	Communions	Viaticum	Confirmations
1770	3									
1771	23									
1772										
1773	165	32	11							
1774	267	36	23	244						
1775	263									
1776	439									
1777	518									
1778	575									181
1779	603									359
1780	638									
1781	662									
1782	763									491
1783	938			614						766
1784	1040	287	395	645						938
1785	1191	329	463	711						
1786	1252	344	536	694						
1787	1315	358	573	707						
1788	1387	368	628	720						
1789	1460	393		732						
1790	1550	408	778	712						1247
1791	1693	432	845	770						1416
1792	1819	468	930	800						1537
1793	1908	490	976	835						1642
1794	1999	513	1038	861						1764
1795	2097	527	1101	876	444	434				1805
1796	2135	549	1167	839						
1797	2192	560	1226	832						
1798	2252	570	1273	738						
1799	2295	586	1338	720						
1800	2343	600	1346	747	367	380				
1801	2383	605	1400	705						
1802	2418	633	1496	688	367	312				
1803	2452	653	1559	591	302	289				
1804	2487	667	1604	591	298	293				
1805	2539	682	1652	587	297	290				
1806	2624	717	1741	550						
1807	2684	737	1786	562						
1808	2728	751	1841	550	285	265	300	230	4	
1809	2760	764	1888	533	272	267	300	230	12	
1810	2795	776	1940	511	255	256	350	240	13	
1811	2831	786	1989	485	252	233	400	250	21	
1812	2865	803	2041	455	245	210	400	230	27	
1813	2905	812	2074	448	243	205	400	250	15	
1814	2934	825	2112	431	235	197	380	230	11	
1815	2978	832	2151	423	227	196	370	200	8	
1816	3017	848	2191	405	226	179	330	150	15	
1817	3064	863	2230	402	226	176	335	147	8	
1818	3101	873	2264	390	218	172	310	130	11	
1819	3154	881	2288	397	219	178	314	112	5	
1820	3195	885	2337	381	205	176	300	145	18	
1821	3239	902	2375	374	200	174	300	113	10	
1822	3267	912	2432	341	182	159	280	102	9	
1823	3317	919	2474	317	170	147	250	92	9	
1824	3358	929	2514	306	166	140	196	80	8	
1825	3411	937	2561	295	161	134	204	90	8	
1826	3466	952	2590	277	155	122	180	70	5	
1827	3533	969	2621	275	153	122	150	50	5	
1828	3587	976	2707	234	134	100	180	50	10	
1829	3648	983	2750	233	134	99				
1830	3713	1002	2782	229	128	101	125	70	8	
1831	3769	1018	2803	209	111	98	164	70	2	
1832	3827	1032	2837	185	96	89				
1845	44529									8710

MATERIAL RESULTS.—AGRICULTURE.—1772-1832.

Year	Wheat		Barley		Corn		Beans		Peas		Total Fanegas		Total Bushels
	Plt.	Hrv.	Plt.	Hrv.	Plt.	Hrv.	Plt.	Hrv.	Plt.	Hrv.	Plt.	Hrv.	Hrv.
1772....	¼	5	....	......	....	......	....	......	....	......	¼	5	8
1773....	5	......	....	......	....	......	....	......	....	......	5	......	......
1774....	3	125	....	......	⅔	150	½	7	....	......	4	182	303
1783....	....	......	....	......	....	......	....	......	....	......			
1784....	....	633	....	700	....	750	....	120	....	108	....	2311	3852
1785....	24	89	33	350	5	760	5	85	4	3	81	1287	2135
1786....	24	440	22	969	8	167	6	79	4	72	64	1727	2868
1787....	22	300	25	1215	3	50	6	43	2	42	58	1650	2750
1788....	32	447	28	1342	7	......	7	17	3	26	77	1832	3053
1789....													
1790....	69	692	62	675	11	820	10	145	8	120	160	2452	3087
1791....	71	221	52	536	11	150	13	211	6	119	153	1357	2262
1792....	73	231	60	204	17	1400	14	31	9	147	173	2013	3355
1793....	68	333	55	476	14	700	11	70	10	115	158	1794	2990
1794....	62	657	48	608	12	500	13	291	11	218	146	2074	3457
1795....	57	15	51	52	13	350	28	264	12	135	161	816	1360
1796....	81	230	65	297	17	400	23	466	12	124	198	1517	2528
1797....	94	1800	55	1728	15	800	21	270	12	320	197	4918	8197
1798....	60	200	10	300	11	1000	20	250	23	310	124	2060	3433
1799....	150	800	50	800	15	1724	20	200	26	476	261	4000	6666
1800....	56	500	81	1025	21	1600	20	127	41	710	219	3962	6603
1801....	68	500	82	1050	18	1200	22	502	61	1134	251	4386	7310
1802....	60	240	80	1000	12	600	12	200	50	840	214	2880	4800
1803....	30	200	70	1000	7	200	8	400	22	290	137	2090	3483
1804....	50	900	60	1900	5	220	5	200	9	403	129	3623	6038
1805....											129	2300	3833
1806....	56	827	55	900	6	25	7	100	14	239	138	2091	4835
1807....	100	464	30	400	9	41	10	125	20	364	169	1394	2323
1808....	40	433	50	744	1	9	14	300	12	380	117	1866	3110
1809....	65	844	58	861	1	18	12	36	17	280	153	2039	3397
1810....	84	682	60	860	1	5	10	250	30	658	185	2455	4092
1811....	80	865	80	975	2	70	5	125	12	229	179	2264	3773
1812....	72	540	45	500	2	30	4	50	8	104	131	1224	2040
1813....	65	770	7	260	2	40	7	200	11	400	92	1670	2793
1814....	60	200	33	320	2	4	6	50	10	205	111	779	1297
1815....	53	511	50	400	2	24	6	130	12	265	123	1330	2220
1816....	61	642	61	900	2	8	7	70	18	358	149	1978	3297
1817....	54	825	61	310	1	50	7	200	12	449	135	1834	3057
1818....	55	715	51	970	1	50	7	200	11	500	125	2435	4058
1819....	70	790	16	800	2	60	2	112	6	588	96	2550	4260
1820....	100	672	....	......	1	25	5	244	9	604	115	1545	2575
1821....	96	720	12	100	1	80	7	196	8	339	124	1435	2392
1822....	96	377	20	323	1	6	8	245	8	406	133	1357	2262
1823....	80	500	30	600	1	......	8	140	9	131	128	1371	2285
1824....											121	1393	2322
1825....											116	1351	2252
1826....	80	321	40	420	1	40	8	366	....	500	138	1647	2762
1827....	60	189	40	318	1	24	8	58	11	285	120	854	1423
1828....	50	400	31	475	1	......	4	128	10	275	96	1278	2130
1829....	50	168	31	240	....	......	6	......	12	70	99	478	797
1830....											102	1878	3130
1831....	50	200	15	215	5	......	4	......	7	62	81	477	796
1832....	96										96	511	852

MATERIAL RESULTS.—LIVESTOCK.—1773-1834.

Year	Cattle	Sheep	Goats	Pigs	Mules	Horses	Total
1773......	47	....	....	28	12	9	96
1774......	61	....	....	32	15	24	131
1783......	500	220	....	25	18	50	813
1784......	500	110	110	26	20	125	991
1785......	600	160	70	28	23	125	1006
1786......	600	180	70	20	16	155	1041
1787......	609	106	90	30	18	170	1023
1788......	710	526	303	24	11	199	1773
1789......	....	....	....	....	....	....	....
1790......	1082	900	353	10	15	393	2753
1791......	1193	1140	399	6	15	272	3025
1792......	1460	1254	306	6	20	309	3355
1793......	2000	1600	400	8	31	512	4651
1794......	2300	1577	200	20	39	610	4746
1795......	2362	1137	244	18	47	721	4529
1796......	2280	1209	400	18	27	913	4847
1797......	1417	1740	100	35	10	840	4142
1798......	730	3200	100	30	30	950	5040
1799......	900	3000	100	40	30	950	5020
1800......	1200	4000	100	60	32	912	6304
1801......	1200	5000	120	60	30	972	7382
1802......	1250	6000	100	40	34	875	8299
1803......	1680	6000	....	....	38	820	8538
1804......	2000	6000	....	....	25	900	8925
1805......	2000	7000	....	....	25	984	10009
1806......	2000	7000	100	25	25	810	10060
1807......	2100	7000	60	25	25	514	9724
1808......	2150	7000	50	23	25	466	9714
1809......	2300	7000	50	20	25	354	9749
1810......	2100	6000	26	20	24	406	8576
1811......	2100	4000	20	10	18	326	6474
1812......	2200	3500	20	10	18	313	6061
1813......	2360	2300	30	10	14	294	5008
1814......	2400	2513	30	10	14	290	5257
1815......	2400	2527	40	20	14	390	5391
1816......	2500	2600	25	12	12	410	5559
1817......	2800	2700	30	13	8	420	5971
1818......	2900	2400	30	12	9	420	5871
1819......	3000	4000	20	10	9	450	7489
1820......	3000	4000	22	10	6	430	7468
1821......	3000	4000	22	4	4	483	7513
1822......	2230	4000	22	16	3	360	6631
1823......	2240	5000	16	20	16	400	7692
1824......	2000	5400	16	20	20	508	7964
1825......	1500	5450	10	19	18	570	7567
1826......	2000	5400	....	8	17	580	8005
1827......	2000	5050	....	7	16	620	7693
1828......	1200	4450	....	7	14	640	6311
1829......	1440	3200	....	3	8	320	4971
1830......	2150	3800	....	....	10	440	6400
1831......	2050	4400	....	....	8	470	6928
1832......	2100	3300	....	....	8	410	5818
1833......	....	....	....	....	....	....	....
1834......	312	....	....	....	9	491	812

C

LIST OF RESIDENT AND OTHER FATHERS.

Fr. Junipero Serra, June 3, 1770, to August 28, 1784.
Fr. Juan Crespi, June 3, 1770, to January 1, 1782.
    Fr. Miguel Pieras, No. 27, Sept. 29, 1772, Nos. 29-30, October 27, 1772.
    Fr. Domingo Juncosa, No. 28, October 18, 1772.
    Fr. Francisco Palóu, Nos. 163-165, Dec. 8, 1773.
Fr. Francisco Dumetz, No. 33, January 1, 1773, to May 18, 1782.
Fr. Jose A. Murguia, No. 207, July 31, 1774, to Nov. 30, 1776.
Fr. Thomas de la Peña Saravia, Febr. 25, 1775, to October 1776, No. 427.
    Fr. José de Nocedál, No. 412, June 23, 1776.
    Fr. José Cavaller, No. 442, Febr. 23, 1777; June 9, 1782, No. 678.
Fr. Matias Antonio de Santa Catarina y Noriega, Nov. 21, 1781,—Sept.
    17, 1787.
Fr. Diego de Noboa, August 9, 1783, to
Fr. Francisco Palóu, August 20, to Sept. 7, 1784.
    Fr. Buenaventura Sitjar No. 1015, August 30, 1784.
Fr. Antonio Paterna, Oct. 3, 1784, to May 23, 1785.
    Fr. Miguel Pieras Aug. 13, 1785, Nos. 1156-1158.
    Fr. Juan Mariner, Sept. 4, 1785, No. 1162.
Fr. Fermín Francisco de Lasuén, January 12, 1786, to
    Fr. José de Arroita, Oct. 8, 1786, No. 1235.
    Fr. Thomas de la Peña, Oct. 31, to Nov. 26, 1786; Aug. 14, 1790.
Fr. Pascual Martinez de Arenaza, Febr. 5, 1787, to January 10, 1797.
    Fr. José de Arroita, No. 1311, Oct. 21, 1787.
Fr. José Francisco de Paula Señan, Oct. 17, 1787, to Sept. 10, 1795.
    Fr. Miguel Pieras June 7, 1788.
    Fr. Francisco Miguel Sanchez, Sept. 4, 1789; July 13, 1793.
    Fr. Benito Cambón, June 10, 1790.
    Fr. Faustino de Solá, July 22-29, 1790.
    Fr. Antonio Dantí, July 27, 1790.
Fr. Estevan Tápis, Aug. 27, 1790, to Oct. 18, 1790.
Fr. Mariano Rubí, Dec. 14, 1790, to May 19, 1791.
    Fr. Bartolomé Gilí, Febr. 1, 1793.—June 18, 1791.
    Fr. Pedro de San José Esteban, January 1795.
    Fr. Antonio Jayme, Sept. 17, to Oct. 1, 1795; Aug. and Oct., 1798.
    Fr. José de la Cruz Espí, March and May, 1796.
Fr. Mariano Payeras, July 10, 1796, to Sept. 7, 1798.
Fr. Francisco Pujol, June 26, 1797, to Dec. 21, 1800.
    Fr. Magín Catalá, No. 2171, June 27, 1797.
    Fr. Antonio de la Conc. Horra, No. 2182, Sept. 18, 1797, (to an adult
    of forty years.)
    Fr. Francisco Gonzalez, May 28, 1798.

Fr. Baltasar Carnicer, Oct. 18, 1798, to April 10, 1799.
  Fr. José Viader, May 19, 1799.
Fr. José Viñals, May 22, 1799, to Febr. 18, 1804.
Fr. José Manuel de Martiarena, Jan., 1800, to—
  Fr. Isidoro Barcenilla, Febr. 13, 1800.
  Fr. Mariano Payeras, April 15, 1800.
  Fr. Jacinto Lopez, April and May, 1800.
  Fr. José Garcia, Sept., 1800.
Fr. Baltasar Carnicer, March 7, 1801, to Nov. 28, 1807.

  Fr. Antonio Jayme, May 1, 1801, No. 2358; Aug. 1801; Dec. 1811.
  Fr. Domingo de Iturrate, June 13, 1801.
  Fr. José Ant. de Uría, July, 1801.
  Fr. Luis Gonzaga Gil de Taboada, Aug. 12, 1801.
  Fr. Florencio Ybañez, Aug., 1801.
  Fr. Ramon Abella, Aug. 23, 1801.
  Fr. Jacinto López, Aug. and Sept., 1801.
Fr. Juan Amorós, Sept. 10, 1804, to June 29, 1819.
Fr. Vicente Francisco de Sarría, Sept. 10, 1809, to Aug. 16, 1829.

  Fr. Felipe Arroyo de la Cuesta, Sept. 14, 1809; April 3, 1813.
  Fr. Jayme Escudé, Jan., 1813; Nov., 1814.
  Fr. Estevan Tápis, Aug. 17, 1813.
  Fr. Pedro Cabot, Dec., 1813.
  Fr. Pedro Cabot, Dec. 18, 1814, to Jan. 22, 1815.
  Fr. Estevan Tápis, March 1, 1815, No. 1945.
  Fr. Juan Sainz de Lucio, June 24, 1816, to Nov. 11, 1816.
  Fr. Pedro Cabot, Dec. 21, 1816, Nos. 3016-3017; Dec., 1825; March
    and April, 1826.

Fr. Ramon Abella, June 30, 1819, No. 3134, to April 21, 1833, No. 3834.
  Fr. Blas Ordáz, Aug. 13, 1820, No. 3167.
  Fr. Thomas Esténaga, Sept. 13, Nov. 23, 1820.
  Fr. Felipe Arroyo, Febr. 1, 1822; June, Dec., 1823; July to Aug.,
    1824; June, 1826.
  Fr. José Altimira, Dec. 14, 1826; Febr. 17, 1827.
  Fr. Juan Moreno, No. 3533, Dec., 1827.

Fr. Antonio Menendez, O. P., (Presidio) Febr. 28, 1830, to April 12,
    1831, No. 3728.
Rev. Patrick Short, July 26, 1832, to Jan. 5, 1835.
Fr. Rafael Moreno, Febr., 1833, to Jan. 6, 1834.
Fr. Diego Garcia, March 3, 1833.
  Fr. Lorenzo Quijas, March 4, 1833.
Fr. José del Reál, Febr. 13, 1834, Nov. 5, 1844.
  Fr. Jesus Maria Vasquez del Mercado, July, 1834.
  Antonio del Reál, April, 1837.
  Fr. José Maria Gutierrez, Oct. 13, 1839, to Jan. 12, 1840.

Fr. Antonio Reál, Nov. 21, 1844, No. 4679, to Oct. 21, 1845, No. 4758.
Fr. José Ant. Anzar, Nov. 30, 1845, No. 4759, to Jan. 14, 1846, No. 4775.
Fr. José Reál, Jan. 23, 1846, to Febr. 3, 1846, No. 4779, (only five).
Rev. Dorotéo Ambrís, Febr. 26, 1846, to March 9, 1849; Dec., 1850.
Rev. Prudencio Santillan, March 6, 1846; Febr. to March, 1848.
Fr. Ignacio Ramirez de Arellano, Febr. 15, 1849, to July 9, 1851,—Febr.
    2, 1853.
Rev. Prud. Santillan, March to July, 1849.
Rev. Dorotéo Ambrís, Jan. 12, to June 2, 1851.
Fr. Sadoc Vilarrasa, O. P., March 21, 1851, to Febr. 28 (26?), 1854.
    Rev. S. B. Loubert, Febr. 25, 1851; June to July, 1851.
Rt. Rev. José Sadoc Alemany, O. P., April 27, 1851.
    Fr. Antonio Jimeno, O. F. M., Aug. 17, 1853, No. 5305.
    Fr. Antonio Agustin Langlois, O. P., Sept. 13, 1853, and later.
Rev. Francisco Foretnick, July, 1854, and later.
Rev. S. Filoteo Nov. 9, 1855-1856.
    Rev. B. Raho, C. M., 1856.
Rev. Cajetanus Sorentini, 1857-1858.
Rev. John Comellas, 1859-1864.
Rev. Michael Racca, 1865-1869.
Rev. Angel Delfino Casanova, 1870-1883.
Very Rev. Angel Delfino Casanova, 1884-1893.
Fr. José Godiol, March 19, 1893-April 5, 1893.
Rev. Ramon Maria Mestres, 1894-1900.
Rev. R. M. Ferrer, rector pro tem., 1901.
Rev. Ramon M. Mestres, 1902-1930.

    Rev. Mathias Cuevas, 1902.
    Rev. Philip Farrelly, 1903-1905.
    Rev. P. Murphy, 1909.
    Rev. A. Serra, 1911.
    Rev. M. Pablos, April 4, 1916-Oct. 21, 1917.
    Rev. Joseph B. Hummert, 1916.
    Rev. Constantinus Garcia, March 18, 1917-April 25, 1920.
    Rev. E. Fiori, June 30, 1918-Aug. 25, 1918.
    Rev. B. H. Harmon, Jan. 1, 1920-May 24, 1920.
    Rev. J. Coma, Oct. 10, 1920-Jan. (June) 8, 1921.
    Rev. William Verhallen, July 3, 1921-Oct. 30, 1921.
    Rev. Ascensio Segarra, Nov. 8, 1921-Nov. 9, 1924.
    Rev. William Stuhlman, March 15, 1925-Dec. 6, 1925.
    Rev. William Guidotti, June 21, 1925.
    Rev. J. R. Ehrenfried, Dec. 20, 1925-March 13, 1927.
    Rev. E. Huebbers, Febr. 5, 1927-July 4, 1927.
    Rev. C. F. McNamara, July 16, 1927-April 28, 1928.
    Rev. Ignacio Romo, Nov. 4, 1927-May 29, 1929.

Rev. James Culleton, D. D., Dec. 25, 1928-March 5, 1929.

Rev. Michael C. Murphy, Febr. 17, 1929-Nov. 25, 1931.

Rev. Michael C. Murphy, had care of Mission Carmel and remained Assistant at Monterey, March 30, 1929-Oct. 31, 1933.

Rev. Gerald Culleton, April 20, 1929-Jan. 20, 1933.

Rev. Paschal Merola, Sept. 7, 1929-June 5, 1931.

Rev. Philip G. Scher, May 30, 1930-Febr. 1, 1933.

Rev. James Culleton, D. D., July 19, 1930.

Rev. George L. Smith, Jan. 24, 1932-June 10, 1933.

Rev. Luke Lynch, Sept. 18, 1932.

Rev. Michael Dunleavy, Nov. 29, 1932-Oct. 20, 1933.

Administrator, Rev. James Culleton, D. D., Febr. 1, 1933-Aug. 15, 1933.

Rev. Matthew O'Brien, Febr. 11, 1933—

Very Rev. Gerald Gay, V. F., Aug. 15, 1933—

Rev. Silvano Baquedano, Oct. 20, 1933—

Rev. Michael O'Connell, Oct. 27, 1933—Pastor of Carmel Mission, made into separate parish.

D

CASADOS Y VELADOS.

A peculiar custom obtained among the Mexican people of the early Mission Days which gave rise to the terms "Casados y Velados"—Married and Veiled. These require some explanation.

After all the formalities had been observed, in accord with the directions of the Catholic Ritual, the couple to be married appeared with the required witnesses before the authorized priest at the altar just before Holy Mass. There the marriage ceremony took place, that is to say, both plighted their troth. After this, in the language and according to the understanding of the Mexican people, the couple were called *Casados*, married. The marriage contract lacked nothing to be valid. Thereupon they left the Sanctuary.

Then the Holy Mass began and continued until just before holy Communion. At this time the couple again entered the sanctuary without witnesses, and knelt on the lower step of the altar platform. The celebrant of the Mass recited a lengthy blessing, called the Nuptial Blessing, over the bride. This blessing, as a rule, was bestowed only in holy Mass. The Nuptial Blessing having been imparted, the couple were considered not only casados but *velados* also.

During the reading of the Nuptial Blessing, a piece of white gauze trimmed with ribbons was thrown over the couple so as to veil them. Hence the term *velados*—veiled. It meant that the couple had been married at holy Mass, or that the couple married before had now received the Nuptial

Blessing. The tying with ribbons and veiling had nothing to do with the rubrics. It was merely a pretty custom in vogue among the Mexicans in California long ago. A noted traveller, Frederick Gerstaecker, described such a scene as late as 1849 at Dolores Church in San Francisco.

It was, and still is, the ardent desire of the Catholic Church that her children contract matrimony in connection with holy Mass, and so receive the solemn Nuptial Blessing. This was the invariable practice in the Missions. If, however, for any important reason the marriage had to take place in the afternoon or evening on account of a hasty journey, etc., the couple could receive the Nuptial Blessing on any suitable occasion.

Micheltorena was an officer in the Mexican Army and subject to orders. It so happened that he and his bride could not attend holy Mass when they were married by the priest outside the usual time, and so had to dispense with the Nuptial Blessing for the time. When they arrived at Santa Barbara, on their way to Monterey, the opportunity was taken by them to receive the Nuptial Blessing there and at the hands of the first Bishop of California, after they had been married eight years. The fact is duly noted in the Marriage Register at the parish church of Santa Barbara as follows: "On July 29, 1843, in this Church of Santa Barbara, I gave the Nuptial Blessing to His Excellency Don Manuel Micheltorena and to Doña Josefa Fuentes, previously married, as is evident to me, and to which Don Felix Valdes and Don Juan Avella, both officers of the army, can testify, and in order that for all time it can be on record I have signed this today, April 20, 1844.—Fr. Francisco, Bishop of California." The entry is written in the hand of Fr. González Rúbio, the Bishop's Secretary; but the signature is in the Bishop's own hand. On the margin of this entry we read these words: "No. 265. Velacion del Exmo. Señor Don Manuel Micheltorena con Doña Josefa Fuentes."

E

TESTAMENT OF HERMENEGILDO SAL.

"I firmly believe in the most Venerated Mystery of the most Holy Trinity, God the Father, God the Son, and God the Holy Ghost, three distinct Persons and only one true God; and in all the other mysteries which are proclaimed and taught us by our Mother, the Roman, Catholic, Apostolic Church, in which faith I have lived and protest that I desire to live and die as a Catholic Christian. I choose for my protectress and advocate, the most holy Virgin Mary, with whom as the Mother of sinners I beseech God to forgive my sins. I trust in her clemency and in the prayers of the Saints, more particularly in those of my patron Saint, of those to whom I had special devotion and of my Guardian Angel. From my heart I call and invoke them that by their supplications my soul may enter into the Court of Salvation. Thus hoping I have made my testament in the following manner:

"1. I give and recommend my soul to God, Our Lord, its Creator, who also has redeemed it with the costly price of His Precious Blood. I beseech the Divine Majesty that my soul may come to Him for Whom it has been created. I give and recommend my body to the earth from which it has been formed.

"2. I order that, after my decease, my body be clothed in the habit of Our Holy Father St. Francis (Third Order) and interred in the Church of the Mission of San Carlos.

"3. I order that the Mission of San Carlos be given three hundred pesos for the most Holy Sacrament in satisfaction for penances badly performed, which may have been imposed upon me.

"4. I order that for my soul one Mass of Requiem be sung, for which I give twenty pesos as stipend. Etc."

This highly edifying and interesting document relates nothing uncommon among the genuine Spanish officials of the early Mission Period.* In any emergency they would give expression to their deep reverence for their Creator and his rights over them. On this subject they were at one with the missionaries, hence their respect for those unselfish and fatherly guides of the Indian converts at the Missions. Would that the paisano leaders influenced by the unspeakable pair—Echeandia and Padrés—had been so faithful to their Creator and God as the loyal Spanish officers; they would not now be covered with infamy and remembered as the brutal destroyers of the most meritorious institutions which the world has ever seen, and the very ruins of which command admiration under the title of California Missions.

The will was made on November 9, 1800.[1] Sal died a month later as the Book of Burials has it: "On December 10, 1800, in the church of this Mission of San Carlos de Monterey, I gave ecclesiastical burial to the body of Don Hermenegildo Sal, Lieutenant-Commander of the Presidio of Monterey. He was a native of Valdemar in the Archbishopric of Toledo. He died on the 8th (1800); all the Sacraments were received by him, etc."—Fr. José Viñals. It is No. 1343 in the First Book of Burials of the Mission and Presidio of San Carlos de Monterey.

F

RESTORATION OF MISSION SAN CARLOS DE BORROMEO.

Save for the roofless church edifice, the buildings of Mission San Carlos, Fr. Junipero Serra's own scene of zealous activities, had at last

---

* See for another edifying sample our *Mission Soledad* in the case of Governor José Joaquin Arrillaga.

[1] *Cal. Arch.*, vol. xxiv, pp. 392-397.

been wiped out to the satisfaction of Pio Pico and his inglorious gang of freebooters. When the Rev. Angelo D. Casanova received the appointment of rector or pastor of the parish of Monterey in 1870, he began planning to restore at least the unsightly church ruins. Tourists as yet seldom visited the place because few only knew much about its most interesting history, and settlers manifested little concern for the project of expensive reconstruction work. Father Casanova, however, was determined to see a roof on the sacred edifice, and to clean out the rubish which covered the floor to a depth of three feet. This would make it easy to locate the graves of Fr. Serra and three other Franciscans who lay buried within the church. The Burial Register clearly named four priests who had been interred within the sanctuary. They were Father Juan Crespi, who died here on January 1, 1782, at the age of sixty-one years; Father Junipero Serra, Presidente of the Missions, who died on August 28, 1784, at the age of seventy-one years; Father Juan Lopez, who died here on July 15, 1797, at the age of thirty-five years; and Father Fermín Francisco de Lasuén, Presidente of the Missions, who died here Sunday June 26, 1803 at the age of eighty-three years.

By January, 1882, the Rev. Angel Casanova had succeeded in collecting sufficient funds to clear out the debris in the sanctuary. Some workmen were engaged to perform the task of laying bare the floor, and so discovered the tomb which contained the remains of the four Franciscans "In the sanctuary, on the Gospel side, fronting the altar of Our Lady of the Seven Dolors," as the Records revealed.

After announcing in the San Francisco papers that an opportunity would be afforded to view the remains of the four missionaries, on July 3, 1882, Father Casanova with more than four hundred people went out to Carmelo. With the Register of Burials in hand, standing before the open grave and beholding the skeletons, he in turn read aloud the entries of Fathers, Crespi, Serra, Lopez and Lasuén. The remains of each had been placed in unplaned redwood coffins, and were still in a good state of preservation, the ribs standing out in proper arch. Parts of the vestments were in good order, likewise the heavy silk stole which is worn only by priests, was in good order; it was in one piece, two and a half yards long with the silk fringes as good as new. The stone slabs were replaced over the whole tomb.

* * * * * * * * * *

In April, 1884, Father Casanova began his work of restoring the church building. An appeal for funds was brought to the notice of the people of California on June 22, 1884. The address was by His Excellency George Stoneman, Governor of California, Hon. Washington Bartlett, Mayor of San Francisco, Ex-Governors Perkins, Burnett, Irwin and Downey, and fifty leading citizens of California, irrespective of Creeds. The amount required was about $20,000.

ANOTHER VIEW OF MISSION SAN CARLOS RESTORED BY FATHER CASANOVA.

The work of restoring the church was heartily approved by the Ecclesiastical Authorities. Father Casanova was gratified to receive the following endorsements.

Very Rev. Father:—With pleasure and gratitude I see that you persevere in your zealous effort of restoring the ruined old church of San Carlos Mission, wherein rest the mortal remains of the venerable pioneer, the Very Rev. Junipero Serra. I need not repeat that I heartily approve your good work, and hope that the friends of Religion and of the glories of our State will assist you substantially.

Yours very truly,
Francis Mora,
Bishop of Monterey and Los Angeles.

San Juan, June 24, 1884.
We cheerfully concur with the above.

J. S. Alemany,
Archbishop of San Francisco.

P. W. Riordan,
Coadjutor Archbishop of San Francisco.

* * * * * * * * * *

In the work of restoration, Father Casanova has adhered as much as possible to the original design of the church. It speaks well for the State of California that men of all Creeds have aided him so that the monument raised over the grave of the State's foremost pioneer could be completed. It was re-dedicated on August 28, 1834.

G

SAN CARLOS SCHOOL AND SAINT JOSEPH'S CONVENT,
MONTEREY, CALIF.

Rev. R. M. Mestres, Pastor of San Carlos Mission, erected the present school building in 1898.

The Sisters of St. Joseph from San Diego opened the school; the attendance was very good up to the 8th grade until 1914 and 1915. They also taught First High and Commercial. For some reason the school was closed in 1915 and remained closed till September, 1917.

Father Mestres frequently engaged the Jesuit Fathers to help out at Christmas and Easter. He communicated to one of the Fathers, Rev. F. Sauer, S. J., from Gonzaga College, Spokane, Washington, his desire to reopen the school. This Father recommended the Franciscan Sisters who were teaching in the school at Chewelah, a Jesuit parish near Spokane, to re-open the school.

At the end of August, 1917, three Sisters arrived. They received a very kind welcome from the Pastor, Rev. R. M. Mestres. Kind friends had provided the necessary furniture, beds, kitchen utensils, etc. To this very day the Sisters are most grateful for the privilege the Rev. Pastor granted them, the day after their arrival, to have the Blessed Sacrament in their little chapel. Two of the pioneer Sisters came from Rome in 1900, where their Motherhouse was till the beginning of the world war, when the Community had to leave Rome, the majority of the Sisters being of German nationality. September 1st, the three Franciscan Sisters opened San Carlos School with an attendance of fifty pupils. Gradually the number increased and the Sisters had to engage a lady teacher.

Through a friend, who is a zealous member of the Little Company of St. Joseph for the Dying, established throughout the East and West of the U. S. by the Very Rev. Hugolinus Storff, O. F. M., the Sisters learned to know of this wonderful devotion and spiritual work.

The Pious Union of St. Joseph for the Dying counts among its millions of members, many Bishops, Priests, Missionaries and Religious, both contemplative and active. The Poor Clares at Oakland, California, have perpetual adoration of the Blessed Sacrament for the Dying. The Sisters at Monterey, by a special privilege of Divine Providence, were called to consecrate their whole life, their teaching, their labors of charity in whatever form or shape for the salvation of the Poor Dying Sinners. They bind themselves to this work when they pronounce their religious vows.

The Most Rev. John J. Cantwell, the newly-elected Bishop of Monterey-Los Angeles, took a fatherly interest in the Sisters and appointed Very Rev. Hugolinus Storff, O. F. M., Provincial at San Francisco, as the Spiritual Director of the community. He obtained in 1918 the affiliation of the community with the Franciscan Sisters of the Immaculate Conception at Rock Island, Ill. The brown habit was adopted while up to this time the Sisters at Monterey wore the black Franciscan habit.

Under the guidance and spiritual direction of Very Rev. Fr. Hugolinus, O. F. M., the zealous son of St. Francis, the community grew in the religious life as well as in numbers.

On December 8, 1920, a great blessing was conferred on the community. Most Rev. John J. Cantwell, signed the Decree of Episcopal Approbation and sent it to the Director, Very Rev. Fr. Hugolinus, O. F. M.

For a clearer understanding of the special purpose of this community there are subjoined a few paragraphs of the decree, translated from the Latin.

"For the greater glory of God and in honor of Our Mother Mary Immaculate and of her chaste Spouse, our most Blessed Father St. Joseph, on the occasion of the Golden Jubilee, which the Catholic Church solemnly celebrates on the Feast Day of the Immaculate Conception of the current year 1920, on which day, fifty years ago, St. Joseph was proclaimed the Patron of the Church by Pope Pius IX, we, by Our Authority, as far as the laws of the Church permit, gladly approve the Congregation of the Sisters of the Third Order Regular of St. Francis, which now leads a religious life in the old town of Monterey, famous by the memory of the Venerable Missionary, Father Junipero Serra, of the Order of Friars Minor.

"As was stated in the petition to the Sacred Congregation of Regulars, the name of the Congregation shall be this: 'Franciscan Sisters of Mary Immaculate and St. Joseph for the Dying.'

"The chief end of this Congregation shall be this: 'That the Sisters consecrate their whole religious life and daily offer up all their works for the Salvation of the Dying, etc.'

"In order to help the increase of the Congregation and the work, we hereby give permission to receive as postulants and novices those who seem to be fitted for the religious life and wish with their whole heart to consecrate themselves and their life to the Salvation of the Dying."—

With grateful hearts do the Sisters treasure the paternal solicitude and kindness of the Most Rev. Bishop Cantwell.

God blessed the humble labors of the Sisters in the classroom and other activities by asking a great sacrifice. The youngest of the pioneers was called to give her young life for the souls of the children and the Salvation of the Dying. After a short illness she died well prepared, January 16, 1923.

Most Rev. Bishop Cantwell delegated Very Rev. H. Storff, O. F. M., to take his place at the different ceremonies of investment and profession.

In 1924, the diocese was divided and Most Rev. John B. McGinley became Bishop of Monterey-Fresno. The Sisters again found a very kind friend in the new Bishop. With Attorney Charles C. Sullivan the Bishop made arrangements for Incorporation and this was accomplished on July 30, 1927. In the same year the Most Rev. Bishop obtained from Mrs. Narcissa Dutra for the Sisters the corner lot for the new Convent. Very Rev. Fr. H. Storff, O. F. M., blessed the ground June 14, 1927, prior to his departure for Rome.

For nearly twelve years the Sisters had their home in the parish school; their numbers increasing, they built with the help of kind friends and with their own savings a plain but substantial convent and a beautiful chapel. The convent is named St. Joseph's convent and the chapel is dedicated to the Immaculate Conception.

On August 15, 1928, the cornerstone was laid by Monsignor Mestres, assisted by Monsignor Crowley and Rev. Father Philip G. Scher and a number of friends. After the blessing of the cornerstone, Monsignor Crowley gave an eloquent talk in the Old Mission Church on the meaning of the ceremony and the labors of the Sisters.

December 8, 1928, Monsignor Mestres celebrated the first Mass in the chapel, and on December 27th, the Feast of St. John, the ceremony of dedication took place, Most Rev. Bishop McGinley officiating. The celebrant of the Mass was Rev. Kerfs; he was assisted by Rev. Humilis Wiese, O. F. M., Rev. P. G. Gay, Rev. J. Culleton, Rev. F. Romo; Wm. Chasagne of St. Joseph's Seminary, Mountain View, California, acted as master of ceremonies. The ceremony closed with the solemn Benediction of the Most Blessed Sacrament.

Due to the illness of Rev. Pastor, Monsignor Mestres, Rev. Philip G. Scher was appointed pastor of San Carlos on May 31, 1930. His coming meant new life and success for the school. The prolonged illness of Monsignor Mestres naturally caused lack of cooperation with the school and the teachers. But the new pastor soon won the hearts of the children, all loved and revered him. On the days he taught Christian Doctrine to the upper grades, his holy influence could be felt all day in the hearts of the children. When giving the monthly reports he encouraged and uplifted all, big and small. Through his kind cooperation the Sisters' labors in the education and training of the children, who are of a variety of nationalities, have geen greatly lightened. The number of pupils increased, so that two more classrooms had to be used. He made many improvements in the building, heating system, more teaching materials, etc. A school bus brings the children from Seaside to school and on Sundays to Mass. Many children attend Mass on school days at 8:30 o'clock.

The new pastor proved himself a real friend of the Sisters community also. They have the great privilege of daily Mass in their chapel, Benediction on Sundays, Wednesdays and Saturdays and on Special Feasts of the Franciscan Order.

August 5, 1930, Monsignor Mestres was called to his eternal reward. Most Rev. Bishop McGinley, on account of illness retired. In 1933, God's Providence by the voice of His Vicar on earth, the Holy Father, called the dearly beloved pastor of Monterey to the episcopal dignity, to be the Father not only of his children of Monterey, but to all his people, to care for the lambs and the sheep. It is the one great prayer of all that God preserve him to his spiritual children in health and strength for many years to come! All need him as their Father but most of all do the Sisters of St. Francis need him.

Should there be any readers of this little history who feel the call to the religious life, they are welcome to communicate with the Superior of the Franciscan Sisters.

St. Joseph Convent,
Monterey, California.

H

FATHER SERRA AND THE GRATEFUL STATE OF CALIFORNIA

The State of California paid tribute to good Father Serra on occasion of the bi-centennial of his birth, 24th of November, 1913. Without any engineering on the part of his Franciscan brethren the commonwealth, through its governor, honored the memory of its acknowledged benefactor in such a manner as has never before been done for a native or adopted Californian. His Excellency, Governor Hiram W. Johnson issued a proclamation worded as follows:

"Executive Department,
  State of California.

"To the memory of Junipero Serra California owes everlasting tribute. He brought civilization to our land, and in character and in deed he deserves a foremost place in the history of our State.

"Monday, November 24th, will be the two hundredth anniversary of the birth of Junipero Serra and I regard the occasion as one that should be observed by all Californians.

"NOW, THEREFORE, I, HIRAM W. JOHNSON, Governor of the State of California, do hereby appoint
  MONDAY,
the 24th day of November, 1913, to be a legal holiday, which shall be known as SERRA DAY!"

"IN WITNESS WHEREOF, I have hereunto set my hand and caused the Great Seal of the State of California to be affixed this 17th day of October, 1913."

SEAL   HIRAM W. JOHNSON,
                                                      Governor.
Attest: Frank C. Jordan,
              Secretary of State.

* * * * * * * * *

An Act of the United States Congress, incorporated in the Resolution of the State Legislature, inspired the bestowal of another signal honor upon Father Junipero Serra. It will be more satisfactory to quote the document on the subject which reads as follows:

"Senate Concurrent Resolution No. 17.—Selecting and designating two illustrious deceased persons whose statues in marble or bronze shall hereafter be provided and furnished by the State of California to be placed in National Statuary Hall.

FATHER JUNIPERO SERRA, THE FOUNDER OF CALIFORNIA
AND OF THE MISSIONS.

"Whereas, The Congress of the United States of America has by statute enacted and declared as follows, to wit: 'The President is hereby authorized to invite each and all the states to provide and furnish statues, in marble or bronze, not exceeding two in number for each State, of deceased persons who have been citizens thereof, and illustrious for their historic renown or for distinguished civic or military service, such as each State shall deem worthy of this national commemoration; and when so furnished the same shall be placed in the old hall of the House of Representatives in the Capitol of the United States, which is hereby set apart, or so much thereof as may be necessary, as National Statuary Hall, for the purpose herein indicated.'

"Whereas, the State of California has never designated the deceased persons whose statues shall be so provided and furnished by the State of California; now, therefore be it

"Resolved, by the Senate and Assembly, jointly, that the Legislature of the State of California hereby selects and designates Junipero Serra and Thomas Starr King as the two deceased persons who have been citizens of the State of California and illustrious for their historic or for distinguished civil or military service whose statues in marble or bronze shall be hereafter provided and furnished by the State of California to be placed in National Statuary Hall, as so provided by Act of Congress."

This Resolution was
    "Adopted in Senate April 1, 1927."
    "Adopted in Assembly April 21, 1927."
    "Received by the Governor April 26, 1927."

The presentation and unveiling of the statues of Junipero Serra and Thomas Starr King, of California, were held in Statuary Hall, United States Capitol, Washington, D. C., on Sunday, March 1, 1931, at three P. M. They were accepted in the name of the United States by the Senate, February 23, 1931, and the House, February 27, 1931, after both had agreed to the following concurrent resolution, (S. Con. Res. 40):

"*Resolved by the Senate (the House of Representatives concurring).* That the statues of Junipero Serra and Thomas Starr King, presented by the State of California, to be placed in Statuary Hall, are accepted in the name of the United States, and that the thanks of Congress be tendered said State for the contribution of the statues of these eminent men, illustrious for their distinguished services as pioneer patriots of said State.

"Resolved further, that a copy of these Resolutions, suitably engrossed and duly authenticated, be transmitted to the Governor of California."

* * * * * * * * * *

This year marks the sesquicentennial of Father Serra's death. The grateful State of California has arisen to the occasion once more as is evident from the official pronouncement:—

"Assembly Concurrent Resolution No. 41—Relative to the establishment of the twenty-eighth day of August, 1934, as "JUNIPERO SERRA DAY."

"Whereas, it is an established historical fact that Fr. Junipero Serra was the founder of California and the Father of the Missions; and—

"Whereas, the twenty-eighth day of August, 1934, is the sesquicentennial of the death of Fr. Junipero Serra; now, therefore, be it

"Resolved by the Assembly of the State of California, the Senate thereof concurring, That the twenty-eighth day of August, 1934, be designated as "Junipero Serra Day" in commemoration of the memory of this truly great man."

Adopted in Assembly May 4, 1933.

Arthur A. Ohnimus,
Chief Clerk of the Assembly.

Walter J. Little,
Speaker of the Assembly.

Adopted in Senate May 12, 1933.

J. A. Beek,
Secretary of the Senate.

Frank F. Merriam,
President of the Senate.

* * * * * * * * * *

"I, FRANK C. JORDAN, Secretary of State of the State of California, do hereby certify that I have carefully compared the transcript to which this certificate is attached, with the record on file in my office of which it purports to be a copy, and that the same is a full, true and correct copy thereof. I further certify that this authentication is in due form and by the proper officer."

"IN WITNESS WHEREOF, I have hereunto set my hand and have caused the Great Seal of the State of California to be affixed hereto this 25th day of May, 1933.

Frank C. Jordan,

SEAL   Secretary of State.

By Charles J. Hagerty,
Deputy.

* * * * * * * * * *

This Resolution was received by the Governor *this 15th day of May, A. D., 1933, at 11 o'clock A. M.*

Wm. A. Smith,
Private Secretary of the Governor.

I

GREY FRIARS AND BROWN FRIARS.

(Anent an article which appeared in the *San Francisco Call-Bulletin*, May 8, 1934, and in other periodicals).

The Franciscan Friars of the Mission Period wore a *grey* habit and the Franciscan Friars of today wear a *brown* habit. Are Grey and Brown Friars members of the same Order or do they belong to different Orders?

It must be borne in mind that though St. Francis of Assisi wore a grey tunic, as early writers assure us, he did not dictate the color of the habit for members of his Order. His Rule merely prescribes that "clothes of probation" be given to candidates; and in his Testament we read: "Those who came to receive this life gave to the poor all that they might have had. And they were content with one tunic mended, within and without." Masseron[1] writes on this point: "We may be sure that the Poverello who regarded the questions of material organization as of secondary interest, did not strictly regulate the habit of his first disciples. The shape and color of the tunic were of small importance in his eyes."

A number of early Franciscans were clothed in grey like their holy Founder, though it is evident from the records of those days that others used the freedom allowed on this point and garbed themselves in a black white or blue habit, or in one which happened to be at hand irrespective of color. Such was the diversity in consequence that the writer, quoted above, declares that "the first brethren of Rivotorto and Portiuncula certainly were not remarkable for the exaggerated uniformity of their garb. . ." It soon became apparent, therefore, to those in authority that the question of shape and color of habit would have to be ventilated.

The Constitutions of Narbonne (1260), issued by authority of St. Bonaventure, whilst he was Minister-General, contained the first legislation of any importance on this matter. They prescribed that the color of the habit be grey and should not be wholly black or white as had been worn hitherto by some. The fact that St. Francis wore grey undoubtedly had some influence in the choice of this color.

Amidst the changes which took place in the Order during the sixteenth and following centuries, grey continued to be the prevalent color of the habit and was prescribed by certain editions of the General Constitutions and Provincial Statutes. Thus, the regulations (1881) for the Province of the Sacred Heart (U. S. A.) defined that the color of the habit be grey. It was to this Province that the venerable Old Mission of Santa Barbara and its community were attached in 1885 to insure continuance

---

[1] Masseron, *The Franciscans*, p. 87.

and increase of members. But uniformity of color had not been established as yet. Dr. Holzapfel, O. F. M., writes, "Franciscans could wear black, brown, and blue habits, according to the *approved customs* of the Provinces.[2]

Brown gradually superseded grey and is the only legitimate color for the Franciscan habit since 1897. In that year Pope Leo XIII approved of the General Constitutions of the Order of Friars Minor or Franciscans, after they had been favorably passed upon by the Congregation of Bishops and Regulars. This sanction was solemnly reiterated by the Holy Father in his famous letter "Felicitate Quadam," which was addressed to the Franciscan Order October 4, 1897. These Constitutions prescribe: "The artificial color of the outer garments shall resemble the color of wool naturally blackish or dark brown which is called *marrone* in Italian and in French *marron*." (No. 107, CC. GG.) This same paragraph has been embodied verbatim as no. 139 in the latest edition of the General Constitutions, 1921.

The mind of the Holy See on this question is quite evident from the following case. His Excellency, the Most Reverend Archbishop of Lima, Peru, addressed a letter to the S. Congregation of Bishops and Regulars in which he recalled that, in a Brief, June 12, 1877, Pope Pius IX had commanded all Franciscans of Colleges in America without any discrimination to wear the grey habit without any dye; that the aforesaid color had been worn by the brethren in all Central America from ancient times. His Excellency, therefore, petitioned the Holy See that the Fathers, members of Franciscan College in the Peruvian Republic be exempt from the prescription as contained in "Felicitate Quadam" regarding uniformity of habit, and that they be free to wear the old and respected grey color because it would redound to the spiritual good of the faithful of those parts.

The S. Congregation of Bishops and Regulars replied, July 8, 1898, that the Apostolic Colleges of Friars Minor (Franciscans) in Peru are not exempt from the prescription of the Apostolic Constitution "Felicitate Quadam." Hence article 107 (quoted above) of the new General Constitutions is to be observed and put into practice not only by the Colleges but by all members of that Religious Order (Franciscans) who reside in any part of America, whether they are affiliated to a college or a Province. And the Bishop is enjoined not to omit bringing this information to the knowledge of all religious of the Order of Friars Minor.[3]

To summarize, grey was worn by the Franciscans of the Mission Period, as is brown by their successors in California today, because different editions of the General Constitutions of the Order prescribed these respec-

---

[2] Holzapfel, O. F. M., *Geschichte des Franziskanerordens*, p. 378. See also *General Constitutions Ord. Min.*, 1890, cap. ii, par. 17, nos. 113, 119.

[3] Act. Ord. Fratrum Min. August, 1898, p. 123.

tive colors. But, though the general norms were changed on this point, as they were on others, to meet the needs of time, place, and custom, all of the editions were issued, with the approval of the Holy See, by the Minister General of the Order of Friars Minor to which the Mission Padres belonged as do the members of the Santa Barbara Province in California today. Indeed, were Father Serra and his companions alive today, they would accept the latest regulation as to the color of habit and, in the spirit of true Franciscan obedience, exchange the grey for the brown habit.

INDEX

A

Rumsen, Indian tribe, 121; Dialect of, 121.
Russians, 11.

S

Saint Augustine, 234.
Saint Joseph, Patron of the expedition, 13.
Sal, Hermenegildo, 117; Death of, 119; 250.
Salinas, River, 14, Town of, 141; Rancho of, 172.
San Agustin, First ship to land, 5; Wrecked, 5.
San Antonio, Mission of, 31, 90, 199; Packet-boat, 11, 22.
San Bernardino, Ranch of, 168.
San Blas, Port of, 37.
San Buenaventura, 37; Survey boat, 6; Mission of, 196.
San Carlos, Mission of, 17; Beginnings of, 26; Patron of, 26, 240; First Missionaries of, 26; First chapel of, 26; Site unsuitable for, 28; First Baptism, 29; Second site of, 32; Distress at, 41; Situation at, 49, 173, 184; New site, 54; Spiritual affairs of, 55; State of, 67; Families and persons in, 70, 148; Internal affairs at, 87; First stone of new church, 115; Retreat place, 138; Headquarters of all Missions, 139; Cañada of Missions, 167; Proposed suppression of, 154; Inventory of, 185; Wealth of, 211; In secular hands, 214; Final disposition of, 215; Patent for, 216.
San Carlos, Presidio of, 25; Packet-boat, 11; Rancheria of, 91, 227.
San Cajetan, Rancho of, 172.
Sanchez, Fr. Francisco, O. F. M., 106.
Sancho, Fr. Guardian, O. F. M., 106.
San Clemente, Plains of, 168.

San Diego, Bay of, 17; Harbor of, 13; Mission of, 33, 153; River of, 13.
Sandoval, Josefa, wife of Gov. Roméu, 196, 237.
Sandwich Islands, 162.
San Fernandino, Religious, 187.
San Fernando, Missionary College of, 30, 63, 85, 120; Mission of, 196.
San Francisco, Bay of, 16, 45; Port of, 20, 51; Mission of, 90; Plains of, 168; Rancheria of, 91, 226.
San Francisco Solano, Mission of, 182.
San Gabriel, Mission of, 33, 180, .196.
Sanjones, 168, 169.
San José, town council for, 150, 162; Mission of, 197; Guadalupe, Station of, 201.
San José, Rancheria of, 91.
San Juan Capistrano, Mission of, 196.
San Lucas, Cape, 12.
San Luis Obispo, Mission of, 31.
San Luis Rey, Mission of, 181, 196.
San Miguel, Bay of, 3; Rancheria of, 91, 226.
San Pedro, Bay of, 6.
San Saba, Rio de, 232.
Santa Anna, Antonio Lopez de, General and President, 194.
Santa Barbara, Mission of, 92, 187; Town of, 153.
Santa Catalina, Fr. Mathias de, O. F. M., 231.
Santa Clara, Mission of, 90, 112, 197.
Santa Cruz, Missionary College of, 42; Mission of, 201, 213.
Santa Inés, Mission of, 197.
Santa Lucía, Sierra de, 14, 17, 31.
Santa Maria, Fr. Vicente de, O. F. M., 45, 52.
Santa Teresa, Rancheria of, 91, 226.

LAUS DEO

Distance from Mission Soledad,—15 leagues.
Distance from Mission San Juan Bautista,—12 leagues.

The Missions of California

(Correct dates of their founding)

San Diego de Alcala, July 16, 1769.

San Carlos Borromeo, or Carmelo, June 3, 1770.

San Antonio de Padua, July 14, 1771.

San Gabriel, Arcangel, September 8, 1771.

San Luis Obispo, September 1, 1772.

San Francisco de Asis, or Dolores, June 29, 1776.

San Juan Capistrano, November 1, 1776.

Santa Clara de Asis, January 12, 1777.

San Buenaventura, March 31, 1782.

Santa Barbara, December 4, 1786.

La Purisima Concepcion, December 2, 1787.

Santa Cruz, August 28, 1791.

La Soledad, October 9, 1791.

San José, June 11, 1797.

San Juan Bautista, June 24, 1797.

San Miguel, Arcangel, July 25, 1797.

San Fernando Rey, September 8, 1797.

San Luis Rey, June 13, 1798.

Santa Inés, September 17, 1804.

San Rafael, Arcangel, December 14, 1817.

San Francisco Solano, July 4, 1823.